PENGUIN BOOK

IN SEARCH OF SHANGRI-LA

Michael McRae is a forming contributing editor to *Outside Magazine*.
He lives in Oregon.

To Andy + Donna —

Best wishes for
epic adventures
& happy trails!

Mike McRae

In

Search

of

Shangri-La

THE EXTRAORDINARY TRUE STORY
OF THE QUEST
FOR THE LOST HORIZON

Michael McRae

PENGUIN BOOKS

PENGUIN BOOKS

Published by the Penguin Group
Penguin Books Ltd, 80 Strand, London WC2R 0RL, England
Penguin Group (USA) Inc., 375 Hudson Street, New York, New York 10014, USA
Penguin Books Australia Ltd, 250 Camberwell Road, Camberwell, Victoria 3124, Australia
Penguin Books Canada Ltd, 10 Alcorn Avenue, Toronto, Ontario, Canada M4V 3B2
Penguin Books India (P) Ltd, 11 Community Centre, Panchsheel Park, New Delhi – 110 017, India
Penguin Books (NZ) Ltd, Cnr Rosedale and Airborne Roads, Albany, Auckland, New Zealand
Penguin Books (South Africa) (Pty) Ltd, 24 Sturdee Avenue, Rosebank 2196, South Africa

Penguin Books Ltd, Registered Offices: 80 Strand, London WC2R 0RL, England

www.penguin.com

First published in the United States of America by Broadway Books as *The Siege of Shangri-La* 2002
First published in Great Britain by Michael Joseph as *In Search of Shangri-La* 2003
Published in Penguin Books 2004

1

Copyright © Michael McRae, 2002
Printed in England by Clays Ltd, St Ives plc

For Ginny

my divinely feminine adventurer,

with love and appreciation

Contents

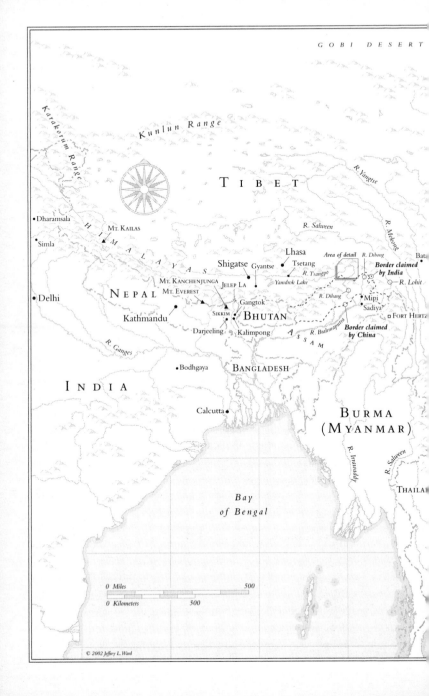

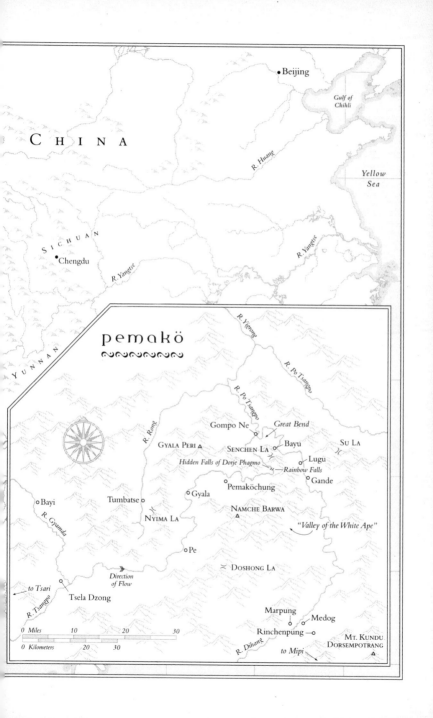

Prologue

The
Riddle
of the
Tsangpo

∾

Page vi: Vale of mystery: the heart of Tibet's Tsangpo River Gorge, now thought to be the world's deepest. To nineteenth-century geographers, the gorge was "one of the last remaining secret places of the earth, which might perhaps conceal a fall rivaling Niagara or Victoria Falls in grandeur" (British political officer, spy, and explorer Capt. F. M. Bailey, 1913). Photo by David Breashears.

Title page: Rainbow Falls as seen from above. Until the modern era, daunting terrain beyond this point turned back all Westerners who attempted to forge through the Tsangpo's inner canyon, including the steel-willed plant hunter Francis Kingdon-Ward on his 1924 Riddle of the Tsangpo Gorges Expedition. Photo by Francis Kingdon-Ward, from the collection of the Royal Geographical Society.

Previous page: The southeastern Himalayas with the Tsangpo River in the foreground. After disappearing into these snow-clad mountains at an elevation of about ten thousand feet, the river emerges in the jungles of northern India at five hundred feet, having lost more than nine thousand feet in less than two hundred river miles. Photo by Gordon Wiltsie.

DURING THE NINETEENTH century's Golden Age of Exploration, the West had a peculiarly Eastern way of relating to far-flung landscapes. The world's remote and uncharted places were initially conjured up in an imaginative process—a kind of geographical meditation—before Europeans went out and "discovered" them. Often based on rumors or sketchy reports from early travelers, the envisioned landscapes gained form and definition through the process of surveying and mapping. In time, after repeated surveys, the world's "white spaces" or "blanks on the map," as they were called, left the realm of imaginative geography and became real.

It was the era of scientific discovery, and the great explorers of the age—Livingstone, Burton, Speke, and Stanley in Africa; Amundsen, Scott, and Shackleton at the poles; and, later in the century, a wave of Himalayan explorers—were the high priests of geography. The maps drawn by these intrepid travelers were "to exploration what scriptures were to theology: the font of authority for ascertaining truths distantly glimpsed," according to historians Karl Meyer and Shareen Brysac.

But an Eastern philosopher might offer that such an empirical method of knowing the world stops short of real discovery, that once the newly found landscape is defined through rational observation, it becomes separate from us, and we lose a vital connection to it. In Tibetan Buddhism, for example, the distinction between the physical landscape and the inner landscape of the mind is blurred. Exploring the former can become a journey into the latter, particularly if the landscape is a sanctified "power place." Geography in such places is said to exist on four levels. The physical realm is obvious to all, but the inner, hidden, and paradisiacal secret levels are accessible only to adepts who are spiritually prepared, and only when the time is auspicious. For them, the journey through the physical landscape becomes an allegory for the path to enlightenment itself.

This is the story of the West's discovery of one such power place, the Yarlung Tsangpo River Gorge of southeastern Tibet. Here, after meandering for nearly a thousand miles across the breadth of the Himalayas, the Tsangpo plunges off the Tibetan Plateau and disappears into a knot of lofty peaks. In the course of less than two hundred miles, the river loses some nine thousand feet of elevation before it spills onto the plains of northern India, where it is renamed the Brahmaputra.

A century and a half ago, geographers were as puzzled about what happened to the Tsangpo after it left the plateau as they were about the source of the Nile. Did it feed the Brahmaputra, as we now know, or did it flow into any of half a dozen other rivers that spill down from Tibet and crash through the jungles east of the Himalayas, in Burma and China? Within about two hundred miles of the Tsangpo are the Yangtze, Mekong, Salween, and Irrawaddy, as well as lesser rivers such as the Lohit, Dibang, and Dihang. The four major rivers bore through the mountains, forming deep, narrow, impassible canyons and, at lower elevations, they rush through subtropical forests with a rich diversity of flora and fauna, from orchids to red pandas and, in the lower Tsangpo Gorge, the last of Tibet's tigers, believed to number fewer than twenty.

Until the middle of the nineteenth century, the Tsangpo Gorge and much of the surrounding region remained a geographical black hole within a black hole: a place of extreme climate and terrain, populated by fierce tribes, and lying within the borders of Tibet, which was then closed to all outsiders. The British had more than an academic interest in penetrating the canyon; there were also strategic and commercial imperatives. At the time, Britain was engaged with Russia in a geopolitical contest called the Great Game. The intrigue had opened earlier in the century when British agents found evidence that Russian emissaries had been in Tibet. Fearing that the tsar would overrun the country and use it as a launching pad to gain control of Central Asia and the crown jewel of India, Britain sent its own spies into Tibet to learn the lay of the land and gather intelligence. The native surveyors, recruited in India and trained by British officers, were the famed pundits (a Hindu word for "learned man"). They were sent into Tibet disguised as religious pilgrims to chart the course of the Tsangpo and determine whether, in fact, it was connected to the Brahmaputra. If so, the river could be followed upstream from India, and both British troops and traders would have a new route over the Himalayas and into Tibet.

But others have told the story of the Great Game; here we are interested not in geopolitics as much as geography, specifically the geography—physical and metaphysical—of the gorge of the Tsangpo. The curtain on our tale goes up in the 1920s, when the link between the Brahmaputra and the Tsangpo was known and much of the gorge had been surveyed. Even so, no one had yet walked the length of the river. The gorge's innermost reaches—the deepest ten miles of canyon, where the river surges and foams between the adjacent peaks of Namche Barwa and Gyala Peri—had repelled every intruder, from the pundits to the British intelligence officers Frederick Bailey and Henry Morshead, who surveyed the gorge in 1913. As all discovered, there were no trails along this portion of the river, no villages, nothing except the Tsangpo hurtling into an apparently impassible void.

But in 1923, the celebrated plant hunter Francis Kingdon-Ward resolved to solve what he called the "riddle" of the Tsangpo: How could it lose so much elevation so rapidly if not for a major waterfall? In Kingdon-Ward's view, and that of many other geographers, the question of the lost falls of the Tsangpo was "the great romance of geography" left unsolved in the preceding decades of Western exploration. The Nile's source was known, the poles had been achieved; now attention was riveted on Tibet, in part because of its growing mystique as a font of occult knowledge and also because of its diplomatic isolation. Tibet was coming into its own as a forbidden land of magic and mystery, and it was a topic of much public speculation.

Kingdon-Ward cared nothing for the occult. A short, careworn, tenacious man, he made a slender living by finding flowering plant species in the Himalayas that would thrive in England's gardens, and by writing about his adventures. He had always wanted to collect in the Tsangpo Gorge, and in 1923 he seized the opportunity to kill two birds: to add to his huge list of botanical discoveries, and to finally lay to rest all questions about the mythical Falls of the Brahmaputra.

The first part of this book, while focusing on Kingdon-Ward's expedition, also looks back at the pundits' journeys and that of Bailey and Morshead. The story of the gorge's early exploration is rooted in questions of topography and natural history, and to a lesser extent the ethnography of the tribes who lived there: the Monpas, the Lopas, and the murderous Abors of the lower gorge. Finding the rumored waterfall was never far from anyone's mind, however, but though all looked, none succeeded. No one, from the pundit Kintup to Bailey and Morshead to Kingdon-Ward himself, managed to close the ten-mile "gap" in the inner canyon. Nonetheless, their survey data indicated that the river channel was steep enough in these unyielding depths to account for the Tsangpo's rapid loss of elevation without a huge waterfall. The existence of a lost falls was almost, but not quite, ruled out after Kingdon-Ward's exploration of the gorge.

Part One concludes with the 1950 Communist takeover of Tibet, after which the country once again became off-limits to foreigners. The gorge slipped behind the Bamboo Curtain for the next four decades, the mysteries of its unexplored physical and spiritual geography still intact.

Part Two chronicles the modern age of exploration in the gorge, beginning with the opening of southeastern Tibet to tourism in the early 1990s. Prior to that, the Chinese had declared the region militarily sensitive, because it abuts the contested border with India. The gorge remained closed to Western travelers even while the rest of Tibet was wide open.

By this point in the story, we meet another breed of explorer interested in a different type of geography than Kingdon-Ward and his contemporaries. Renegade scholars fluent in Tibetan and schooled in

Eastern religions, these adventurers shared an appreciation for the mythology of Tibetan Buddhism, with its cosmology of mountain gods and demons to rival anything in Greek mythology. Hitchhiking and walking across the country, they found that ordinary Tibetans, not just well-educated clerics and monastics, enjoyed a spiritual connection to the natural world that the West, with its focus on rational observation, seemed to have misplaced. Magic was an everyday reality in Tibet, they discovered, and inexplicable phenomena part of the norm in power places such as the Tsangpo Gorge, the most famous of Tibet's sacred hidden lands, or *beyul*. The origins of the fictional kingdom of Shangri-La sprang from tales of such hidden lands collected by some of the first missionaries and explorers to penetrate Tibet's formidable physical and political defenses.

Among the most ardent spiritual geographers were two expatriate scholars living in Kathmandu, Ian Baker and Hamid Sardar. Baker, a student of Asian art and religion with a degree in English literature from Oxford, and Sardar, an American-Iranian Tibetologist schooled at Harvard, conducted the most thorough investigation of the gorge's physical and supernatural realms ever undertaken. Between 1993 and 1998, the two explored the gorge eight times, together and separately. They came as religious pilgrims and academics, following spiritual guidebooks written centuries ago in an esoteric "twilight language," as Baker calls it. At first, neither of them cared to revisit the question of a lost falls, but their quest for the secret center of the *beyul*—the legendary *yangsang ney* (literally, "innermost secret place")—ultimately brought them to the same unexplored gap that had defeated all previous explorers. What they found there—and the ensuing dispute over the "discovery" of a large hidden waterfall—made headlines around the world and ignited a controversy over the nature of discovery in the modern age.

The final section of the book is devoted to this thoroughgoing inquiry, but it is also partly based on my own attempt to reach the gorge with Sardar. We hoped to trek into what he believes to be the *beyul*'s secret sanctuary, an uninhabited subvalley that no one from the outside world (and few who live in the gorge) has ever seen. That journey remains to be made.

. . .

I FIRST CAME to the story of the Tsangpo Gorge in the summer of 1994, when a men's magazine offered me a pressing assignment: Could I drop everything to write an article about an important geographical discovery being claimed by Richard D. Fisher, a little-known wilderness guide from Tucson, Arizona? I had never heard of him during fifteen years of covering exploration and discovery, but the forty-two-year-old Fisher claimed to have completed "the first ever exploration and documentary of . . . the earth's largest and deepest canyon" in southeastern Tibet.

But wait, I thought. Wasn't the deepest canyon in the Peruvian Andes, along the Rio Colca? Indeed it was, according to a recent article in *National Geographic.* Beyond that discrepancy, I found it far-fetched that Fisher could have made such a find in the late twentieth century, long after the remotest, least accessible, and most forbidding blanks on the map had been filled in. Was he insinuating that several centuries of explorers, geographers, and cartographers had been oblivious to the gorge's stupendous depth, or that his survey had left them with egg on their faces? It was as if some obscure climber had just returned from the back of beyond to announce that he had found a summit taller than Everest.

On the other hand, Fisher's altitude readings in the gorge had satisfied the *Guinness Book of World Records.* The book's editors had contacted him after reading articles about his findings, and their consulting geographer had concurred with him on all but one point: what to call the great trench carved by the Yarlung Tsangpo River. The expert did not consider it to be narrow or steep-sided enough to qualify as a canyon. Rather, he felt that it should appear in future editions of the record book as the world's deepest *valley,* besting by some 1,200 feet the previous entry, the 14,436-foot-deep Kali Gandaki Valley in the Nepal Himalayas. At its narrowest, deepest point, where the Tsangpo tumbles between the closely adjacent peaks of Namche Barwa and Gyala Peri, the gorge (or valley, or whatever one wanted to call it) was more than three miles deep. That made it at least a mile deeper than Colca Canyon and more than three times the depth of our own Grand Canyon.

Could the *Geographic* possibly be wrong? That seemed unlikely, and yet another item in Fisher's media kit suggested that he and the *Guinness* editors really might be on to something. It was a dispatch from the official Chinese Xinhua News Agency, dated May 4, 1994, in which geologists from the Chinese Academy of Sciences were claiming the new depth record as their own discovery. Their data differed slightly from Fisher's, but the Chinese researchers had fixed the chasm's depth at an average of about three miles over its 198-mile course. The story noted that, by comparison, the Grand Canyon is "a mere 1 mile deep."

The timing of the Chinese announcement might have been a co-incidence, but the whole affair had the distinct odor of historical revisionism, if not one-upmanship—a competition between a prestigious international scientific body and a brash American outfitter. To me, the controversy (or rather tempest in a teapot) spoke volumes about the diminished state of exploration as the millennium approached. Determining the depth of a river gorge in Tibet was a long way from reaching the poles or the source of the Nile. Had we run so short of genuine discoveries that the whole point of exploration had been reduced to refining topographical statistics?

The next day, I booked a flight to Tucson, little imagining that the project I had taken on would occupy me on and off for the next six years before leading to this book. Rick Fisher was to play a pivotal part in the unfolding tale: It was through his invitation, after all, that Ian Baker reached the gorge in the first place. But though Fisher would place himself at the center of the story, he is no protagonist—if in fact there is one to be found. Fisher's role—his destiny, some might say—is to play the dark and slighted captain of adventure in a drama of intrigue, rivalry, and Faustian ambition that has been playing out in the sequestered Himalayan realm since outsiders first set foot in it. Like Tibet itself, the gorge has retained a shimmering aura of mystery and magic despite (or perhaps because of) the best efforts of the Western world to define and quantify the place. As was the case in the early years of its exploration, the gorge stands as a blank slate for the dreams and fantasies of the Western imagination.

James Hilton's 1933 novel *Lost Horizon* evokes a secret mountain valley called Shangri-La located somewhere in Tibet's mountains. With its weedless gardens, painted teahouses, and a monastery over-looking all, the valley is a sanctuary of learning and culture, an Eden where time stands still. That vision of paradise conformed to the escapist dreams of a war-weary Europe. Beyul Pemakö, as the Tsangpo Gorge is known, bears little resemblance to Hilton's utopia. It is a Tantric Buddhist paradise in which bad weather, near-vertical slopes, trackless jungles, and lethal white water serve a higher purpose: to increase mindfulness and hasten the passage to self-enlightenment.

Like Shangri-La, the gorge of the Tsangpo was once isolated from the West. But given the recent invasion of competitive outsiders—from spiritual seekers to chauvinistic Chinese researchers to white-water adventurers, each seeking some reward—it has been transformed into a vale of rancor and controversy. Only a few have understood the difficulty they were taking on in Pemakö. All have returned home profoundly transformed—if they survived to return at all.

Part One

The Lost
Waterfall

∽

Small wonder . . . that Tibet has captured the imagination
of mankind. Its peculiar aloofness, its remote unruffled
calm, and the mystery shrouding its great rivers and
mountains make an irresistible appeal to the explorer.
There are large areas of Tibet where no white man has
ever trod.

FRANCIS KINGDON-WARD, *The Riddle of the Tsangpo Gorges*

࿇

IN EARLY 1924, when Francis Kingdon-Ward set sail from London bound for Calcutta and, eventually, the Tsangpo River Gorge in southeastern Tibet, he was under no illusions about the challenges ahead. At thirty-nine, Kingdon-Ward was among the world's most experienced and successful plant collectors. Having served for thirteen years as a field agent in Asia for the Cheshire seed firm of Bees & Company, he was responsible for having introduced scores of exotic species to the gardens of England, from the showy yellow-bloomed rhododendron *R. wardii,* named in his honor, to numerous primroses, lilies, and poppies. His first commission for Bees, in 1911 as a young man of twenty-five, had taken him to the mountains of south-central China's Yunnan Province and the adjoining ranges of Tibet, not far from his intended destination on this expedition. Traveling with a personal servant and an enormous Tibetan mastiff called Ah-poh that he had found as a stray, he had spent the better part of 1911 hunting for hardy alpine species that he felt would thrive in England's temperate climate. The work was time-consuming and, because he was toiling at a breathtaking altitude, exceptionally demanding. After locating likely candidates while they were still in flower, he would have to return months later to collect their seeds, sometimes having to excavate marked specimens from beneath several feet of snow at ten thousand feet above sea level. Afterward, the seeds and plants—he was also collecting whole specimens for private herbariums and for the Royal Botanic Gardens in Edinburgh—had to be painstakingly dried, cataloged, and packed for shipment home to England. And he had to record his field notes faithfully, every night.

By the end of a year, Kingdon-Ward had collected some two hundred species, twenty-two of them new to science. He completed his fieldwork with a forced march of three weeks, finally straggling into the Chinese town of T'eng-yueh, where he'd started out. He looked frightful: "My hair was long and unkempt, my . . . feet were sticking out of my boots, my riding breeches torn and my coat worn through at the elbows," he wrote in *The Land of the Blue Poppy,* the second of his twenty-five books and, according to his biographer Charles Lyte, his best work. For six months after exhausting his food stores, Kingdon-Ward had managed on meager rations of native fare: *tsampa* (the roasted barley flour that is the staple of Tibetan diets), bitter brick tea, yak milk and butter, mushrooms, bamboo shoots, and eggs when he could find them. He and his servant, Kin, had suffered illnesses, awful weather, mutinous muleteers and porters, landslides, and loneliness (especially Kingdon-Ward, who waged a lifelong battle against bouts of black depression). A revolution that rocked Yunnan Province after the fall of the Manchu Dynasty in 1911 had filled the hills with army deserters, who turned to banditry for survival. As a foreigner traveling with loaded pack animals, Kingdon-Ward was a prime target, and he was also subject to repeated questioning by wary officials. After all, it had been only seven years since British forces under Col. Francis Younghusband had made a bloody march on Lhasa, Tibet's capital, to impose British will over the recalcitrant nation. Until then Tibet had rebuffed British overtures to align with the empire and to resist Russian advances in Central Asia, and had sealed its borders.

Younghusband, an archimperialist and key player in a political intrigue known as the Great Game, led a force of twelve hundred soldiers, ten thousand porters, and as many pack animals from Darjeeling, India, over the Himalayas and into the "Forbidden Kingdom." His troops slaughtered seven hundred poorly armed Tibetans in one infamous skirmish alone, and ultimately forced the government to sign a treaty of cooperation.

While Tibet was a perilous place for foreigners in 1911, its great river gorges were a plant hunter's nirvana. As Kingdon-Ward explained, there are actually two Tibets: the high, arid plateau where rivers such as the Tsangpo, Salween, and Mekong trace their upper courses, and the more formidable gorge country that comprises the rivers' middle sections. It is in the latter regions, after having meandered eastward and southeastward across the plateau, that the rivers turn south and cut through the Himalayas and barrier ranges east of Namche Barwa, the last major peak in the chain. After rampaging down through the mountains, the rivers spill out onto the plains of northern India, Burma, and Laos to eventually make their way to the sea.

Waxing eloquent, Kingdon-Ward described the gorge country as a land "of dim forest and fragrant meadow, of snow-capped mountains and alpine slopes sparkling with flowers, of crawling glaciers and mountain lakes and brawling rivers which crash and roar through the mountain gorges; . . . of lonely monasteries plastered like swallows' nests against the cliffs, and of frowning forts perched upon rocky steeples, whence they look down on villages clustered in the cultivated valleys at their feet."

In this prettified, Shangri-La-esque portrait, however, he neglects to point out that the gorges are also nightmarishly inhospitable. Their jungles teem with leeches, gnats, stinging nettles, venomous snakes, and large, dangerous animals, including Bengal tigers. The densely forested slopes are horrifically steep and often trackless. There are few villages, little cultivation, and not much food to be had. The weather is abominable for most of the year—wilting heat, pouring rain, snow and ice at higher elevations. Catastrophic floods and land-slides rearrange the landscape with alarming regularity.

The idea of a Tibetan jungle might seem incongruous given the semidesert conditions that prevail north of the Himalayas. But Tibet lies in the rain shadow of the Himalayas, just as Death Valley does in that of the Sierra Nevada. The range forms a barrier to monsoons that batter the Indian subcontinent with rain. By the time their moisture-laden winds have been deflected up and over the mountains and sweep down onto the Tibetan Plateau, they have dropped their burden and turned dry and hostile to plant life.

But at the eastern end of the Himalayas, east of Namche Barwa's icy ramparts, the monsoon is able to find a way through the mountains by funneling up the gorges. Kingdon-Ward called the roughly two hundred miles between Namche Barwa and the foot of the Yunnan Plateau "the Achilles' heel in that otherwise impenetrable mountain defence which rings Tibet like a wall." Storms rush furiously up through the chasms, dumping quantities of rain and snow as they rise. Thus drenched, the canyon lands are thick with rhododendrons and giant bamboo; higher up, they are blanketed with lovely woodlands of pine, cedar, and poplar, which spread out in fanlike formations behind the Himalayas and then quickly disappear as the arid conditions on the plateau take hold. This breach in the mountains was Kingdon-Ward's lifelong hunting ground, the source of most of the twenty-three thousand species he collected during his career.

In the thirteen years that Kingdon-Ward had been tramping the divide, he had explored every major watershed in it except the Tsangpo's. Approaching its gorge, either from the top by traversing the Tibetan Plateau and following the river downstream or from the bottom by marching upstream from the state of Assam in northeastern India, posed serious problems, due not least to the political upheaval in China and the presence of hostile aborigines in the Abor and Mishimi foothills below the gorge. Still, it was not for lack of trying that he had failed to reach his hoped-for destination.

In 1913, for instance, after chronicling his first expedition in *The*

Land of the Blue Poppy, Kingdon-Ward had returned to China uncertain of his itinerary. But now he had the added support of the Royal Geographical Society (RGS), which had made him a fellow and was eager to have him survey the region. One of his missions, in addition to mapmaking for the RGS and collecting seeds for Bees & Co., the Cheshire plant firm that launched his career as a plant hunter, was to trace the middle course of the Brahmaputra River, or Tsangpo as it is called in Tibet, through the gorge. The connection between the two rivers had been a matter of guesswork until around the turn of the century, when British survey expeditions determined that the Tsangpo fed the Brahmaputra. Yet none of these teams had managed to penetrate the Tsangpo's rugged central canyon. In 1913, it remained a black hole to geographers.

The name Brahmaputra had been fixed in Kingdon-Ward's mind since he had heard it as a boy. His father, Harry Marshall Ward, was a distinguished botanist at Cambridge, and scholars and explorers returning from abroad would often stop at the university to see him. One whom young Frank met had been to India and spoke of the Brahmaputra as a river of mystery. "There are places up the Brahmaputra where no white man has ever been," he is reported to have told the boy. The remark captured Kingdon-Ward's imagination and stayed with him for years. In 1925, when he was writing *The Riddle of the Tsangpo Gorges,* he would repeat very nearly the same line about Tibet as a whole.

It was on the 1913 expedition that Kingdon-Ward wanted to solve the "riddle" that had been a source of fascination from the drawing rooms of Mayfair to the meeting halls at the RGS: How could the same river that flowed past Lhasa at an altitude of about twelve thousand feet lose so much elevation so rapidly after spilling off the Tibetan Plateau? By the time the river emerges in the Abor Hills at the bottom of the gorge, roughly two hundred miles from the top, it has dropped more than nine thousand feet. Somewhere in the depths of the Tsangpo's canyon, the speculation went, there must exist a waterfall to rival or surpass Niagara, or even Victoria Falls on Africa's mighty

Zambezi River. Indeed, the idea of a great lost waterfall in the gorge gained further credibility after the link between the Tsangpo and Brahmaputra was established. Were the Tsangpo connected to a more distant river such as the Irrawaddy or Salween, which lie east of the Brahmaputra, its mysterious journey through the mountains would be long enough to bring it down to the foothills without a waterfall. But the prevailing theory in 1913 was that the Tsangpo formed the headwaters of the Brahmaputra, and the only way the two rivers could be linked was if there was a monumental drop somewhere in the gorge.

Thus was born the legend of the Falls of the Brahmaputra—"the great romance of geography," as Kingdon-Ward called it. With typical pluck, he took a crash course at the RGS in surveying and mapmaking before embarking for China in late 1912. But in the field, surveying was for him a distraction from botanizing, and he had little aptitude for the tools of the surveyor's trade—the plane table, which looks like a ruled drawing board mounted on a tripod and is used for recording the lay of the land; the theodolite, a kind of transit to measure vertical and horizontal angles; and various sextants, barometers, clinometers, and compasses. All these instruments were heavy and complicated, and attracted unwanted attention. Anyone, especially a European, found with a plane table and theodolite in Tibet would be suspected of spying.

During the nineteenth century, the British administration's Survey of India had gone to elaborate lengths to develop equipment and methods for its native surveyor-spies, called pundits, to use on covert mapping missions in Tibet. Unlike Kingdon-Ward, with his fair looks, they could disguise themselves as religious pilgrims or traders. Among their few possessions, the pundits carried innocuous-looking prayer wheels in which they concealed compasses and coded route notes; walking staffs that held thermometers for measuring the boiling point of water and converting the results into altitude readings; rosaries strung with a mathematically convenient 100 beads rather than the usual 108, the better to keep track of their uniformly long paces, which they counted carefully, slipping a bead every hundred paces, day after day after day.

In 1874 the pundit Nain Singh was dispatched from India with orders to follow the length of the Tsangpo. Walking west to east, he reached the riverside town of Tsetang, about 250 miles short of the gorge, where he ran out of funds and was forced to return home by a southern route across the Himalayas. Four years later, the Great Trigonometrical Survey of India recruited a lama named Nem Singh— code-named "G.M.N" in survey reports (the middle consonants of his name scrambled)—to carry on beyond Tsetang. After training in clandestine surveying techniques, he set out from Darjeeling with a stout-hearted Sikkimese tailor, Kintup, or "K.P." The pair succeeded in reaching the upper end of the gorge and the village of Gyala, but extreme terrain below the hamlet forced them to abandon the effort.

After their journey, about a hundred miles of the river was left uncharted—the stretch between Gyala and the British outpost of Sadiya, in Assam. The river's plumbing in that hundred-mile gap was still unverified. Any one of the three rivers that converged near Sadyia—the Dihang, Dibong, and Lohit Brahmaputra—might have been connected to the Tsangpo, as far as was known in the 1870s. British survey parties had also been working upriver from Assam to find out which of the three it was and, they hoped, to close the hundred-mile gap. Abor guerillas and a dense jungle slowed them to a pathetic pace; some days they could manage only a hundred yards. Lt. Henry Harman, who commanded the surveys, reported that even his dog could not make it through the wall of vegetation and had to be carried. Harman became so debilitated by the tropical climate that he had to return to the Indian hill station of Mussoorie to recuperate.

Harman chose Kintup again for the next mission—to survey the hundred-mile gap—and paired him with a new pundit, a Chinese lama. They crossed into Tibet in 1880 and reached Tsetang without incident. Here the lama fell ill for three weeks, during which time he treated Kintup "very badly," Kintup would later report. Further downriver, they stopped at a village called Thun Tsung and found lodging. The lama, evidently a worldly fellow, developed an eye for the innkeeper's wife and struck up an affair with the woman—that lasted four months. The adulterers were found out, and only when Kintup offered to pay the cuckolded husband twenty-five rupees were the pundits allowed to proceed.

Things went from bad to worse for poor Kintup. By March of 1881, he and the lama had reached Gyala in the gorge. They trekked beyond the village for several miles to the little monastery at Pemaköchung. In a report of his debriefing published some years later, Kintup was quoted as saying that two miles below the monastery the Tsangpo fell over a cliff about one hundred and fifty feet high. Beyond this point, the trail along the river peters out, and one must detour up onto the steep, rhododendron-choked slopes above. Kintup and the lama could manage no more and retraced their steps to a fort called Tongkyuk Dzong (*dzong* means fort), where the lama promptly vanished. Kintup discovered that the scoundrel had sold him into slavery, to the *dzongpon* (district administrator), and then made a hurried exit.

Kintup spent ten months in indentured servitude before he managed to give his captors the slip. In March 1882, he struck out for the lower gorge, traveling along trails high above the river (and thus skirting the unexplored gap). But the *dzongpon*'s men were in hot pursuit. They caught up to him about thirty-five miles from Tongkyuk, at the monastery of Marpung, where the abbot took pity on Kintup and bought him for fifty rupees.

Harman's plan to verify that the Tsangpo fed the Dihang and thus the Brahmaputra was still foremost in Kintup's mind. The pundit had been directed to cut five hundred logs each a foot long, bore holes into them, and insert into each a tin tube. Then, somehow, he was to send word to Harman to position spotters on the Dihang where it enters Assam. Beginning on the appointed day, Kintup would toss his logs into the Tsangpo fifty at a time. If the observers spotted them, Harman's conviction that the Dihang linked the Tsangpo to the Brahmaputra would be borne out, thus solving part of the river's mystery.

The abbot of Marpung was a kindly sort and occasionally allowed Kintup to visit sacred sites in the gorge, recognizing him to be a devout Buddhist. On one such absence, Kintup cut the logs and stashed them in a cave. Another time, the abbot allowed him to go on a pilgrimage to Lhasa. There Kintup met a Sikkimese judge who was returning to Darjeeling. He dictated a letter to the man with instructions to make sure that it reached Harman. Then he trekked back to Marpung to await the first launch date.

Harman meanwhile had fallen gravely ill, and he left India in December 1882. (He died five months later of pneumonia.) Kintup's letter never reached him. And the logs? If they did make it as far as the Dihang, they passed unnoticed.

Kintup eventually received his freedom from the abbot. Still mindful of his mission, he followed the Tsangpo down toward Assam but soon entered territory controlled by the Abors. The natives were "almost naked, wearing nothing but a wrapper over the lower part of the body," he reported. They were always armed with bow and arrow, and were said "to eat dogs, snakes, tigers, leopards, monkeys, etc." Friendly villagers told him that he would certainly be killed if he proceeded. Still miles short of the border between Tibet and Assam, Kintup was forced to turn around. He returned to the Tibetan Plateau and made his way back to Darjeeling, arriving there in December 1884. He had been away four years.

Kintup's return did not immediately come to the attention of Harman's replacement, Col. Henry Charles Baskerville Tanner. In fact, two years would pass before Kintup was summoned to survey headquarters for a debriefing. Being illiterate, he had kept no notes while in the gorge. Instead he dictated his account entirely from memory, in Hindustani, which Tanner did not speak. The narrative was then translated, edited to remove any militarily sensitive information, and published finally in 1889, in a limited edition of one hundred and fifty copies.

In it, Kintup reportedly recalled that the big waterfall was about two miles from the Pemaköchung monastery, the point where he and the dastardly Chinese lama had run out of trail and turned around. The report indicated that the Tsangpo fell over a cliff called Sinji-Chogyal and, at the foot of the precipice, pooled up into a large lake. On sunny days, rainbows were always visible at the foot of the cascade.

Eight years earlier, in 1881, the *Proceedings of the Royal Geographical Society* had reported on the travels of a French missionary, Père Desgodins, who spoke of "an immense waterfall on the boundary of eastern Tibet." Could there now be any doubt about the Tibetan Niagara?

. . .

THE APPEARANCE OF Kintup's report in 1889 rekindled the initiative to find the lost waterfall. Several plans to penetrate the gorge from above were abandoned as being too risky—supply lines were too tenuous, the journey from Lhasa too far. Reconnaissance parties were also sent up from Assam. They ran into the Abors and were driven back. The initiative stalled for some years, but in 1911, when Capt. Frederick M. "Eric" Bailey set out to solve the mystery by himself, the search took on new life.

If anyone stood a chance of success in the gorge, it was Bailey. Tall, statesmanlike, and ruggedly built, he was an avid sportsman and naturalist, and fluent in colloquial Tibetan. He never traveled without his butterfly net and hunting rifles, and had earned the nickname "Hatter" because of his habit of stopping in the most precarious situations to collect a new species of insect or flower or bird. Younghusband regarded him as a "keen and adventurous officer" and "an excellent fellow," and detached him to explore western Tibet after the Lhasa campaign. Bailey was toughened by the elements—temperatures of twenty-five below, altitudes exceeding eighteen thousand feet—and he loved the spectacular landscape and the people that it bred. He remained in Tibet after his tour of duty in the west, befriending everyone from the lowest peasant to the Panchen Lama and reading everything that had been written about the country. The conundrum of the Tsangpo's falls especially captivated him.

After nine years of hard duty in Central Asia, Bailey had earned a two-year furlough. In August 1909, he sailed from Bombay to Edinburgh aboard the steamer *Egypt* and was soon home among friends and family. When he was not fishing or hunting, or partying in London at the Trocadero or the Ritz, he was concocting a bold plan to tackle the question of the waterfall alone, as a private citizen, while on leave from the military.

By January 1911, Bailey was ready. He crossed the Channel and boarded a train in Paris, bound for Moscow and eventually Peking. His sixteen-year-old former Tibetan servant boy, Putamdu, had traveled all the way from Tibet to Peking at his behest, and the two took a steamer up the Yangtze to Wanhsien, where they switched to sedan chairs for a two-week, 450-mile journey to Chengdu. (Bailey had been urged to take the chairs to give the appearance of prestige, but he scorned his and walked much of the time.) From Chengdu they set a course west and south, heading for the Tsangpo, with Bailey netting butterflies and shooting partridge and hares as they went.

Meanwhile, all was not well in the jungles ahead. Around the time that Bailey and Putamdu were sailing up the Yangtze, Abor tribesmen murdered the British political officer in Assam, Noel Williamson, and thirty-nine of his men. Williamson had been well liked by the natives—"largely cupboard love, I'm afraid," Bailey explains, "for he used to give them large presents of opium and other things." Nevertheless, Williamson knew how unpredictable the Abors could be; he was under orders not to trespass on their territory. The last thing the British wanted was to stir up trouble on the far borders of the empire, only to have to mount a costly punitive expedition. Williamson had ignored the order.

News of the massacre reached Bailey in Chengdu in the form of a cryptic four-word telegram that his father sent to the consul-general: "Warn Bailey massacre Sadiya." That was all, and the consulate could provide no further news. "It was an alarming message," Bailey wrote, "because it failed to say who had massacred whom and why, and I had to proceed with great caution."

Later, he learned what had happened: Williamson and his men had crossed the Dihang into Abor territory despite warnings from friendly locals that the party risked being attacked. Brushing aside the advice, he marched upriver for several days until a number of his Nepalese coolies became sick. Williamson's medical officer, Dr. Gregorson, sent the three worst cases back for treatment, along with a courier bearing letters about the progress of the expedition. The men backtracked to the Abor village of Rotung, where they were welcomed. But that night the self-aggrandizing messenger decided to impress his hosts and took out the letters, flourishing them for all to see—a huge mistake.

The envelopes were white but bordered in black, to mourn the death of Edward VII. Each had been sealed with red wax. The village chiefs asked the significance of the colors, and as Bailey explains, the messenger answered:

" 'You see this white? That is for the two white men [Williamson and Dr. Gregorson]. And this black line round them is Indian Military Police guard which surrounds them.'

'And the red,' said the Abor, knowing that in his own tribe the symbol for anger was the red of scarlet chilies, "that means anger?"

'Yes,' said the letter carrier. 'Great anger.' "

The letters, the village headman decided, must not be delivered to British authorities. After the coolies and courier left Rotung the next morning, they were ambushed and killed. Then the Abors chased down and slaughtered Williamson, Gregorson, and most of the remaining porters.

"The whole affair in fact was caused by the foolish boasting of the Miri letter-carrier," Bailey wrote. "It was altogether a concatenation of foolish blunderings, though no more foolish perhaps than the events which precipitate most wars." To make the situation stickier, matters between Tibet and China were at a crisis stage. In Lhasa, the widely loathed Chinese viceroy and a hundred of his minions had been murdered. The Chinese reaction was swift and brutal. Scores of Tibetans—men, women and children—were beheaded or beaten to death. (Kingdon-Ward, it will be recalled, was in Yunnan province at the same time as Bailey and met a minor Tibetan prince who had been beaten with heavy clubs—fifteen hundred times. Bailey, in the Chinese town of Batang, met a lama who had suffered twelve hundred blows one day and three hundred the next.) The whole of the gorge country ahead was crawling with Chinese soldiers bent on revenge.

But Bailey had a passport from Peking that allowed him to be in Yunnan and Sichuan provinces, and decided to take his chances. Traveling now by pony, with a New Zealand missionary from Batang that he refers to only as Mr. Edgar, Bailey and his entourage reached the Tibetan frontier at the Mekong River. Chinese soldiers were not inclined to let Bailey use the cable crossing, but Edgar argued persuasively with them in Chinese and they relented. The ponies were blindfolded, lashed to a wooden trolley that was hooked atop the stout "cable" of twisted bamboo bark, and pushed off into space above the muddy Mekong. The hundred-yard crossing took only seconds, and Bailey writes, "There was something comic in their terror as they felt the ground disappearing from under their feet, and as they flew across they stretched out their feet pathetically in all directions feeling for solid earth."

The crossing—five men, three ponies, and six loads of luggage—took two hours. Finally, in darkness, they stood on the opposite shore, now outside the bounds of Bailey's passport, in a war zone.

The deeply furrowed gorge country had them marching over fifteen-thousand-foot passes in ice and snow, then descending into forests of colossal fir and cedar trees, some eleven feet around at the trunk. Bears and goral, a kind of mountain goat with coarse reddish hair, roamed the rugged slopes; overhead, noisy parrots darted through the forest canopy. The group crossed into the Salween drainage and by June 15, 1911, they had reached the village of Menkong, with its garrison of Chinese soldiers. Ironically, two days after they left, heading for the Tsangpo, Kingdon-Ward pitched up in Menkong on his first prospecting expedition for Bees & Company.

Edgar returned to Batang from Menkong, leaving Bailey alone

with his men. For the next two months, Bailey noted in his memoir, he did not see another white face. Chinese troops had destroyed a number of monasteries that Bailey passed, and killed hundreds of monks, but in the end it was not the Chinese who were his undoing. By the first of July, he had reached the surviving monastery of Shugden Gompa, "on the very verge of the country into which it had been my object to enter." Streams flowing past the monastery fed a major tributary of the Tsangpo called the Po Tsangpo, which flows south to join the main river at the Tsangpo's "Great Bend." This confluence is not far from the location of Kintup's reputed waterfall, but to get there meant traversing territory controlled by the treacherous Poba tribesmen, who were battling the Chinese and had killed five hundred of their troops. The district administrator at Shugden Gompa refused to take responsibility for Bailey's safety. "[He] said I was certain to be killed," Bailey wrote, ". . . [that] the Chinese would kill me for a British spy, and the Pobas . . . because they thought I was some kind of Chinese or because they were in the habit of killing all strangers."

When the administrator refused to supply Bailey with ponies and porters, there was nothing left to do but turn back. "My disappointment when so near my goal can be imagined," Bailey wrote. "I spent the morning arguing about this, and it was not till two o'clock that I reluctantly started on my return."

Bailey's furlough was nearly up, and he had to return to India by the most direct route—straight down to Assam, or if the hill tribes along the route were still acting up, through Burma. His plan was daring in its vagueness, especially considering that he still did not know which tribe had been responsible for the Williamson massacre. To reach Sadiya, he would pass right through the region where the murders had occurred.

He struck a course down the Zayul River with Putamdu, a second servant, and seven coolies. The heat was oppressive: eighty-six degrees at five o'clock in the afternoon—and this at an elevation of almost seven thousand feet. Bailey stuffed tobacco leaves in his puttees to repel leeches, but to little avail. After one especially hard march, he discovered his legs crawling with leeches—one hundred and fifty, and still counting when daylight failed and he quit trying to remove them.

Along one trail, the party passed several wooden cages: display cases for the heads of criminals decapitated by Chinese soldiers. "Though the heads had been removed, gruesome traces were still left," Bailey noted. At the village of Chikong, he discovered a garrison of two hundred Chinese troops, but one of them recognized him from Batang and invited him for a meal. Bailey treated several of the men with quinine, and the captain of the garrison reciprocated by breaking out a bottle of champagne, putting him up in a comfortable hut, and sending him on his way with two soldiers as escorts. Several months later, he learned that the Poba tribesmen massacred the whole force and threw their bodies in the river.

Lower down in the hills, he met his first Mishimis—"three dull, morose men with very few clothes and wearing necklaces of dogs' teeth, with long hair tied in a topknot on their heads." These were the "barbarians" the Chinese in Peking had told him about. They were rumored to have tails, like monkeys. The closer he came to Mishimi country, however, the shorter the reputed tails grew. Now they were said not to be "a luxurious curly thing . . . [but] a short stump about three inches long and very awkward to sit down upon. In fact, you could always tell where a party of Mishimis had rested, as they were obliged to make holes in the ground with sticks to tuck their tails into."

Finally, he understood the source of the story: The Mishimis travel the hills with loads of tea, and to take the weight off their backs, they lean on T-shaped sticks. The trails were pitted with the holes of these walking staffs. The two Chinese soldiers escorting Bailey refused to accept this explanation, pointing out that the three morose Mishimis were wearing jackets just long enough to conceal a three-inch tail.

The Mishimi people were cordial to Bailey. They told him that the Abors had murdered Noel Williamson and his party, which was a relief since the Mishimis were widely known to have murdered two French missionaries sixty years earlier. Still, Bailey was wary and became all the more so when he awoke one morning to see his Tibetan coolies slipping quietly across a rope bridge and hustling up the trail toward home. Now it was just Bailey and his faithful Putamdu.

The Mishimis wanted opium in exchange for replacement coolies, and Bailey was able to oblige them. He had bought two pounds of it in China just for this eventuality. Under way again, the small band proceeded along trails that Williamson had trod only five months earlier. Bailey's boots wore out, and he patched the soles with the hide of a takin—a sort of mountain musk ox—that he had shot for his collection. In time the boots failed completely and he had to resort to cutting up his canvas bathtub and strapping the pieces to his feet, like mukluks. He developed a fever, his leech bites festered, and, he confessed, he "was in a rather low state of health."

Finally he reached Sadiya—clothing in rags, unshaven, scuffling along in his sorry mukluks. The wife of a Captain Robinson invited him for tea. Luckily, Bailey noted, he still had in the bottom of one tin box a blue serge suit, clean shirt, collar, and handkerchief—"and to my delight, a pair of bedroom slippers that I had completely forgotten.

"Washed and shaved and thus perfectly attired except for the bedroom slippers, I went to call on Mrs. Robinson," Bailey writes, "and the way I demolished her delicious but flimsy cake must have astonished and dismayed her."

Bailey was in hot water when he returned to India—officially, anyway. He was reprimanded for having overstayed his leave and lost twenty days' pay. But privately he earned the congratulations of many in the Foreign Service, as well as medals from the Royal Geographical Society and the United Service Institution of India. He had covered a broad swath of uncharted and very strategic territory on his freelance journey, making maps and picking up all sorts of intelligence about the region and its tribes. This was critical information because the empire was about to strike back for the massacre of Noel Williamson. The Indian government had decided to punish the Abors by sending a force under the command of Sir Hamilton Bower, who even then was preparing to launch his operation.

Bower's avenging army was skilled in jungle warfare. Apart from seven hundred and twenty-five Gurkha regulars, he recruited some three thousand five hundred Naga coolies, who were the Abors' blood enemies. The fierce Nagas went naked except for loincloths, and each carried a long spear. Marching six abreast, they chanted a chilling war cry that sounded like "He-hah! He-hoh!" It could be heard far ahead and was "calculated to put the fear of God into all who heard it."

Bailey had been a spy before, and he would be one again during his illustrious career in Central Asia. For now, the foreign secretary, Sir Henry McMahon, knew an opportunity when he saw one; he arranged for Bailey to return to the front to do "some quietly useful work" as the punitive mission's intelligence officer. This was the first opportunity anyone had had in years to enter Tibet from Assam, McMahon realized, and Bailey was the ideal man for the job. By October 1912 Bailey was back in Sadiya, itching to trek into the gorge and find Kintup's waterfall.

He would need a surveyor, and found a perfect match for himself in Capt. Henry Morshead, a six-year veteran of the Survey of India who, Bailey could see, possessed "extraordinary powers of physical endurance" and great enthusiasm for the project. When the punitive mission began wrapping up, in the spring of 1913, he and Morshead began scrounging supplies for their trek into the gorge—coincidentally at about the same time that Frank Kingdon-Ward was collecting plants in neighboring China but entertaining visions of lost Tibetan waterfalls. It was Kindgon-Ward's great hope to put to rest all questions about the Falls of the Brahmaputra during his 1913 expedition. But partway through it, he learned in a letter from the RGS that Bailey and Morshead were intent on doing the same. Rather than being let down or miffed, Kingdon-Ward applauded their effort. "[Bailey] will have got to the falls by this time," he wrote in an interim report to the RGS about his own progress, "and he is not a man to fail."

. . .

IN DECIDING WHICH route to take into the central gorge, where the falls was reputed to be, Bailey and Morshead relied on the recollections of Tibetans from the village of Mipi, in the lower canyon. These were the leftovers from a larger contingent of refugees who had fled eastern Tibet in 1903, when the Chinese were overrunning them. Buddhist texts from the seventeenth century refer to the gorge as Beyul Pemakö, the "hidden land of the opening lotus," and prophesy that during times of strife it will serve as a sanctuary—an earthly paradise where giant fruits grow that can feed a whole family, and crops flourish without need for cultivation. Instead, the refugees found only a miserably inhospitable jungle and hostile neighbors. Most of the immigrants had abandoned Mipi to return to the plateau, perishing in droves on the homeward journey. About a hundred people had stayed behind, too sick or too elderly to travel, and their headman, Gyamtso, became Bailey's confidant and route advisor (with the help of the village's oracles).

The group—Bailey, Morshead, ten coolies from Mipi, and three jungle guides—set out in the middle of May, traveling north. Morshead worked tirelessly and seemed utterly fearless. "I believe he thought so little about danger that he didn't realize that there was such a thing as risk," wrote Bailey. "[H]e would stand there covered with leeches and with blood oozing out of his boots as oblivious as a small child whose face is smeared with jam. It worried me, because I felt that I had to be responsible for Morshead's tropical hygiene as well as my own." Some years later, on Mount Everest, Morshead's cavalier attitude about his health would cost him several fingers.

Advancing up the gorge, they came across a camp of "fleshless skeletons in rotting clothes"—the remains of the Tibetan immigrants on their fatal retreat. The track vanished into claustrophobic thickets of bamboo where the trees grew so close together that it was impossible for a man to squeeze between them. Hacking their way through in pouring rain, they trudged uphill to passes covered with waist-deep snow. Five of the coolies went temporarily snow-blind, and Bailey touched off an avalanche but arrested his fall with the handle of his butterfly net.

"I am often asked how Morshead and I *planned* our itinerary,"

Bailey would write about the trek years later, in *No Passport to Tibet.* "[I]n 1913 the idea never occurred to us that any expedition should be routed and highly organized. There was so much to discover that once we left Mipi, wherever we went and whatever we saw was important . . . We were happy in being opportunists . . . [but] if we had been granted a vision of all that lay ahead of us, we might well have flinched."

When they neared the country of the savage Pobas, local officials again refused them passage because of the danger of being murdered as Chinese collaborators. Instead, they detoured around the region, planning to hit the Tsangpo again higher up and march down the river looking for the waterfall. They reached Gyala on July 17 and saw a stream that fell over a cliff the villagers called Singche Cho Gye. This was surely the waterfall to which Kintup had referred, but it was just as surely not located on the Tsangpo. At Gyala, on a rare clear day, they were treated to a spectacular view of Gyala Peri's gleaming white 23,460-foot summit.

"In itself, it was one of the great mountains of the world," Bailey wrote, "but what made it so astonishing was that only thirteen miles away was the peak of Namche Barwa, 25,445 feet, and between them flows the Tsangpo over 14,000 feet below Gyala Peri and 16,000 feet below Namche Barwa." It did not occur to Bailey that a canyon so deep might set a world record. That "discovery" would be left for adventurers who would follow his footsteps eighty years later, thinking of themselves as pioneers.

Each day below Gyala, the going became more difficult. At one point, nearing the Pemaköchung monastery, Bailey found a path leading down to the river and saw a waterfall of about thirty feet, whose spray towered fifty feet above the riverbed. Morshead spotted a rainbow in it and named it Rainbow Falls. Yet by that point, short on food, exhausted, and feverish, they did not have high hopes for making much more progress. "We did not admit it to one another, but each of us knew in his heart that we should never get right through the gorges along the river bank," Bailey confided. "It was getting worse and worse . . . as far as the western world was concerned, we were exploring country of which nothing was known but much was speculated; one of the last remaining secret places of the earth, which might perhaps conceal a fall rivaling the Niagara or Victoria Falls in grandeur. The thought of what we might find in the next few days would anyway have kept me awake, even if it had not been for the pain and throbbing of the cuts in my knees."

But the discovery was not to be. Beyond the forlorn monastery, they were forced to claw through the rhododendron thickets above the river, where the plants' trunks were as thick as a man's leg. Their hands were raw and blistered from the constant chopping, and they were now down to several days' rations.

"Reluctantly we had to admit ourselves beaten," Bailey writes. Although he and a guide managed to go a few miles further into the canyon, he was in no shape to continue and had to turn around. Their journey was far from over, however. Remarkably, Bailey and Morshead surveyed the Tsangpo all the way back up to Tsetang, where Kintup and the Chinese lama had started their survey. Then the two bedraggled explorers turned south and crossed the Himalayas to India. After traveling more than sixteen hundred miles, mostly on foot, they boarded the Eastern Bengal State Railroad at Rangiya looking more like tramps than officers in the Indian government service. They reached Calcutta on November 17, 1913, and went straight to the Grand Hotel to celebrate with a hot bath and a meal.

When Bailey returned to London, he made a formal report to the RGS. "The falls reported to be 150 feet in height have been proved to be merely an exaggerated rapid of 30 feet," he told a well-attended meeting on June 22, 1914. Yet at the same time, he acknowledged that there remained an unexplored gap in the very heart of the gorge—in the very deepest, darkest section, where the river disappeared as if it were pouring down a drain to the center of the earth. The ten-mile-long gap was lined on one side by an almost sheer cliff rising thousands of feet and on the other by a series of knife-edged ridges that sliced down from the heights of Namche Barwa and plunged into the Tsangpo's boiling white water. Trying to work down into the gap from upstream or to penetrate it from below was simply more than Bailey could contemplate, and he was made of tough stuff. To traverse those ridges and follow the river into the inner gorge would have been like scaling the pleats of some giant accordion, then rappelling down the other side, only to begin again.

In China, mucking about in the Mekong-Salween divide, Kingdon-Ward learned in a letter from the RGS of Bailey's uncertain findings on the Tsangpo. By leaving an unexplored gap of ten miles in the Tsangpo Gorge, Bailey had left the door slightly ajar to the plant hunter to make a name for himself as the discoverer of the Falls of the Brahmaputra. Kingdon-Ward wrote back to the RGS and vowed to one day "solve some of the Indo-China puzzles" himself, even if it meant dying in the attempt. A decade would pass—ten years that began with a world war and ended with his marriage to a pretty blond socialite twelve years younger than he—before he was able to make good his promise to carry on the search for the mythical waterfall.

. . .

IN THE YEARS during and immediately after the Great War, Kingdon-Ward had shifted around widely. He saw noncombat duty with the 116th Mahrattas in Mesopotamia (now Iraq), spent several years in Burma botanizing, then in 1920 returned to England for home leave. At thirty-five years old, he was already going gray, due partly to genetics but also to the stresses of prolonged work in the Himalayas. Terrible fevers had flattened him for weeks at a time, and he was forever turning up at some godforsaken outpost of the empire such as Fort Hpimaw on the Burma-Yunnan border, his boots flapping, his beard long and matted, his green eyes looking haggard. Plant collecting and soldiering had forged him into a lithe, wiry, five-foot-eight welterweight. His face was prematurely lined but ruggedly handsome, and he had an eye for the ladies.

For all his stoicism in the field, Kingdon-Ward was quite the romancer while on furlough. He seemed to be perpetually falling in love and proposing, only to be disappointed. On the voyage back to England in 1920, he was smitten with a beauty named Alice and composed an odd lyric about her:

> *Alice in wonderland,*
> *Alice through the looking glass,*
> *Alice for short*
> *Alice,*
> *Alice where art thou, (hiding?)*
> *Alice blue gown*

When he reached England, he would have pursued marrying Alice had not his letters to her been intercepted by a meddlesome relative. Ultimately, Alice's parents forbade their daughter from carrying on with a vagabond botanist who barely eked out a livelihood hunting for plants in China. Soon afterward a resilient Kingdon-Ward was carrying a torch for another woman and decided to propose to her. She not only turned him down but eloped with another suitor (the *second* time that had happened to Kingdon-Ward). Then he fell for a golden-haired goddess named Florinda Norman-Thompson. She, too, turned him down but after seeing him off to China in 1921 reconsidered his offer.

Florinda was twenty-three when the two met. Taller than Kingdon-Ward, she was fine-boned, energetic, and charming. She usually wore her hair up, and she dressed in long skirts and big hats—not particularly à la mode for the Roaring Twenties, but still alluring. Although she had declined Kingdon-Ward's hand in marriage, she thought him "extraordinarily brave" and longed for his company while he was away. So, on the first day of 1922, after taking a long early-morning walk, she sat down to write Kingdon-Ward, who was then in Asia. "My Dearest," she began, "In case you did not get last week's letter, I am making an amplification of it. My Dear, I wrote to ask if you would marry me when you came home."

It's miraculous that any letters or cables could reach someone working in the wilderness at the ends of the earth. But to the British, the reliability of the imperial mails was a point of national pride. No destination was too remote, from the bush outposts of Rhodesia (where mail was borne by runners in khaki shorts and fezzes) or the jungles of Burma to the hill stations perched on the verge of the Indian Himalayas. The British historian James Morris observed that regular mail service to the colonies "strongly appealed to the British sense of far-flung order" if not their romanticism. Even before the turn of the century, a letter to India took but seventeen days to travel from London to Calcutta by rail and steamer.

Florinda had mixed luck with the mails. Her first proposal of marriage seems to have gone astray, even though it was sent via the celebrated travel firm of Thomas Cook & Son, which had worldwide offices and was so adept at logistics and communication that in 1884 the British government hired it to organize an expedition up the Nile to rescue Maj. Gen. Charles Gordon, the head of the British government in war-torn Sudan, from which Britain was withdrawing. The second missive reiterating her proposal she dispatched to a boyhood friend of Kingdon-Ward's, Kenneth Ward, who was then teaching mathematics at Rangoon University. That letter found the plant hunter preparing to embark on an expedition that would start in Yunnan province and finish in India. Kingdon-Ward had hoped to make this arduous traverse in 1913 but had been foiled by political unrest in the region. This time it was fever, probably malaria, that felled him in the mountainous jungles of northern Burma not long after he started. Unable to take any food except a few raw eggs, Kingdon-Ward grew so weak that his porters had to carry him back to Fort Hertz on a bamboo stretcher. He was on the verge of death when he was admitted to the small field hospital there and was still tremendously debilitated when he returned to England.

Florinda nursed him back to a reasonable state of health, and the couple was married in a civil ceremony in April 1923. Yet even as they were settling into domestic bliss, Kingdon-Ward was already planning his return to Tibet, this time to find the lost waterfall—"to go right through the gorge and tear this last secret from its heart," as he put it. So soon after slipping the ring on Florinda's finger did he immerse himself in the logistics of the expedition that it seems doubtful that the mission (or any other that he would plan in the years to come) was ever far from his mind. In any case, Mrs. Kingdon-Ward found herself at the docks again in February 1924, wishing her new husband God-speed and a safe return. They had been married less than a year.

. . .

THE VOYAGE OUT to India took about a month. With Kingdon-Ward was Lord Cawdor, a game twenty-four-year-old Scot-tish earl who had attended Cambridge. The fifth earl of Cawdor—John, or Jack to his friends—was athletic, keen for natural history, and gung ho for adventure, and Kingdon-Ward had recruited him for his brains, eagerness, and money. The young peer had agreed to finance part of the expedition and also to be responsible for the dreaded chore of surveying. He also willingly took on the task of studying the local tribes in the gorge while Kingdon-Ward busied himself with finding and collecting plants and seeds. In the end, Cawdor contributed the final two chapters of Kingdon-Ward's *The Riddle of the Tsangpo Gorges*, about the tribes: the Monpas, descendants of Bhutanese refugees who resettled in the region in the early nineteenth century; the Lopas, a local term loosely meaning "aborigines" (Kingdon-Ward describes them as short and "simian"-looking); and the fierce and jungly Abors, who had murdered Williamson and his men.

The pair landed in Calcutta just as a crushing heat wave settled over the Gangetic Plain. With daytime temperatures hovering around ninety degrees in the shade, and little respite after sundown, they rushed to get out of "the city of dreadful night" as soon as possible. On March 9, after four unbearable days, they boarded the night train for Darjeeling, the hill station three hundred and fifty miles to the north and seven thousand feet higher, where the British administration had its summer capital. At six o'clock the next morning, while switching to the toylike narrow-gauge train that to this day makes the wheezing six-hour, eighty-mile-long climb to the city, they caught their first glimpse of the Himalayas, hazy in the distance.

Darjeeling was the traditional staging area for expeditions to Tibet. Younghusband had launched his assault on Lhasa from there in 1904, and the ill-fated 1922 and 1924 British expeditions to Mount Everest—whose numbers included George Leigh-Mallory and Andrew Irvine—also used the so-called queen of hill stations as a staging area. It's a lovely spot: cool, misty, and surrounded by endless acres of tea plantations (a landscape that Kingdon-Ward deemed "picturesque but monotonous"), and strategically located near the main pass leading into Tibet, the Jelap La (*la* means "pass" in Tibetan) in nearby Sikkim.

The expedition stores had been held up in customs in Calcutta, so Kingdon-Ward and Cawdor had a few days to linger in Darjeeling. They may have taken pleasant walks on the Mall or drinks at the Rockville Hotel, but Kingdon-Ward's account of the sojourn is all business—checking on the delayed equipment, changing money for the expedition into silver rupees, and hiring muleteers, among them an eager-to-please fellow that Kingdon-Ward nicknamed Sunny Jim, whom he describes as a "cheerful idiot." Gen. Charles Bruce, the leader of the 1924 Everest expedition, met Kingdon-Ward and Cawdor in Darjeeling and helped them find pack animals for the first leg of their journey and hire the camp staff.

Kingdon-Ward could be wickedly derisive of natives. He once observed gratuitously that two Tibetan boys he had hired as collecting assistants "showed symptoms of intelligence." One senses, however, that his barbs grew out of a general frustration at not being able to accomplish everything he set out to do. Cawdor, on the other hand, displayed the sort of racist superiority that infected the Raj. Waiting for the expedition gear to arrive at the railhead village of Kalimpong, near Darjeeling, he was disturbed in his sleep by a raucous religious festival. "The local coons made a beastly wailing noise and beat drums far into the night," he grumbled in his journal.

In Kalimpong, the pair did some eleventh-hour shopping for spices and other foodstuffs, but Kingdon-Ward knew better than to

stock up for the full year that they would be gone. Finding transportation via mule or yak couldn't be guaranteed in the remote reaches
of Tibet, but in any case traveling heavy was not Kingdon-Ward's
style. "The essence of traveling rapidly in Asia is undoubtedly to travel
light," he observed in a 1936 lecture delivered at the Royal Geographical Society. "For the most part, my servants and I lived on the
country. It is always possible to get butter and milk in Tibet, and the
older I get the more easy I find it to live on milk. In fact, in my fifti-
eth year, I lived chiefly on milk just as I did in my first year."

A hardworking stoic, he placed no premium on fine dining in
the field and rarely lingered over meals before turning back to botanical work. Still, by his usual standards, this expedition was lavishly
stocked. Before leaving London, he had stopped in at Fortnum &
Mason and ordered six cases of provisions—a variety of jams, tinned
butter, Quaker oats, mincemeat, Heinz baked beans, dehydrated soup,
Yorkshire relish, tinned pâté de foie gras, a smoked ham, bacon, Mexican chocolate bars, coffee, tea, and cocoa. Each case weighed sixty
pounds, the maximum load a porter could reasonably carry.

Because the provisions and equipment were slow to arrive from
Calcutta, their host in Kalimpong, the director of the Scottish mission, offered to forward the stuff to Phari or Gyantse in Tibet, two
trade posts where Cawdor and Kingdon-Ward would be stopping.
Kingdon-Ward was itching to cross into Sikkim. The country's political officer—conveniently enough—was now Eric Bailey, a veteran of
two expeditions to the Tsangpo Gorge. Bailey promised to be an invaluable source about routes in the gorge and would be full of stories
about his 1913 search for the lost waterfall. More important, though,
he was holding Kingdon-Ward's and Cawdor's Tibetan passports.
Without the documents, the two would go nowhere.

Permission to enter Tibet was easier to obtain than it had been
ten years earlier, but entry was by no means guaranteed, in part because of what Kingdon-Ward refers to as the "antics of certain English
travelers." While he does not elaborate in *The Riddle of the Tsangpo*

Gorges, the "travelers" were the members of the 1921 Mount Everest reconnaissance team, whose numbers included a geologist. Shortly after the team had finished its work and left Tibet, in September 1921, Tibet's prime minister had lodged a diplomatic complaint: Local officials had reported to him that members of the team had desecrated the sacred hills around Everest by digging turquoise and rubies and carrying the stones away. To the Tibetans, Everest is Chomolungma, Goddess Mother of the World. The lands around the massif are protected by malevolent deities, and, the minister explained, it was now feared that they would seek revenge by causing epidemics to spread among the local people and livestock. The prime minister suggested that future expeditions to Tibet might be barred.

Had it not been for Bailey's intervention, along with that of Sir Charles Bell, a former political officer in Sikkim and old Tibet hand himself, Everest might have remained off-limits to the British until a later date. In that event, the lives of seven Sherpas lost during the 1922 expedition, as well as those of Mallory and Irvine in 1924, would have been spared. As it was, Bailey appealed directly to the thirteenth Dalai Lama, assuring him that any reports of gemstone mining were false and that future teams would observe all Tibetan customs. Bailey and Bell were among the few political officers in the Raj who could speak fluent Tibetan, and both were on especially good terms with the godking. They had helped orchestrate his narrow escape from Lhasa in 1910, when two thousand Chinese troops marched into the city to reassert Chinese control over Tibet. Bailey had come up with the idea of disguising His Holiness as a *dak wallah,* a postal runner. The Dalai Lama—carrying the official mailbag that Bailey had procured for him—slipped into India and spent the next two years in Darjeeling as the guest of the British before the situation at home cooled down enough for him to return.

Bailey and his wife were stationed in Gangtok, Sikkim's capital. Kingdon-Ward and Cawdor spent two "delightful" days with them, but Kingdon-Ward is otherwise unrevealing about the meeting. In *The*

Riddle of the Tsangpo Gorges, he offers up some boilerplate flattery about Bailey being a "distinguished Tibetan explorer himself" but sheds no light on Bailey's heroic 1913 expedition to the gorge with Morshead, who coincidentally went on to join the 1921 Everest reconnaissance team. In 1922, climbing with Mallory on the first attempt at Everest's upper slopes, Morshead lost three fingers to frostbite.

Kingdon-Ward is hardly more illuminating about Cawdor. During their brief sojourn in Sikkim, the great plant hunter was much more interested in observing the country's "wonderland" of alpine forests—strewn with white orchids, scarlet rhododendrons, and mauve primroses—than he was in nattering with his young protégé. Cawdor was already having second thoughts about traveling with a botanist as focused and dry as Kingdon-Ward.

Riding ponies, the two crossed the pass into Tibet and made good time to Gyantse, located about one hundred and fifty miles west of Lhasa. Kingdon-Ward was happy to be back in Tibet, even to smell the familiar odor of the Tibetans, who never bathed and smelled of campfire smoke and rancid yak butter. "Raw and monotonous as the landscape is," he wrote, "these wide, open empty spaces with the thin keen air rushing over them, and the crude generous colouring of earth and sky, beckon man on and on, to investigate and explore and enjoy."

At Gyantse, while Kingdon-Ward was nursing an ulcerated tongue, Cawdor boisterously fell in with the little community of British and Indian soldiers and administrators. The Europeans numbered six, including a trade agent, medical officer, commander of the guard, and principal of the school for Tibetans. Cawdor played soccer with them (on the Tibetan team, facing the Sikhs), and finally encouraged Kingdon-Ward to stand for a couple of matches of tennis and four chukkas of polo. In spite of a painful tongue and his seriousness of purpose, Kingdon-Ward was a good sport. He had a ripping good time at polo, his first taste of that sport. "Great fun," he wrote. "First pony wouldn't gallop, second wouldn't go near the ball." He also made time to botanize around the town.

After a week, their equipment and food stores caught up with them. They loaded everything on yaks, mules, oxen, and ponies, and on April 11, 1924, set out on the long journey to the gorge. Bailey had given them directions, but in any event Kingdon-Ward knew where he was going from his earlier expeditions to Yunnan and Burma. Still, once they had passed Yamdrok Lake and left the northerly road to Lhasa, as Kingdon-Ward notes, they quite literally rode "off the map."

. . .

IN A STRICT sense, Kingdon-Ward and Cawdor were not entering entirely uncharted territory when they left Yamdrok Lake and rode into the great wastes of eastern Tibet. Although the region was certainly not well known in 1924, it had been partially mapped by the pundits and Bailey and Morshead, and written about by various clerics, military men, civilian explorers, and the odd plant collector or two, including himself. But theirs was a small fraternity: In the six centuries preceding the British invasion of Lhasa in 1904, fewer than two hundred Europeans—invited guests and gate-crashers alike—had managed to penetrate Tibet's diplomatic isolation and return home to write about their travels.

Their maps and written accounts gave shape first to the country's physical and cultural geography. But there were stories, too, that conjured up a rich supernatural landscape in Tibet and the relationship to it enjoyed by Tibetan Buddhists. By the time Kingdon-Ward and Cawdor began their journey, Tibet was perceived not just as a land of high mountains and vast open spaces, as it had been, but now also as a realm of magic and mystery. Here were lamas capable of levitation, flying mountains and magic lakes, reincarnated deities whose excrement was packed into sacramental pills, poison cults, oracles who selected the nation's maximum leaders by divination, and cave-dwelling hermits who endured subzero temperatures purely through the power of meditation. Tibet was imagined to be a kind of Buddhist Arcadia, an island of enlightenment hovering in the sky, where lamas retained esoteric knowledge lost to the modern world. That it was cut off by stupendous mountains and vigilant border guards simply fed the fantasy.

The Australian cultural historian Peter Bishop has called Tibet an "imaginable complexity," arguing that it has been embroidered out of travelers' tales over the centuries and transformed into a sacred place. "Travel writing is not concerned only with the discovery of places but also with their creation," Bishop writes in *The Myth of Shangri-La*. In devouring the literature on Tibet—and his bibliography is massive, encompassing references on everything from Jungian dream analysis to Western fantasy making—Bishop concludes that the country began almost as "a mere rumor in the mid-eighteenth century, but a hundred years later had evolved into one of the last great sacred places of Victorian Romanticism. Its significance still reverberates strongly through European fantasies to this day."

Consider the contribution to this myth by Alexandra David-Neel, the French orientalist, explorer, and author who in 1923 became the first European woman to reach Lhasa. Her difficult four-month journey took place while Kingdon-Ward and Cawdor were making final preparations in England for their Tsangpo expedition, and her book about the trip, *My Journey to Lhasa*, came out in 1927, the year after *The Riddle of the Tsangpo Gorges*. A sensation in its day and now a cult classic, *My Journey to Lhasa* is a window onto Western perceptions of Tibet during the Jazz Age, when all things occult were in vogue, from Ouija boards to Theosophy. It brims with stories about paranormal phenomena and esoteric meditative practices, one of which—called *thumo reskiang,* or the art of increasing one's body temperature—kept her alive one bitter night en route to Lhasa. ("I saw flames arising around me," she writes. "They enveloped me, curling their tongues above my head. I felt deliciously comfortable.")

David-Neel was a respected scholar of Tibetan Buddhism. She had met the Dalai Lama in Darjeeling during his 1910–1912 exile and so impressed him with her knowledge of Sanskrit that he urged her to further her studies. So in 1914, while the First World War was raging at home, she crossed illegally into Tibet from India and spent a year at a monastery several miles inside the frontier. In 1916, after living with a hermit-tutor in a cave in Sikkim, she crossed the border again, this time visiting Shigatse, the seat of the Panchen Lama, who is considered by some Tibetan religious leaders to be the spiritual superior of the Dalai Lama. Because David-Neel had violated both the British administration's ban on crossing into Tibet and Tibet's own ban on travel, Sir Charles Bell himself ordered her thrown out of Sikkim and fined her. That only stiffened her resolve to reach Lhasa and meet the Dalai Lama, which she ultimately succeeded in doing—by traveling as a beggar, dressed in rags and carrying a revolver under her robes. As a rogue Frenchwoman, she did not have the consent of the British or the Tibetans that Kingdon-Ward and Cawdor enjoyed on their officially sanctioned expedition. This galled her no end.

Several years after the appearance of *My Journey to Lhasa,* David-Neel published *With Mystics and Magicians in Tibet.* In it, she recounts a story that embodies the enduring fantasy that all things might be possible in Tibet. The tale concerns an encounter with one of Tibet's legendary wind runners, or *lung-gom-pa,* who appeared one day while she and her servants were crossing northern Tibet:

"Towards the end of the afternoon . . . I noticed, far away in front of us, a moving black spot which my field-glasses showed to be a man [proceeding] at an unusual gait and, especially, with an extraordinary swiftness," she begins. A servant takes a closer look through her binoculars and pronounces the figure to be a lama *lung-gom-pa.* He warns David-Neel not to break the lama's trance, for if suddenly roused, the man might perish. When the runner approaches, David-Neel could see

> his perfectly calm impassive face and wide-open eyes with their gaze fixed on some invisible far-distant object situated somewhere high up in space. The man did not run. He seemed to lift himself from the ground, proceeding by leaps. It looked as if he had been endowed with the elasticity of a ball and rebounded each time his feet touched the ground. . . . His right hand held a *phurba* [magic dagger]. His right arm moved slightly

at each step as if leaning on a stick, just as though the *phurba,* whose pointed extremity was far above the ground, had touched it and were actually a support.

After the lama passes by, they pursue him for about two miles, but he vaults up a steep slope and disappears into the mountains. "Riders could not follow that way, and our observations came to an end," she writes. "We could only turn back and continue our journey."

On the strength of such enchanting tales, David-Neel became, according to sinologist and journalist Orville Schell, "the guru of choice for those Westerners with a yearning to believe in an idealized Eastern never-never land." Kingdon-Ward was not much interested in all this mumbo jumbo. He was seeking flowering plants first and a waterfall second. The mythology of Tibet and in particular that of the gorge as a sacred hidden land, or *beyul,* would play into his story, but not to any great extent. It would take another generation of more spiritually minded explorers to actually go looking for the entrance to the never-never land in the Tsangpo Gorge, which according to some accounts lay within the ten-mile gap that had defeated Bailey and which Kingdon-Ward and Cawdor were about to face. Ironically, the object of their search in the gap, the elusive waterfall, would play a central role in the latter-day hunt for the earthly paradise that Tibetans know as Beyul Pemakö.

On their expedition, Kingdon-Ward and Cawdor were driven by questions about the physical geography of the gorge, not its spiritual landscape. As the pair rode east toward the gorge, they were filled with hope that they would finally lay to rest all questions about the lost waterfall.

"We approached the matter with open minds and were prepared for almost anything," Kingdon-Ward wrote, "except the possibility of failure."

. . .

CAWDOR AND KINGDON-WARD were not a great match as traveling companions, and not long after leaving the small comforts and companionship of Gyantse, the young lord had grown prickly. Four days into the trip, in the midst of an awful dust storm, a piece of Cawdor's pony's tack had broken. Kingdon-Ward, perhaps being phlegmatic or maybe just lost in thought, had not stopped to offer a hand, and Cawdor lit into him, cursing "quite unreasonably," he lamented to himself later that evening in his journal.

Although only a brief row, it revealed a tension between the two men. They "made it up" right away, Cawdor notes, "and felt the atmosphere lift immediately," but it would soon darken again.

"There's not much companionship to be got out of such a chap," Cawdor recorded in his journal some months later. "In my whole life, I've never seen such an incredibly slow mover . . . [and] if I ever travel again, I'll make damned sure it's not with a botanist. They are always stopping to gape at weeds.

"Evidently," he concluded, "God never intended him to be a companion to anyone."

That was an impression others took away as well, not least Ronald Kaulback, who joined Kingdon-Ward as surveyor on a 1933 collecting trip to the hill country of Assam just below the gorge. Kaulback, who was twenty-three, recalls feeling slightly unnerved by Kingdon-Ward when the two first met in London, and as their train clattered east from Calcutta toward Assam, he felt that Kingdon-Ward was studying him. The stoniness rarely cracked, not even after the two reached their base camp in the lush hills of Assam. As Kaulback told Charles Lyte, Kingdon-Ward's biographer, "He was, to start with at any rate, until I got to know him, a very, very difficult man to travel with, simply because he could so easily fall into total silence, which would last for two or three days. Not a damn thing. He might say, 'Good Morning,' [but] otherwise he would just march along, and at the end of the day sit down and have a meal, but nothing, not a word."

In time, Kaulback stopped worrying about Kingdon-Ward's silences. They were stress-related, he decided, the product of the intense strain Kingdon-Ward put himself under while working in the field. "He always felt he could have done better, and should have done better," Kaulback said. "He was never satisfied." Progress reports that Kingdon-Ward regularly sent back to the RGS display a trace of this anxiousness, perhaps even a tinge of insecurity. His letters are relentlessly upbeat, except when he is being hard on himself.

Nevertheless, Kaulback never made an issue of the silences. Kingdon-Ward was the classic loner, Kaulback decided, and one tough, self-sufficient loner at that. But he was not always dour. After a few days of moodiness, he would "snap out of it and be great fun," Kaulback noted. Once, while celebrating Easter at a boozy dinner with a provincial official, Kingdon-Ward broke out his ukulele and tore through a medley of minstrel tunes while Kaulback danced the Black Bottom and the Charleston. They were an immense hit with the villagers.

"It was one of the only times I saw him laugh," Kaulback recalled. "He was laughing away like mad at a table piled with that godawful Chinese spirit, and twanging away at this evilly played ukulele."

Kingdon-Ward never showed this side of himself to Cawdor. The younger man grew homesick and physically ill, and he had to rely on Kingdon-Ward to communicate with the camp staff, since he spoke no Hindustani. The food was not to Cawdor's liking, either, in spite of Kingdon-Ward's efforts at Fortnum & Mason. He grumbled in his journal about the toughness of a locally procured chicken. "It was such hard work to eat that one was hungrier at the end than at the start," Cawdor wrote. "By God I could do justice to a damned slice of Figgy Duff [a baked desert] tonight."

Beyond Yamdrok Lake, they traveled through a valley of sparkling streams and April's green pastures, where "birds sang in groves of budding trees and whitewashed houses loomed through a pink mist of almond blossom," Kingdon-Ward rhapsodized. "If this is the real Tibet, what a maligned country it is! Could anything be more charming and peaceful, more full of spring grace and freshness?"

But the trees soon vanished as they pushed east, leaving a landscape of bare brown hills. Their route intersected the Tsangpo River at Tsetang, roughly fifty miles southwest of Lhasa. Wet snow fell there, leaving the streets ankle-deep in slush and mud. The river was "mooning sluggishly along between harsh barren mountains," the wind was roaring, and the air was thick with blowing sand from the dunes piled up alongside the river. Though wide and sluggish, the river carried an enormous volume of water that acted like a great mill, grinding together granite boulders in the riverbed and producing an "inexhaustible supply of sand." Several villages on the river below Tsetang had been abandoned after blowing sand smothered their croplands.

By this time, Kingdon-Ward and Cawdor had fallen into their routines. Cawdor was surveyor, but he had also become, as he put it, "head transport wallah, Quartermaster, Good Samaritan and Pioneer Sergeant." In other words, he did all the scut work that Kingdon-Ward couldn't be bothered with. The great plant hunter was there to look for plants. He had commissions to fulfill, including one as a favor for the Dalai Lama, who had a green thumb and wanted Kingdon-Ward to bring him seeds for the gardens around his house in Lhasa. "KW," as Cawdor referred to him in journal entries, was also collecting for the British Natural History Museum and the Royal Botanic Gardens at Kew, a massive job that required him to put up specimens of just about every plant along their route, whether or not it had any ornamental value for gardeners back home.

Downstream from Tsetang, earthquakes had destroyed trails along the south or right side of the Tsangpo, so they ferried across to the north bank in a flotilla of five coracles, little circular boats with willow frames and yak-leather hulls. From there, they walked over the breathtaking Lung La in a driving snowstorm, postholing into knee-deep snow at the sixteen-thousand-foot summit of the pass. Their transport fell far behind, and by nightfall, the two were resigned to spending a long night out. Just then, they heard a shout and saw a torch through the swirling snow: the monastery of Chokorchye. Hot buttered tea and a night's sleep next to a charcoal fire revived them.

The caravan crept forward at an exasperating pace—as slow as the sluggish Tsangpo, Kingdon-Ward complained. According to local custom, they had to stop and change pack animals in every village.

Their retinue took on a dozen women and girls to carry the bundles that could not be piled on the "kicking ponies and sleepy oxen." The women were short and sturdy, and as Kingdon-Ward remarked, "their habit of smearing black varnish over their faces does nothing either to conceal a latent comeliness or to intensify their ugliness."

At the village of Trungsasho, they were introduced to the Dalai Lama's sister, who was taking her ponies to water. "She was just a simple country wench, with a rather pronounced goiter, living on in the old village, completely unaffected by the knowledge that her brother was the ruler of all Tibet, and venerated as a god by millions outside the country," Kingdon-Ward wrote. State oracles had sought the boy out and proclaimed him to be the reincarnation of the previous Dalai Lama after he recognized certain holy objects.

Unlike the hostile natives of the lower Tsangpo, villagers in this region were welcoming. They brought gifts of milk, butter, and eggs, sticking out their tongues in greeting to show that they were not demons. (In the pre-Buddhist Bon tradition, all demons were said to possess black tongues.) Living on the verge of Pemakö, the locals were well aware of the spiritual significance of Kingdon-Ward and Cawdor's destination. In both Buddhist and Bon mythology, the gorge and mountains guarding it are gateways to a promised land beyond time and space, where one might break free from the endless cycle of death and reincarnation. According to scripture, only those with pure intentions and sufficient merit can enter the hidden land; all others will find only empty mountains, blinding storms, landslides, floods, and perhaps even death.

It was an unusually bleak spring—wet and very windy, with many passes to the south still closed by snow. The wind howled all day, kicking up a maze of dust devils that danced across the riverside dunes and gradually flowed together into what Kingdon-Ward described as a "dense fog" of sand. "Fierce draughts spun the sand aloft, rasping the cliffs," he wrote, "and under the pewter-coloured skies, the leaden water, dully gleaming, nosing its way amongst the wet dunes and snow-clad mountains, looked very forlorn."

Cawdor came down with fever, a dog bit one of the staff, and the ponies bolted repeatedly, strewing stoved-in packing cases and ripped-up valises along the trail. "[A]ltogether, we were in a bad way," Kingdon-Ward confessed.

Everyone needed a rest, he decided. He called a halt at the fortress of Tsela Dzong, where he and Cawdor settled into a comfortable house, much relieved by the thought of not having to repack their kit for the next two weeks. For Kingdon-Ward also came the excitement of planning his first botanical reconnaissance of the expedition. The fort overlooked the confluence of the clear-running Gyamda River and the muddy Tsangpo, and the surrounding hills were splashed with rhododendrons smothered in blooms of lemon yellow, salmon pink, mahogany, and bright purple. Once the wind died in the evening, you could stand on the ramparts of the fort and see the distant, snowbound summit of Namche Barwa towering above the deepest part of the gorge.

In fact, they stayed in this idyllic spot for three weeks before moving a couple of days east to the village of Tumbatse, which Bailey had recommended using as a base of operations. Situated up in the fir forests at about twelve thousand feet, Tumbatse was a smart choice: close to the gorge, with a fine climate and picturesque scenery, and with masses of flowering plants to collect locally. It was June when they arrived, and the alpine meadows were bursting with spring flowers. Snow-white clematis hung in frozen cascades from the treetops, rhododendrons bloomed profusely in the boggy clearings, and along the rushing brooks an especially beautiful poppy was just opening its sky-blue flowers. This was the soon-to-be-celebrated *Meconopsis baileyi*, named after Eric Bailey.

Bailey had collected one specimen of the poppy during his and Morshead's 1913 expedition. They were riding out from the fort where Kintup had been enslaved, hoping to find the fabled waterfall, when they passed through a series of grassy meadows below the fifteen-thousand-foot Nyima La north of the Tsangpo's upper gorge. It was July 10, and Bailey made this entry in his journal: "Among the flowers were blue poppies I had not seen before." He'd been riding on a hard, uncomfortable Tibetan saddle for sixteen and a half hours that day before sitting down to write in his journal. Forty-four years later, he ribbed himself about the glancing reference to the plant that made him famous: "What a pedestrian way to record one's assignation with the immortality of a seedman's catalogue!" he wrote in *No Passport to Tibet*. "If I had been a plant hunter, I might have been struck by the possibility of growing these blue poppies elsewhere. But I could have done no more than I did, because I saw them in the glory of the flowering season and there was no means of gathering seed."

On this trip Kingdon-Ward was on the lookout for *M. baileyi*. He first spotted it blooming under some bushes near Tumbatse and mistook it for a bird with exotic plumage. "This fine plant grows in clumps, half a dozen leafy stems rising from the perennial rootstock to a height of 4 feet," he wrote. "The flowers flutter out from amongst the sea-green leaves like blue-and-gold butterflies; each is borne singly on a pedicle, the plant carrying half a dozen nodding, incredibly blue four-petalled flowers, with a wad of golden anthers in the center."

Kingdon-Ward recognized immediately that *M. baileyi* would be a winner back home. "Never have I seen a blue poppy which held out such high hopes of being hardy, and of easy cultivation in Britain," he predicted. Most of the seeds that he later collected and sent back to Britain survived the trip, and produced fabulous blooms in fifty different test gardens around England and Scotland. The flower became a sensation, earning awards from horticulture societies across Europe. Seedlings of Bailey's blue poppy sold for five dollars apiece at the 1927 Chelsea Garden Show.

Kingdon-Ward and Cawdor set up a temporary base at the Temo monastery, a half day's ride from Tumbatse and not far from the Nyima La into the Tsangpo drainage. The blockish, imposing *gompa* stood on a low hill surrounded by emerald pastures, and its guest house had a well-tended garden shaded by willow trees. Striding out in the morning for a day in the hills, "with larks singing overhead and butterflies playing underfoot," Kingdon-Ward was "fresh and eager" to see what new plants he could find. "After the long journey by sea and land," he wrote, "it is immensely refreshing to settle down to a serious job."

After several days of botanizing above the monastery, Kingdon-Ward and Cawdor moved back to Tumbatse and rented two rooms in a peasant family's house, a shingled, two-story structure with the living quarters one flight up from the ground-level stables. Big barnyard dogs snarled at the men, and the cocks crowed incessantly. But the roof did not leak, and while their rooms were dark and drafty, Kingdon-Ward considered their circumstances "pretty comfortable." For the next five months, they would spend about a week each month at this base, sorting and preserving specimens and drying themselves out as well. The rest of the time, they would be slogging around in the gorge.

Their first serious collecting expedition, they decided, would be to the Doshong La, a well-traveled pass at the head of the Tsangpo Gorge. The Doshong La was and still is a key trading route between the Tibetan Plateau and the hill country at the bottom of the gorge. It links the village of Pe at the mouth of the canyon to the settlements scattered along the lower Tsangpo, where the river tumbles through the jungle, heading for the plains of Assam. British surveyors had walked across the pass in 1913 but made no notes about the flora. For Kingdon-Ward, this was virgin collecting territory.

He and Cawdor pulled out of Tumbatse on June 20 with several porters and crossed into the Tsangpo drainage. It was a fine day, and as they clambered down the trail from the heights they could see straight across the top of the abyss swallowing the Tsangpo to the snowy mountains on the horizon. Cawdor spotted a new species of dwarf poppy with sky-blue flowers and a heady fragrance. Kingdon-Ward named it *M. cawdoriana* and entered it in his field notes as K.W. 5751.

The ferry across the Tsangpo to Pe consisted of two dugout canoes supporting a deck big enough for three ponies. After spending the night in Pe, Kingdon-Ward, Cawdor, and their coolies trudged up the boggy trail to the top of the Doshong La in a perpetual drizzle. Topping out at a relatively low thirteen thousand five hundred feet, the pass forms a dip in the Himalayas between Namche Barwa and peaks to the southwest, and is constantly battered by storms shrieking up from Assam. (Kingdon-Ward referred to the weather on the pass as "rain-wind.") From the top, on a rare clear day, you can look down on the Tsangpo flowing north from Pe and pouring into the gorge, then turn around and see the river, only thirty miles away, heading south through the jungle as the Dihang. What's not visible is the river's steepest, narrowest section, where it carves through the Himalayas and makes a big loop whose apex is the Great Bend. Somewhere in that "knee-bend" Kingdon-Ward and Cawdor hoped to find the waterfall that had eluded Bailey and Morshead.

The Doshong La was a fairyland of rhododendrons and prim-roses. One day Kingdon-Ward spotted three new species of rhodo-dendrons without moving from camp. At upper elevations "a turmoil" of dwarf rhododendrons grew amid the sloppy snow. "There was nothing but rhododendron in fact," Kingdon-Ward wrote, exulting about the "sulphur seas of Yellow Peril (K.W. 5853), lakes of pink 'Lacteum' (K.W. 5863) and a vast confusion of 'Anthopogons' of all sizes and colours." One species consisted of a mat of miniscule red flowers that hugged the rocks and spread out like "tongues of fire." Kingdon-Ward dubbed the plant "Scarlet Runner." No part of it grew to a height of more than two inches, indicating the severity of the wind and cold.

Clouds poured over the top of the pass from the Assam side. From time to time they parted to reveal the snowy valleys below in Pemakö. Peering down into the mists, Kingdon-Ward could see that they were standing on top of "a giant stairway of smooth rock, whose steps, ice-carved, ledge by ledge, were filled with dwarf rhododendron in astonishing variety." He and Cawdor returned on another day with two local guides and started down the staircase. It had been sunny coming up the Doshong La from their camp, but that was only because the howling wind was keeping a lid on the dirty weather trying to rise out of Pemakö. The four dropped into the sea of heaving black clouds and made their way downhill, traversing glaciers that ended in sheer cliffs and wading through thickets of flowering rhododendrons.

Streams of meltwater spilled down from the heights, cascading through these colorful thickets.

At the bottom, a wide amphitheater was piled with snow fifty feet deep—avalanches, Kingdon-Ward explained, that had been "vomited into the valley" from above. They went about five miles, marking the location of plants whose seed they would return to collect in late October. Where the snow stopped and forest began, they ran into an immense swamp and decided to turn back. It was raining steadily now, the wind had turned raw, and a three-thousand-foot snow-covered wall stood between them and their camp. They never did get warm during the two-and-a-half-hour climb to regain the pass. Standing at the windy crest, thoroughly soaked and freezing, they looked down toward Pe to see the sun still shining over their camp.

The day was a great success in Kingdon-Ward's view. What had struck him most about Pemakö, apart from the constant rain, was its riotous botanical diversity. He and Cawdor had collected forty species of rhododendrons alone on their short exploration, and expected to find another twenty in Pemakö's gorge country. Yet it was also clear what they were up against in the coming months. Kingdon-Ward thought the prophecy about Pemakö being a promised land rather quaint, but he had no doubt about why it had been chosen as a hidden land: "Pemakö consists entirely of ranges of lofty mountains separated by deep and narrow valleys," he wrote in perhaps the best description of the landscape ever written:

> The Assam Himalaya, with its mighty peaks Namche Barwa and Sanglung, forms as it were the solar plexus, and from this, great ranges radiate in every direction, throwing off in turn a confusion of spurs; and the whole, from the snow-line to the river gorge is covered with dense forest.
>
> Add to this a scanty population confined to the main valleys; a climate that varies from sub-tropical to arctic, the only thing common to the whole region being perpetual rain; snakes and wild animals, giant stinging nettles and myriads of biting and blood-sucking ticks, hornets, flies

and leeches, and you have some idea of what the traveller has to contend with.

. . .

J U N E   I S   A strenuous month for the plant collector. To keep
up with the flush of spring flowers, Kingdon-Ward put in twelve-hour
days collecting, cataloging, and preserving specimens. After a couple
of months of this, he knew from experience, his batteries would run
down. The rain and altitude would start to grate on his nerves; he
would grow peevish.

"You must keep yourself well in hand, and keep a firm grip on
things," he explained. "If you can get through August with your flag
still nailed to the mast, you are all right." The rain tapers off, the
weather grows finer as September approaches, autumn flowers are
blooming, and seeds are ripening. All is well until winter, when "a
tiredness which knows no equal" sets in. This is not a tiredness that
can be cured by a night's rest or even a week's rest, he wrote. "Every
cell and fibre in one's body seems worn out."

Not until November would there be time to go looking for the
waterfall—just about the time Kingdon-Ward's and Cawdor's batteries would be at their lowest ebb. Even when they trekked down the
canyon to Gyala in July, Kingdon-Ward was more concerned about
finding new plants than investigating the big waterfall that Kintup's
report mentioned. They made a stab at hiking down below Gyala for
a close look at a large rapid, but the river was at flood stage and the
trails downstream were submerged in waist-deep water. Some days
later, after the Tsangpo had dropped by ten feet, their second attempt
to reach the spot also failed. The trail simply stopped at an insur-
mountable cliff.

After toiling all summer and into the autumn, Kingdon-Ward
was fired up about his collection of new plants: almost fifty species of
rhododendrons, forty of primroses, and ten of poppies. The yellow
blooms of one dwarf poppy reminded him of Florinda's blond hair,
and he named the species *M. florindae*. The seeds of these plants were

ready for harvesting in October, just about the time the weather once again acquired the "sting of winter." Some days on the Doshong La, Kingdon-Ward dug down into the snow to rhododendrons that he'd spotted the preceding June, only to discover that they had set no seeds. But his success rate was much better than expected, and with his bountiful seed harvest safely stored, he and Cawdor could at last turn their attention to the unexplored gap.

Trekking out of Gyala on November 16, their caravan included twenty-three porters, the cook and headman from Darjeeling (now nicknamed Dick and Tom), an energetic lama from Pemaköchung ("the Walrus") to guide them, two dogs, and a sheep. Instead of trying to walk downstream, they climbed straight uphill through the pines until they were about three thousand feet above the river, then began moving laterally, undulating up and down across spurs that plunged into the river far below. One minute they would be thrashing through a mixed forest of maples and birches, the next clawing up through a grove of forty-foot-tall bamboo trees. The grades were so harrowingly steep that the porters had to build platforms on which to sleep.

When they descended again to the Tsangpo some miles downstream, they found a river that was "all foam and fury." The breakwater of house-sized boulders lining the channel bristled with shattered tree trunks, and even at low water the river's roar was deafening. "The great river was plunging down, down, boring ever more deeply into the bowels of the earth," Kingdon-Ward wrote about the scene. "The snow peaks enclosed us in a ring of ice. Dense jungle surged over the cliffs, filled the glens and marched boldly up to battle with the snow."

Four days after leaving Gyala, the entourage arrived at the Pemaköchung monastery. Kingdon-Ward was still preoccupied with rhododendrons and did not join Cawdor on a hike down to see Morshead's so-called Rainbow Falls and to take a boiling-point reading beside it with his hypsometer (the temperature at which water boils can then be converted to a quite accurate altitude reading). The drop at Rainbow Falls—actually more of a rapid this late in the season, Cawdor reported—is about eighty-five hundred feet above sea level, and the river at that point is galloping downhill at more than a hundred feet per mile. (The Colorado River, by comparison, loses about eight feet per mile through the Grand Canyon). At high water, the rapid would probably resemble the thirty-foot waterfall that Kintup, Bailey, and Morshead had seen.

In *The Riddle of the Tsangpo Gorges,* Kingdon-Ward refers to the rainbow-crowned cascade by Pemaköchung as "Kinthup's Fall." It is the same drop that Morshead named Rainbow Falls. Downstream from it, the riverside trail was impassable, so the caravan took to the hills again, now so steep that, facing one pitch, several of the women porters sat down and cried. Eight grueling days of climbing up and down brought them to a spot where they could descend to the river again. From their camp among the boulders, Kingdon-Ward and Cawdor could see that about a quarter of a mile ahead, the river ran headlong into the foot of a thousand-foot cliff, turned sharply left, and disappeared from view. The earth shook from the river's power.

Scrambling downstream over giant boulders, the two reached the base of the cliff and turned a corner. A half mile ahead, billowing above the lip of a big drop, was a "great cloud of spray" decorated with rainbows. "The falls at last!" Kingdon-Ward thought. But it wasn't. As they climbed higher above the river, it became apparent that the drop was just another forty-footer, which they also dubbed Rainbow Falls.

Photographs that the pair made show why their progress was blocked. Below the falls, the river rushes along calamitously for several hundred yards before smashing into another spur that angles sharply down from the right. The obstruction sends the river zigging to the left out of sight, but how it zags back is not clear. Directly behind the spur, an awesome monolith of glistening black rock seems to block all further progress. The wall juts up half a mile or more, and high up against the skyline, "a few trees cling like fur to the worn rock surface," Kingdon-Ward wrote. "Obviously we could get no further down the gorge; to scale the cliff seemed equally impossible."

Their only recourse was to backtrack and then detour up and around the impasse. "Of that climb, I have only an indistinct recollection, beyond that it was a nightmare," Kingdon-Ward wrote. Slabs of near-vertical rock above them were riven with upward-slanting cracks and horizontal crevices, from which bushes grew. Often, the only way to ascend a pitch was to grab hold of a bush and haul oneself straight up. The porters inched across bare rock streaming with meltwater, where one slip meant a fatal fall into the maelstrom hundreds of feet below. Higher up, the party reached forest and felt more secure in the trees—though no less exhausted as they clawed their way uphill. The fastest route, they discovered, was along tracks that the immensely muscular takin had bulldozed through the undergrowth. An oxlike species *(Budorcas taxicolor)* that weighs about five hundred pounds as an adult but stands just three feet at the shoulder, a takin can crash through rhododendron thickets with no more apparent effort than a rabbit expends scampering across an overgrown meadow.

Exhausted as they were after eight months in the field, it is little wonder that Kingdon-Ward and Cawdor failed to make much more headway downriver than Bailey and Morshead. But they were not completely done in. At the crest of the ridge, now almost four thousand feet above the river, they saw in the distance a cultivated field—the village of Bayi. From there, they would mount another assault on the gap from below. "A last effort was required," Kingdon-Ward wrote.

From Bayi, they moved up toward the Great Bend, where the Po Tsangpo joins the main Tsangpo, with a platoon of eight barefoot coolies—short, sturdily built men with mops of shingled black hair. Kingdon-Ward made them out to be Lopas and noted that they were "dwarf in stature and had almost simian faces; nor was their intelligence much ahead of their looks."

In a village near the confluence of the two mighty rivers, they met a Monpa hunter who told them that no one ever went where they wanted to go. There were no trails along the river leading into the gap, he said, and none into the hills above it from which one could peer down into the canyon. But Cawdor went exploring and found a trail leading in precisely the direction they needed to go. The hunter had been lying, as it turned out, because the Monpas were afraid to trespass on Poba hunting grounds in that part of the gorge.

"No sooner did we call the bluff than the opposition collapsed," wrote Kingdon-Ward. "The Monpas were delighted to come with us!" Eight men were recruited. Descended from the original Bhutanese refugees to Pemakö, they had chiseled features and were as lean and strong as the game they pursued through the mountains. They wore Tibetan boots and capes of goral (the nimble goatlike species *Nemorhaedus cranbrooki*) with the coarse reddish fur turned out against the rain, and carried crude matchlock rifles and powder flasks made of takin horn. And as long as they were going to trespass on the Pobas, they figured, they might as well poach a takin or two.

Cawdor was not well when they broke camp on December 12, in a steady drizzle. He'd been plagued by a bad toothache for days and had not been sleeping well. The Monpas led them straight uphill, rising out of the rain forest, where vines and orchids twined through gigantic bamboo and fig trees, into a band of temperate forest of maple, birch, magnolias, and huge old oaks. Above eight thousand feet they entered an evergreen forest where Himalayan hemlocks dripping with epiphytic orchids and rhododendrons towered two hundred feet overhead. The orchids seemed to thrive even up in the snow zone.

The Monpas were consummate woodsmen. They could have a fire going in no time, even in the rain with wet wood, and could always come up with a pheasant or two for dinner. One night they shot a goral; on another, two takin. Up and down ridges they led Kingdon-Ward and the suffering Cawdor. One camp was on a landslide scar so steep that they had to dig themselves in to avoid rolling downhill to the river, surging along two thousand feet below.

"We presented an odd spectacle dotted about the hillside, a man under a tree stump here, two huddled under a rock there, like a lot of rabbits," Kingdon-Ward wrote.

The mist and drizzle the next morning gave way to clear skies at about ten o'clock. Cawdor was done in. He stayed in camp, such as it was, while Kingdon-Ward started down toward the river with four Monpas. The hunters "moved with the stealth of policemen on night duty," Kingdon-Ward wrote, stopping now and then to remark among themselves about some distant object or animal. The hill fell away so precipitously that they could not see the river, only hear it.

After an "unpleasant" descent, the group came out on a boulder-strewn beach and witnessed the frightening power of the Tsangpo. Just where the riverbed tilted down sharply, the river turned its full force onto a wall-sided spur that jutted across from the opposite bank. The Tsangpo had blown a hole fifteen feet wide right through the middle of solid rock and was pouring through the breach. At flood stage, the water would be forty or fifty feet higher and jetting over the top of the obstruction, creating a thirty- to forty-foot waterfall, Kingdon-Ward reckoned.

Below that point, they could only guess what happened to the Tsangpo. After hurtling through the fifteen-foot-wide breach, wrote Kingdon-Ward, "[it] rushes headlong into a gorge so deep and narrow that one could hardly see any sky overhead; then it disappeared."

In order to gain a view downstream, they climbed off the beach using a makeshift ladder that the hunters fashioned from a small tree, then struggled up through the bushes for about a hundred feet. The river, they could see, flowed fast and green into the dark abyss, leaping in sleek waves over ledges forty feet high, then surged away around another corner.

Back on the beach, they took a boiling-point reading to determine their altitude. The river had dropped about thirteen hundred feet from the point of their last reading, at Rainbow Falls, and it was another five hundred feet down to the confluence, for a total elevation loss of about eighteen hundred feet. According to sacred texts at the Pemaköchung monastery, there were seventy-five waterfalls in those fourteen miles of gorge. If that were true, and if each of the seventy-five drops was only about twenty feet high, altogether they would account for almost the entire drop.

Kingdon-Ward and Cawdor had been able to look down into all but about five miles of the canyon's "narrowest and most profound depths." Based on their calculations, they could not imagine a waterfall of a hundred feet or more in the five-mile gap, but they left the possibility open, if only by a crack:

"We are, therefore, unable to believe that there is any likelihood" is Kingdon-Ward's tentative phrasing.

On the way back to Bayi, the hunters butchered one of their takin and presented a slab of its meat and a pheasant to Cawdor and Kingdon-Ward as a parting gift. "They were a most remarkable body of men, and had behaved splendidly," Kingdon-Ward wrote. "It was with real regret that we bade goodbye to [them]. They were intelligent, loyal and hard-working; once they had made up their minds to take us to the hunting preserves, they did everything they could to help us."

Or so he thought. What he neglected to list among the Monpas' qualities was that they also were very cunning, and they guarded their secrets closely.

. . .

THE TRIBUTES FOR Kingdon-Ward were warm and free-flowing at the Royal Geographical Society's meeting of May 25, 1925. Cawdor was congratulated, too, but in absentia. He had only just arrived in England the day before and sent regrets that he was committed to attend the Royal Caledonian Ball on the night of the lecture. Of course, he had also just finished a year in the field with Kingdon-Ward and was probably in no mood to relive the experience.

Lucky for Cawdor that he skipped the meeting. While he was hobnobbing with royals and dancing set reels at the charity ball, across town at the RGS, the society's president, Lord Ronaldshay, lauded Kingdon-Ward as "the seasoned traveller of the two."

Kingdon-Ward's long, plodding lecture that night pretty well popped whatever remained of the romantic bubble about the Falls of the Brahmaputra. Twenty years earlier, when the dream of a Tibetan

Niagara was fully alive and the British were eager to open new routes into Tibet, the distinguished geographer and former surveyor general of India, Sir Thomas Holdich, had rhapsodized about the possibilities that lay within the unknown canyon. Holdich envisioned a Tibetan branch of the Assam railway chuffing up through the gorge to the Tibetan Plateau, with an intermediate stop at "a spacious hotel for sightseers and sportsmen" overlooking the imagined waterfall.

Holdich had been loath to give up this vision. When Bailey and Morshead had returned to India discounting the likelihood of a huge waterfall on the Tsangpo, Sir Thomas had told the London *Morning Post*, "Unless Captains Bailey and Moorsom [*sic*] have been able to visit the supposed site of the falls . . . and have seen for themselves that there are no falls . . . , the evidence of their non-existence is imperfect." Holdich went on to cite a Tibetan lama who claimed to have visited the waterfall and later sketched it for one of the Raj's most trusted frontier officers. "This rough sketch bears out what the survey of the Indian explorer Kintup proved about those falls," Holdich said. "Until Captain Moorsom . . . can give us a full account of the extreme point to which his exploring party penetrated, and the exact route followed, the question of the falls must remain still in the air."

But Bailey won the day. Using his extensive sources in the native community, he managed to track Kintup down. The pundit, now in his fifties, was living in Darjeeling, making ends meet as a tailor. Bailey was eager to meet the man in whose footsteps he had just trod, and arranged for him to come to Simla for another debriefing. Kintup was built like a takin. He wore a graying goatee and had a steady, proud, distinguished look about him—clearly a man of character. One survey officer who'd hired him to help map Kangchenjunga, the snowy peak visible from Darjeeling, described him as a "thick-set, active man with a look of dogged determination on his rugged, weather-beaten features:

"His deep-chested voice I have often heard calling clearly from a hill-top some miles away, like a ship's captain in a storm. He has all the alertness of a mountaineer, and with the strength of a lion he is a host in himself."

After thirty years, Kintup's memories of Pemakö were still acute, and he recalled details of the gorge's topography that Bailey knew to be accurate, having just covered the same ground. Kintup denied saying that he'd seen any waterfall on the Tsangpo higher than about thirty feet, roughly the height of the house in which their meeting occurred. The 150-foot waterfall was on a small tributary stream near Gyala, he told Bailey, and the deity Singche Chogye was carved or painted on a rock behind the cascade. The "lake" at the foot of the falls was probably the calm, wide stretch of the Tsangpo below Gyala, where it pooled up before rampaging into the inner gorge. Somehow, all this had gotten garbled in the original debriefing, either because Kintup's interviewers had misunderstood him, Bailey figured, or because the Hindustani transcript of the interview had been mistranslated.

Six months later, in June 1914, Bailey and Morshead returned to London to address the RGS. By then, Holdich had changed his tune: "I am afraid we must give up any idea of magnificent falls in the Brahmaputra," he told the lecture hall following Bailey's presentation. "We expected magnificent falls there, and we are to a certain extent, I think, disappointed that we have not found them."

The RGS awarded Bailey a gold medal in 1916, elevating him to a league of luminary explorers that included David Livingstone (who won the medal in 1850 and 1855), Richard Burton (1859), John Hanning Speke (1861), Samuel Baker (1865), and the ill-fated polar specialist Robert Scott (1904, and posthumously in 1913). Bailey's old commander in Tibet, Francis Younghusband (who won it in 1890), nominated him for the honor, and Sir Thomas Holdich (a recipient in 1887) supported it.

Younghusband was on hand for Kingdon-Ward's lecture to the RGS in 1925. Then in his early sixties, and a prolific author himself, he reacted with delight at seeing photographs of the inner gorge from the comfort of an armchair. "We now have in detail, right from one end to the other, the whole [natural] history of the Tsangpo," he said after the talk, overlooking the five-mile gap that no one had been able to traverse. Lord Ronaldshay, the society's president, was equally effusive, noting that it had "fallen to [Kingdon-Ward's] fortune to solve finally one of the few problems of exploration which the nineteenth century left to the twentieth century."

The long-held dream of a huge waterfall on the Tsangpo was pronounced dead that night. It was, the august body of explorers concluded, the end of an era.

. . .

IN 1930 KINGDON-WARD won the RGS's Founder's Gold Medal, "for geographical exploration, and work on botanical distribution in China and Tibet." He told a fellow plant collector, E. M. H. Cox, that he was prouder of that award than any other received during his long career. "There is no doubt that pure exploration is his first love," Cox said, "but alas . . . one cannot live by exploration alone."

Indeed, indulging his infatuation with the wilderness came at a high cost. Kingdon-Ward's health suffered, and he was perpetually on the brink of financial calamity, right up until his final days. His income from writing books and magazine articles was pitful: *The Mystery Rivers of Tibet*, for example, earned him an advance of thirty pounds, and his total income from writing in 1944 brought in the equivalent of roughly a thousand dollars.

His marriage was another casualty. He was away in Burma for the birth of both his daughters, and he never stayed in England for very long. Kingdon-Ward was at home with Florinda for perhaps four of their fourteen years as husband and wife. Money was always a worry, but Florinda spent it at a rate that alarmed and irritated him. After the girls were born she moved into an Edwardian mansion overlooking the Thames, with seven acres, a lake, and a domestic staff, and she entertained lavishly whenever Kingdon-Ward was at home. The atmosphere around the house was strained, with Kingdon-Ward sequestered in his study or sulking at the breakfast table. Friends noticed a lack of affection between them.

The couple nearly divorced in 1934 but decided not to for the children's sake. By the following spring, Kingdon-Ward was drawn back to the Tsangpo Gorge area, to botanize and survey north of the river into the Yigrong Valley, which he and Cawdor had not been able to reach in 1924 because of severe weather. The clouds parted one day as he and his porters were cresting a pass, and he was rewarded with a brief glimpse of the Yigrong's source, in a high valley "gripped by a ring of ice." The frosted pinnacles enclosing the valley reminded him of a Gothic cathedral. "If I had waited, and dreamed, for ten years for that brief glimpse only, I had not lived in vain," he wrote. "It epitomized a life's ambition; a worthwhile discovery in Asia, truly finished."

He and his porters trekked eight hundred miles across southern Tibet on that expedition before turning for home. When he arrived in England, it was clear that his marriage was over. "I should . . . think it highly unlikely that either of [us] will venture again into the perilous and uncharted seas of matrimony," he wrote to his sister while sailing again for Burma and Yunnan in 1937, soon after the split was finalized. "For my part, I am too old, too wedded to exploration, too poor and perhaps too wise."

Some years later, Florinda had her gardener burn some of Kingdon-Ward's field journals that she felt were cluttering up the attic. Fortunately, the Tsangpo diaries were not among them.

Kingdon-Ward did anything he could to stay in the field—teaching jungle survival to airmen during World War II, searching the Burmese highlands for downed U.S. planes, managing a tea plantation in Assam after the war. He was unemployed at times, and his letters home reveal loneliness and depression, but finally, in 1947, he found lasting happiness. That year, at the age of sixty-two, he married again, to a woman of twenty-six named Jean Macklin. The two had met in 1944 over lunch in Bombay, where her father was a distinguished judge. Her parents were staunchly opposed to the marriage; Kingdon-Ward was poor, divorced, and thirty-six years older than their daughter—"a rather small, shrunken, shriveled little man," as one observer described him. But he and Jean realized they were soul mates and took the plunge.

Unlike Florinda, Jean was not averse to living in a soggy tent in a leech-infested jungle. A month after their wedding, they sailed to India for a collecting expedition, and in 1950 they lived through the devastating Assam earthquake while camped in the foothills below the lower Tsangpo Gorge. (Among the ten most violent quakes ever recorded, it registered 8.6 on the Richter scale. Whole mountainsides crashed down into the Tsangpo, blocking its course, causing floods and debris flows, and completely rearranging the landscape. According to Kingdon-Ward's measurements the next day, the spot where they were camped had risen two hundred feet in elevation.) The two were sure they were done for, but survived and made it back to England.

They traveled together through the 1950s—to Burma mostly—collecting for nurserymen and private benefactors. Kingdon-Ward celebrated his sixty-seventh birthday on the road to northern Burma with Jean. He might have considered returning to the Tsangpo Gorge had it not been for the Communist takeover of eastern Tibet in 1950 and the virtual closure of the country to all foreigners. By the mid-fifties, the Communists were assaulting Burma, too, and the country was in turmoil: "violence everywhere, deliberate provocation to war," he wrote. "In such a world plant hunting and peaceful gardening seem to have no place."

Their final expedition was to Ceylon, in 1957, to collect orchids. Back in England, Kingdon-Ward considered mounting expeditions to New Guinea and Vietnam—at age seventy-three. But on Easter Sunday 1958, while sharing a drink with Jean in a London pub, he felt a tingling in his right foot. This had happened before, and he stood up to shake it off but collapsed after a few staggering steps—a stroke. Rushed to a hospital, he slipped into a coma and never regained consciousness.

The stroke felled him twenty-five years to the day after he and Ronald Kaulback performed their wacky ukulele-and-dance routine during their 1933 expedition to the region east of the Tsangpo Gorge. "He was the toughest fellow I ever knew," Kaulback recalled. "He always used to tell me that I was an old-fashioned kind of explorer, but he really was in the mould of the old time mid-nineteenth century explorers.

"He was tough, really tough, and a great man."

. . .

AND OF THE others who explored the gorge? Kintup returned to Darjeeling after meeting with Bailey in Simla and died several months later. Bailey had urged that the distinguished pundit should be given a pension, but the government of India refused, arguing that Kintup might live to be ninety. The best Bailey could manage was an award of a thousand rupees and a parchment certificate of honor, presented by the viceroy, which greatly pleased Kintup.

Bailey himself went on to live a long life. He served in Kashmir and Nepal during the thirties, in the latter post with the grand title of His Majesty's envoy extraordinary and minister plenipotentiary at the court of Nepal. During his residency, he continued to collect flora and fauna avidly, and when he finally retired, in 1938, he donated his collection of more than two thousand specimens of Nepalese birds to the British Museum of Natural History. Returning to Scotland, he turned to writing and produced three books before his death in 1967 at the age of eighty-five. Surely, he was among the greatest explorers of his age—a skillful diplomat, daring explorer, secret agent, linguist, and naturalist par excellence. The London *Times'* obituary compared him to Sir Richard Burton but noted that he would most likely be remembered for his incidental discovery of the magnificent blue poppy (which, in fact, had been discovered first in western Yunnan in 1886 by a Catholic missionary and naturalist, Père Delavay).

In his old age, Bailey became "more and more like a Tibetan sage," according to the historian James Morris, who met him in 1958. "It seemed to me that he had been physically Tibetanized by his experiences, for his cheekbones were high, his eyes were slightly slanted, his skin was like brown parchment, and he even moved, it seems to me in retrospect, in a indefinably remote or monkish way."

And Bailey's great companion, Henry Morshead? "I was always

afraid that the sort of carelessness [about his personal hygiene and safety] would kill him one day," Bailey wrote in his account of their Tsangpo adventures. "But I was wrong. He was taking a peaceful ride one morning in Burma [in 1931] when he was murdered" by unknown assailants.

. . .

WHEN BAILEY HAD delivered his address on the Tsangpo Gorge to the RGS in 1913, the political situation in Tibet was becoming increasingly grave. "The Dead Hand of China" was again being extended over the country, and its grip would grow increasingly tight as the years passed.

After Kingdon-Ward and Cawdor's 1924 expedition, activity in the Tsangpo Gorge was limited to a few expeditions, none of them to the unexplored five-mile gap in search of the falls. Kingdon-Ward prospected for plants along the Po Tsangpo's tributary, the Yigrong River, north of the gorge in 1935, and so did the renowned botanist Sir George Taylor in 1938, on an expedition led by Frank Ludlow and George Sherriff, two naturalists who were every bit as tough and adventurous as Eric Bailey and Kingdon-Ward, and who covered as much or more ground in the gorge as any previous explorer had.

Ludlow and Sherriff made repeated forays to the gorge and into the adjoining mountains between 1936 and 1947. Ludlow was a superb botanist who had studied at Cambridge under Kingdon-Ward's father. Fond of quoting Shakespeare and concocting ditties in the style of Gilbert and Sullivan, Ludlow went to Tibet first in 1922, to serve as headmaster of the little school at Gyantse, where Cawdor and Kingdon-Ward met him during their stopover in 1924 on the way to the gorge. Sherriff, a Scottish ornithologist, met Ludlow in Kashgar in 1930, while the two were guests of the consul general, Noel Williamson. The two scientists became fast friends and went on to explore the remotest corners of Central Asia together for the next twenty years.

Sherriff was a brilliant traveler. Going out on long expeditions, he had villagers around their base camps plant vegetables and bring the produce to advance camps. As Taylor notes about their 1938 expedition, "We frequently had tomatoes, lettuce, turnips and radishes in superb Russian salads." Sherriff knew the importance of creature comforts to the success of any expedition, and to that end meals were fortified with powerful Jamaican rum or "Treasure Whisky" from his family's distillery at Islay. Christmas dinner on their 1946 expedition to the gorge consisted of clear soup, roast stuffed goose, plum pudding, and a bottle of French champagne. He always traveled with a massive shortwave radio and a small library of classics. Like Bailey, he was a crack marksman, a valuable skill to have when collecting birds. (It was said, for instance, that he could bring down a diving swift with one shot.)

During the 1938 expedition to the Tsangpo, Taylor and Ludlow made the largest and most comprehensive collection of plants ever to have come out of Tibet in one season—more than four thousand specimens. They reached Gyala on that trip, and in 1946, Ludlow and Sherriff returned to the gorge along with Sherriff's wife, Betty, and a medical officer from India, Col. Henry Elliot. While the Sherriffs split off to explore the Po Tsangpo and Yigrong Rivers, Elliot and Ludlow joined a pilgrimage of villagers from Gyala to the Pemaköchung monastery. While there, they took a day off from botanizing to visit Kintup's Fall. They had allowed themselves only five days to collect around the monastery, so they did not attempt to go further into the chasm. But Ludlow was so amazed by the rich diversity of plants that he resolved to return in 1948 to spend the whole flowering season in and around the gorge, using Pemaköchung as his base camp.

That was never to happen. Officials in Lhasa were worried about the impending Communist "liberation" of Tibet and refused Ludlow a visa. And indeed, the Chinese did occupy eastern Tibet in 1950. Tibet fell behind the Bamboo Curtain (or, as Mao Zedong would have it, was reunited with the mother country) and entered a period of "democratic reforms" to rid the country of its feudal ways. Finally, in 1959, the Dalai Lama fled his homeland for good and Lhasa fell to the

People's Liberation Army. Once again, Tibet became the Forbidden Kingdom. Its isolation would continue for the next three decades—and the gorge for longer still, because of its strategic position along the disputed border with India. Not until 1992 would the first groups be allowed to try their luck at closing the five-mile gap that Kingdon-Ward and Cawdor had left.

. . .

THE TIBETANS LIVING in Pemakö would have had no doubt about why no one had been able to penetrate the gorge's deepest recesses. The failures were due not to terrain, weather, or lack of stamina on the part of explorers, they would tell you, but for more esoteric reasons. A prophecy holds that the holiest, innermost sanctum of the *beyul* will remain closed until three *tertons* (finders of the "treasure texts") come together at Gompo Ne, at the confluence of the Tsangpo and Po Tsangpo, just below the gap. Only if they determine that the time is auspicious will the *beyul*'s nether regions be opened. Until then, it is written, all who attempt to enter the ultimate sanctuary will do so at their own peril.

Part Two

Perceptions
of Paradise

∽

*One of the final and most complete embodiments of Tibet
as a sacred place in the Western imagination was the
utopia of Shangri-La described in [James] Hilton's famous
1933 novel,* Lost Horizon.

PETER BISHOP, *The Myth of Shangri-La*

∽

T HE MODERN AGE of exploration in the gorge dawned in 1992,
when China lifted the travel ban in southeast Tibet. China's perennial
tensions with India over the disputed border running across the lower
gorge had simmered down, and tourism elsewhere in Tibet was generating quantities of foreign exchange. There was money to be made
from tourism in Pemakö, Chinese officials realized, and the West's interest in Tibet was never greater.

By the 1990s, the idealization of Tibet as a pure land of peace and
enlightened consciousness was complete, due in part to a brilliant public relations campaign by the Tibetan government in exile but also because of real concerns about the continuing threat to Tibetan culture
and religion under the Chinese. In *Prisoners of Shangri-La,* an insight-
ful analysis of how the West has shaped the mythology of Tibet from
afar, Donald Lopez, a University of Michigan professor of Buddhist
and Tibetan studies, writes that in addition to Tibet's long-venerated
image as "the cure for an ever-dissolving Western civilization," the
country was now also seen as a "sacrificial victim" threatened by "the
horror of Chinese invasion and occupation."

The ominous language is not Lopez's but comes from a 1992

tract published by an organization called World Service Network. This manifesto urged that Tibet be transformed into a "New Age mission field," and it extolled Tibet's hoped-for role as the "headquarters of a global utopia." "It is time for the unveiling of Shangri-La . . . [w]here sister/brotherhood, compassion, respect for each other and all life forms, sharing and interdependence are the foundation stones for a Great New Society . . . [and a] lasting global transformation to World Peace," read the group's call to arms.

Western projections of Tibet as a threatened repository of ancient and occult knowledge are nothing new. They date back more than a century, most notably to the Theosophical Society, which grew out of the imaginings of a self-styled psychic named Helena Petrovna von Hahn, aka Madame Blavatsky. Born in Russia in 1831, she was introduced to Tibetan Buddhism as a child and, after a brief marriage of convenience to an older gentleman named Blavatsky, found herself drawn to the East in search of secret wisdom. She traveled through India and Ceylon, devoured the literature of the occult, and met with the learned pundit Sarat Chandra Das, among others, who had written about Tibetan mysticism. Somewhere along the way, she cooked up the story that she was receiving telepathic and written teachings from spiritual masters called Mahatmas, whose ephemeral overlords lived somewhere behind the Himalayas in the invisible kingdom of Shambhala. The myth of Shambhala is closely related to a Hindu prophecy in which a divine hero named Kalki, the tenth and final incarnation of Vishnu, defeats barbarians who tyrannize the world, ushering in a golden age of purity. Scholars have identified Kalki's birthplace as an actual Indian village called Sambhala. But in Tibetan texts, the location of Shambhala varies, and directions to it are always vaguely worded. In some accounts, it lies far north of Tibet—an island guarded by a ring of icy mountains. Others put it at the North Pole, while Blavatsky said it was somewhere in the Gobi Desert.

Following her mystical sojourn in the East, Blavatsky migrated to New York, where in 1875 she and her disciples officially launched the Theosophical Society. The movement gained a following in the

United States and in Europe, and a decade after its founding Blavatsky could boast of more than a hundred chapters around the world, many of them in India, where the society's mystical precepts appealed to Hindus. She lectured around the world, conducted séances, and communed with the departed. And she wrote prodigiously. Her 1877 *Isis Unveiled* fills two volumes and weighs almost five pounds; *The Secret Doctrine,* which appeared in 1888, three years before her death, is even longer and more daunting. Blavatsky claimed not to be the source of the material but simply a channel for the enlightened Mahatmas, who spoke to her in a secret language that she translated into English. *The Secret Doctrine*'s subtitle is *The Synthesis of Science, Religion and Philosophy,* but its contents betray an amalgamation of pseudoscience, Eastern mysticism, and a generous helping of paranormal claptrap: Blavatsky's masterwork discourses on such topics as the inhabitants of the lost continents of Atlantis and Lemuria, the esoteric knowledge of Mesopotamia and ancient Egypt, and a "root race" of Aryan Asiatics, highly evolved spirits who emanated as Tibetan mystics.

(Years later, Germany's Third Reich would seize upon the notion of a pure, Aryan race originating somewhere in Central Asia. In 1935, the head of the German secret service, Heinrich Himmler, ordered the founding of an institute of ancestral heritage. Several of its research associates firmly believed that Tibet was the homeland of the master race and that the Aryans' overlords, the Mahatmas, ruled an underground kingdom called Shambhala. In an expedition to Tibet in 1938 and 1939, the institute's ethnologist, Bruno Berger, was prepared to search for skeletal remains of a Nordic race. He found no such bones or any Aryan-looking Tibetans. On the contrary, Berger considered some Tibetan beggars he met to be racially "inharmonious.")

However laudable the Theosophists' stated goals, from promoting universal brotherhood to encouraging scientific inquiry, Blavatsky was branded a quack. The society nonetheless flourished in the atmosphere of the times, with the public's great interest in spiritualism and the occult arts, and its fascination with Tibet's many mysteries.

(Recall that this was the era that produced geographers who envisioned a colossal waterfall in the Tsangpo Gorge.) The Theosophical Society attracted avant-garde artists and intellectuals on both sides of the Atlantic. Albert Einstein and Thomas Edison were reportedly avid readers of *The Secret Doctrine,* and in Russia author Boris Pasternak, composer Alexander Scriabin, and painter Wasily Kandinsky were disciples. In 1913, as war loomed in Europe, a Buddhist-Theosophical temple opened in St. Petersburg.

No Theosophist was more possessed by the idea of a secret Tibetan utopia called Shambhala than the Russian visionary artist and mystic Nicholas Konstantin Roerich. Roerich collaborated with Igor Stravinsky in designing costumes and painting sets for Stravinsky's ballet *Le Sacre du Printemps*—sets that depicted landscapes of enchanted hills and sacred trees. As a boy, he had spent summers at his family's country manor, on whose living room wall hung a luminous painting of Kanchenjunga, the holy peak visible from Darjeeling. Later, in his thirties, after joining the St. Petersburg Theosophical Society, he received the commission to design the skylight for the city's new Buddhist-Theosophical temple and incorporated into it symbols representing the eightfold path to enlightenment.

It was in St. Petersburg that Roerich met the Russian Buddhist lama Agvan Dorzhiev, who was a tutor to the thirteenth Dalai Lama and Tibet's envoy to the Russian court. On one of his missions shuttling between Lhasa and St. Petersburg, Dorzhiev had brought with him a copy of the ancient *The Prayer of Shambhala* and a "guidebook" on how to reach the holy land, and showed them to Roerich. The painter became obsessed with making a pilgrimage to find the sacred hidden kingdom, and in 1923 he and his wife, Helena, set out for India and Tibet.

By this time, Roerich was referring to himself as "Professor Roerich." Wearing a full white beard and skullcap, he resembled a Russian Orthodox prelate and cut an imposing figure. The professor's vividly colored impressionistic paintings were visions transmitted to him by the Mahatmas, he said, and his overarching mission was to foster a world order of peace and brotherhood. There would be no room for the colonial policies of the past in Roerich's New Age, especially those of imperialist Britain. British agents in India were understandably suspicious when the Roerichs—Russian nationals, anti-imperialists, and possibly spies—pitched up in Darjeeling talking of an expedition in search of Shambhala. The Foreign Office dispatched none other than Eric Bailey to sniff them out. Bailey came down from neighboring Sikkim, where he was the political officer; after listening to Roerich outline his grand plan, he left with an unfavorable impression. Some years later, in an official report, Bailey called Roerich "a humbug, a bad painter, afflicted with megalomania but in character rather agreeable in a vague way."

Ultimately, the professor received permission from the British to enter Tibet from India and carry out his search for Shambhala. In 1926 he, his wife, and their son, George, formed the core of a massive expedition that took them from India to western China, Mongolia, and finally Tibet. When the entourage made a sudden detour to Moscow, however, British agents grew alarmed, suspecting that Roerich was in fact a Bolshevik agent bent on swaying the Tibetans to the Russian cause. The Foreign Office cabled Bailey in Sikkim to exert whatever influence he could on the Tibetan government to sabotage Roerich's expedition.

In the spring of 1927, intelligence reached Bailey that Roerich's team had left Moscow and was once more on the move. Bailey cabled a warning to Lhasa that they would soon cross into Tibet, attempting to reach the holy city. That September, when the expedition approached the northern most Tibetan outpost of Nagchu Dzong they were halted and told to wait for permission from Lhasa to proceed.

"The place will forever remain in our memory," wrote Roerich. "The cheerless upland, arctic in character, was full of small mounds and was bordered by the drear outlines of scree slopes." At the suggestion of the commanding general, the entourage camped in the middle of a marshy plain overgrown with thin, prickly weeds, with a lake and "dead mountains" on the horizon. Here, at fifteen thousand feet, there was "not a bird, not an animal," Roerich wrote, only the bleak view and unrelenting, bitterly cold winds.

A month later, winter had begun to set in, but permission had not arrived. It became clear that, in fact, the party was under arrest. In early November, George Roerich posted a letter to Bailey imploring him to do something to help. The younger Roerich reported that the expedition's supplies were running low, their horses and camels had little to eat, and he himself had nearly died of acute mountain sickness. It was so cold that cognac froze.

"Each night the freezing, starved animals approached our tents as though knocking for the last time before their deaths," recalled Nicholas Roerich in one of his memoirs. "And in the morning we found them dead near our tents. Our Mongols dragged them beyond the camp, where packs of wild dogs and condors and vultures were already awaiting their prey. Of 102 animals, we lost 92. On the Tibetan uplands, we also left five of our fellow travelers. . . . Even the natives could not withstand the severe conditions." George Roerich's pleas for help never reached Bailey, but five months after being detained, the party received the okay to proceed—not to Lhasa but to Sikkim via a roundabout route. Apparently they never suspected that Eric Bailey was personally responsible for the misery they had just endured, and may have had a hand in their liberation as well.

Nicholas Roerich chronicled the extraordinary expedition in three books, including one titled simply *Shambhala*. During their trek through Central Asia, he reckoned, they had crossed three dozen mountain passes above fourteen thousand feet. Despite the difficulty of the journey, he produced some five hundred paintings depicting various Himalayan landscapes and deities linked to the king of Shambhala. He failed to discover the hidden valley of peace and plenty, but the quest was largely metaphorical, anyway—"a search for a new era," as he put it in the subtitle of *Shambhala*.

Still, at one point crossing the Mongolian desert toward Tibet, a lama who was guiding the expedition covered his mouth and nose with a scarf, warning that the party would soon encounter poisonous gas that guarded the frontiers of Shambhala. Later, the party spotted a "huge spheroid body" streaking across the sky that disappeared over the Humboldt Mountains. "The whole camp follows the unusual apparition," wrote Roerich, "and the lamas whisper: 'The Sign of Shambhala!'"

At the end of their grueling trek, the family settled in India in 1928, in the Himalayan foothills, where they established a research institute dedicated to Central Asian studies, Tibetan medicine, and archaeological exploration. Here Roerich wrote his memoirs, and although they were rather obscure works, some literary scholars have speculated that they may have been among the sources for a bestselling novel that would appear in 1933 and introduce a synonym for the Tibetan utopia that Roerich never found: Shangri-La.

. . .

THE NOVEL, OF course, was *Lost Horizon,* by the British author James Hilton. It was largely Hilton's 1933 book and the 1937 Frank Capra film based on it that cemented Tibet's reputation in the popular imagination as the ultimate utopia.

Hilton's Shangri-La—the paradisiacal Valley of the Blue Moon— bears a striking resemblance to the hidden kingdom that Blavatsky and Roerich conjured up. It is discovered by four hostages, three British and one American, being evacuated by air from a revolution in Baskul, a fictional country based on Afghanistan. Their mysteriously hijacked plane never reaches its destination of Peshawar, Pakistan. The plane flies far off course and crash-lands amid the snowy peaks of the Kunlun Mountains on the northern rim of the Tibetan Plateau. Stranded in the "loftiest and least hospitable part of the earth's surface," the four despair of ever reaching civilization again. Then a procession of men appears through the snows bearing a sedan chair.

"I am from the lamasery of Shangri-La," the elderly lama within announces in almost too-perfect English, offering to guide the bewildered group to safety. They trek through snowfields and over a high pass to reach the monastery, which, with its colored pavilions and milk-blue roofs, clings impossibly to a mountainside like "flower-petals impaled on a crag." Soaring above is a twenty-eight-thousand-foot fang of rock and ice called Karakal, and far below, visible through the mists, lies a sheltered, sunny, intoxicatingly beautiful valley.

The monastery is a storehouse of learning, religion, and culture from both East and West. It has a collection of Chinese art, a vast library of books and music, maps, and—best of all—an abundance of time to pursue any course of study that one might choose.

"You will have Time," the monastery's high lama tells Hugh Conway, the gifted but world-weary hero of the story, who turns out to have been hand-picked to succeed the dying old man (thus the hijacking). "Think for a moment," the lama tells him. "Never again will you skim pages to save minutes or avoid some study lest it prove too engrossing." That is because in Shangri-La, Conway learns, time and the aging process have been magically arrested. Isolated in space and suspended in time, the sanctuary is a time capsule of culture and wisdom that will weather a holocaust such "as the world has not seen before," the lama explains. "There will be no safety by arms, no help from authority, no answer in science. It will rage until every flower of culture is trampled and all human things are leveled in a vast chaos." And afterward, Shangri-La will survive to reseed civilization.

"The utopia (u-topia, or non-place) of Shangri-La was an ideal fantasy world at a time when geographical mystery had not yet totally vanished from the surface of the earth," writes Peter Bishop in *The Myth of Shangri-La*. "[I]t stood midway between the Victorian quest for the Holy City and the mid-twentieth-century concern with metaphysical and psychological systems." The ground was especially fertile for the idea of a peaceful, all-enduring kingdom isolated from the conditions in Europe that had caused one world war and were about to ignite another. Here was a place far removed from political and economic calamity, where sanity reigned under the benevolent guidance of Mahatma-like lamas and time stood still.

In the preface to the eighteenth edition of *Lost Horizon* (published in 1936, just three years after the first edition), Hilton explained that the story's message was about "the peril of war to all that we mean by the word 'civilization.'" But with war again threatening, Hilton lamented, "How much happier one would be to dismiss all this as thoroughly out-of-date, than to admit, as one must, that in 1936 it has become more terrifyingly up-to-date than ever!"

In Britain *Lost Horizon* won the 1934 Hawthendorn Prize for the best work of imaginative literature by a young author. Like Hilton's sentimental *Goodbye Mr. Chips,* which came out that year, the story of Shangri-La "wistfully evokes a rosy image of Victorian and Edwardian life . . . that humane, genteel, balanced atmosphere which Hilton— and his readers—felt was destroyed in the ferocity and barbarism of world war," one critic wrote. Hilton told another critic, "The next war will be more than a waste—it will mean practically total annihilation of everything decent and beautiful."

Director Frank Capra hired Hilton to consult on the film version and brought him to Hollywood. Once the movie was finished, Hilton passed through New York on his way to London and was snagged by the *Times* film gossip columnist, who asked him if he had ever been to Tibet. Hilton confessed that he had not; he had seriously considered making the pilgrimage once filming had ended, he explained, but somehow by then "the thrill had gone." It was his conviction that he did not need to see a place to write about it. In the long run, he explained, "imagination will get you further than knowledge or first-hand experience." Nevertheless, his inspiration for the story, apart from the mood of the times, did not spring full-blown from his muses. Hilton found it in the British Museum's library.

Among Hilton's most valuable resources, he told the *Times*, was the travelog *Recollections of a Journey Through Tartary, Thibet and China, 1844–5–6,* by the French missionary Abbé Evariste-Regis Huc. Huc's memoir was republished in English in 1928, five years before *Lost Horizon,* and told of a prophecy that he and his cohort Joseph Gabet had heard while crossing northern Tibet, about a sacred hidden land called Shambhala. In this version, the paradise was said to be located somewhere north of the Kunlun Range, between the Altai and Tien

Shan mountains. It was a sanctuary for a society of "Kelans," followers of the Panchen Lama and keepers of the most secret teachings of Buddhism. The legend foretold of a day when barbarians would overrun Tibet and seize control. A period of darkness would ensue, during which Buddhism would wither. But at the Panchen Lama's summons, an army of Kelans would rise up from among the living and the dead, crush the infidels, and go on to spread Buddhism throughout the world, thus ushering in a golden age. (In some versions of the legend, the forces of darkness are Chinese, but another has them as rampaging Muslims led by a king who "madly rules like a wild elephant.")

Huc and Gabet were not the first to have heard about Shambhala. George Bogle, the first Englishman to enter Tibet, learned of the hidden kingdom on his diplomatic mission from Calcutta to meet the sixth Panchen Lama in 1774. Another principal source was the Hungarian Tibetologist Alexander Csoma de Koros, who traveled through Central Asia in 1819 to search for his presumed ancestral homeland. In Tibet, de Koros obtained texts about Shambhala that described it as a sanctuary where the deepest secrets of Tibetan Buddhism—known as the Kalacakra or Wheel of Time—are closely guarded. His writings were among those that inspired Madame Blavatsky and her disciples, and, directly or indirectly, James Hilton.

The myth of the savior king who leads the devout against the forces of evil is common to many Eastern and Western cultures. But it is particularly well known to Tibetans. Centuries-old Buddhist texts refer to the hidden valleys, or *beyuls,* that were scattered throughout the Himalayas by Padmasambava, the Indian yogin who brought Buddhism to Tibet in the eighth century. Like Shangri-La and Shambhala, *beyuls* are sacred places of mystical retreat, pilgrimage, and refuge during times of strife. Directions to each of them are generally revealed in the form of a *terma,* or "treasure text," also hidden by Padmasambava, perhaps in a cave or prominent outcrop of rock. Every *beyul* would have to be found and "opened" by a yogin known as a *terton*, a "treasure finder," and he would be led to the task only when the time was propitious. Certain hidden lands remain unopened to this day. Their discovery awaits the time when they are needed.

If the name Shambhala had come back from Tibet on the lips of numerous early travelers, so also had that of a *beyul* known as Pemakö, located in the shadow of Namche Barwa, where the Tsangpo River flows into an impenetrable gorge. In his 1912 book *Le Tibet Revolte,* the French traveler Jacques Bacot writes of "Nepemako" as "*la terre promise des Tibetains*" the promised land of Tibetans. The Bhutanese forbears of Pemakö's Monpa people settled in the gorge at the end of the eighteenth century out of obedience to this prophecy. In 1909, while traveling across the Tibetan province of Kham, Huc had met hundreds of families fleeing a Chinese warlord. They were going to Pemakö, they told him, and gave him a copy of their guidebook.

Even as late as the 1950s, when the Chinese like to think they "liberated" Tibet from the yoke of feudal lamaism, the gorge was an escape route in the Tibetan diaspora. Like their predecessors, however, the latter-day refugees were unable to locate the proverbial land of milk and honey in the lower gorge, and they suffered mightily in the jungle heat. Disillusioned, most of them continued south to India and settled into refugee camps, spinning tales of their futile search for the legendary Padma-shel-ri, or Lotus Crystal Mountain, the otherworldly citadel that Father Huc and Eric Bailey had heard about.

During the decades of religious suppression under the Chinese, Tibetans continued to make ritual journeys to Pemakö and other sacred mountains, but in far fewer numbers than in the past. In Tsari, a renowned *beyul* bordering Pemakö's western regions, ritual events staged in holy years would attract as many as twenty thousand pilgrims from all levels of society. Following the Dalai Lama's flight to India in 1959, all religious activity in Tsari was officially banned (but continued nevertheless, and in spite of the on-again, off-again border war with nearby India). The easing of state and military controls since the reopening of Tibet has restored some of the allure of *beyuls* such as Tsari and Pemakö, not only to Tibetans but also—important to our story—to a small band of vagabond scholars, hard-core travelers, and spiritual adventurers who began traipsing across Tibet as soon as the Bamboo Curtain parted.

Tibet's sacred geography has been illuminated as never before by researchers such as Edwin Bernbaum *(The Way to Shambhala)*, Charles Ramble ("The Creation of the Bon Mountain of Kongbo"), Keith Dowman *(The Sacred Life of Tibet,* with its gazetteer on Tibetan power places), and Victor Chan *(Tibet Handbook)*. In researching Beyul Tsari's role as a pilgrimage site, Tibetologist Toni Huber learned that the yoga of "mystic heat" or "internal fire" that the French traveler Alexandra David-Neel claimed to have mastered is, in fact, still practiced in Tsari. Groups of yogins dressed only in light cotton underwear and shawls would survive a January night outdoors at ten thousand feet, emerging from their deep trances at sunrise. For their disciples, the spectacle is said to demonstrate the triumph of a worshiper's inner world over the hostilities and discomforts of the outer world.

Stories brought back by Huber and his colleagues found an eager audience. Life in the "real" world outside of Tibet had grown more chaotic and unsettling during Tibet's dark age under the Chinese. As the millennium came to a close, the West faced wars, environmental calamities, rampant materialism, and a general spiritual malaise. There was a sense that advances of science and technology had further divorced us from nature and spirituality. Indeed, the situation was not so different from the one James Hilton had contemplated as he sat down to conjure up his dream world.

In the 1990s, Tibet became a mecca for the New Age—a spiritual wonderland where package tourists booked at the Lhasa Holiday Inn had their choice of pilgrimage sites from Kailas in western Tibet to Pemakö at the far opposite end of the Himalayas. While not as renowned as Kailas, and far less accessible, Pemakö nonetheless captured the imagination of a small group of aficionados and adventurers, but none were so captivated as Ian Baker and Hamid Sardar, two students of Tantric (or Tibetan) Buddhism who had left behind what Baker calls "the air-conditioned nightmare" of the West to embrace the esoteric wisdom of the East. Both erudite, well educated, and boldly adventurous, Baker and Sardar spent the better part of the millennium's final decade conducting the most thorough investigation of Pemakö's inner and outer geography ever undertaken. Their research of oral and written sources indicated that the canyon's crumpled topography concealed a sacred landscape visible only to those of adequate spiritual preparation, and that the path to this holy realm of peace and plenty would lead them, as Baker explains, "beyond geography."

. . .

An old Tibetan story tells of a young man who set off on the quest for Shambhala. After crossing many mountains, he came to the cave of an old hermit, who asked him, "Where are you going across these wastes of snow?"

"To find Shambhala," the youth replied.

"Ah, well then, you need not travel far," the hermit said. "The kingdom of Shambhala is in your own heart."

From *The Way to Shambhala,* by Edwin Bernbaum

"Lama, how does it happen that Shambhala on earth is still undiscovered by travelers? On maps you see many routes of expeditions. It appears that all heights are already marked and all valleys and rivers explored."

"Many people try to reach Shambhala uncalled [replied the lama]. *Some of them have disappeared forever. Only few of them reach the holy place, and only if their karma is ready."*

From "Shambhala the Resplendent," by Nicholas Roerich

IN TIBETAN COSMOLOGY, the supernatural realms of a *beyul* occupy spaces parallel to the world of three dimensions. As the Tibet scholar Edwin Bernbaum explains, the spaces are like "paintings stacked against a wall; as long as we look only at the first, or top one, we would fail to see the others behind it—or even suspect that they existed. Shambhala could conceivably be hidden right here, an inch away from us, in another world that we do not perceive because we focus all our attention on the familiar one we know."

Not everyone has access to the hidden dimensions. To be able to see beyond the world of physical reality, Tibetans believe, you must have the proper karma—the sum of all previous thoughts and actions. If a person's karma is lacking, his or her vision may be obscured by ego and illusions of reality. Looking for the supernatural dimensions would be like trying to peer through a window clouded with an accumulation of karmic residue. Until it is cleaned through meditation, the window will block a clear view of the mystical geography.

Someone such as Francis Kingdon-Ward or Frederick Bailey would have regarded all this as quaint poppycock. For them, the world of Pemakö existed strictly in three dimensions. Ian Baker and Hamid Sardar, on the other hand, have spent years "cleaning their windows," retreating annually to caves and hermitages in the Nepali Himalayas to meditate, recite mantras, practice esoteric rituals and otherwise prepare themselves for pilgrimages to Pemakö. While both were educated in the tradition of scientific rationalism, they question the ability of logic to account for all phenomena. Pemakö's inner realms do exist, they believe, and access to them is a matter of faith, proper karma, and pure vision, not rational thought.

Like many converts to Buddhism, Baker and Sardar do not look the part. They shun the shaved heads, maroon robes, and other trappings of the orthodox, and for a night on the town in Kathmandu might look as wordly as boulevardiers on Park Avenue. Baker, who is six foot one and solidly built, with a mane of dark, curly hair and a youthful face, might be dressed in linen pants, a stylish shirt, and a pair of beautifully made walking shoes that he picked up in London at Holland & Holland, the exclusive hunting outfitters. Sardar owns a pair, too, and sheepishly confesses to buying a Prada parka when he and an erstwhile girlfriend, a member of Nepal's former ruling family, went on a shopping spree in London. He is handsome, with a square, jutting jaw and flashing white smile, and like Baker is socially in demand. But they are not dilettantes or faux Buddhists. To hear the two describe the mental and spiritual preparation for their "Buddhist adventures" in Pemakö leaves little doubt about their faith or commitment to the quest for inner worlds.

In the gorge, the two go by Buddhist names bestowed by their Tibetan gurus. Baker is Konchok Wangyal, "precious powerful conqueror," while Sardar is Lekdrup Dorje, "accomplished thunderbolt." Over the years, they have developed a kind of Socratic dialog for discussing Buddhist theology, and their notes and e-mails often close with a valediction such as "Prosper and reveal the secrets" or "May the mandala unfold." As practitioners of the Nyingma tradition, the "original" order of Tibetan Buddhism, they seek to reshape emotions such as fear and anxiety that might paralyze a nonpractitioner in a place as arduous as Pemakö. Rather than resist or ignore such emotions, initiates embrace and transform them to achieve enlightenment in one lifetime. It's a quick but risky path to higher consciousness that adepts say is like trying to lick honey from a razor's edge: One either tastes the sweetness or lacerates the tongue.

The two first met in Kathmandu in 1987. Baker, then twenty-nine, was directing the School for International Training, a semester-abroad program that he had attended ten years earlier as a college junior. Sardar, at twenty-one, was a history and religion major at Tufts University who enrolled in the program that year. The routes they had taken to Nepal were vastly dissimilar, but the two recognized at once their common interest in Eastern mysticism and shared horror of living a conventional life in America.

Baker was raised in the environs of New York City, the son of a noted architect, John Milnes Baker. From an early age, Baker displayed a talent for art and a taste for the fantastic. Precociously imaginative, he once tried to persuade several schoolmates that he could see fish swimming outside the family's apartment windows in New York. Later, at boarding school, his doodles were rendered in a cartoonish, Maurice Sendak–like style and filled with goblins and castles. Waterfalls were a recurring theme in his art—the sea pouring off the edge of the earth, or a cascade spilling down from the heights of a medieval village perched on the heights of a mountain and cut off from the surrounding lowlands by a drawbridge. The latter hangs in his father and stepmother's home in a woodsy suburb north of the city.

But it was among the dunes and beach grasses bordering Long Island's Great South Bay where Baker's imagination took flight. The family had a home on an estuary of the Carmans River, and their next-door neighbor was the late Dennis Puleston, a British-born transglobal sailor, sometime treasure hunter, keen ornithologist, painter, author, scientist, and cofounder of the Environmental Defense Fund. Puleston had a profound influence on the young Baker, according to his father. The craggy-looking adventurer would take him and his own children sailing in his yawl, sometimes running a Jolly Roger up the flagpole and landing on an island to hunt for "treasure" that Puleston had earlier buried. At Puleston's home, Baker was exposed to a "house full of writers, film makers, archaeologists—interesting people" with a worldview beyond the limits of Long Island.

Baker's horizons expanded further when he moved to Norway at the age of thirteen with his mother and Norwegian stepfather, who introduced him to mountaineering. Later, he attended Middlebury College in Vermont, where he studied art and English Literature and, according to a classmate, was "at the center of a bohemian fringe that fused intellectual curiosity with creative party spirit." (In his senior year, he reportedly staged a pagan bacchanalia in the woods that featured a live animal sacrifice.) In the spirit of experimentalism that infused the late 1970s, Baker borrowed the motto "Further" from the Merry Pranksters, and like them was known for pushing the edge. Barely two months out of college, while big-wall climbing in Norway, Baker fell seventy feet to a ledge and smashed his knee and head. He was lucky not to have died. When he peeled off the rock face, he was some twenty-five feet above his last piece of protective hardware, and he was not wearing a helmet. After the fall, he looked like "Jesus coming down off the cross," his father said. With blood streaming down his face onto his beard, he was flown by helicopter to a hospital on an island off the coast of Norway. Doctors were not optimistic about his chances of walking normally again.

During his convalescence in New York, Baker recalled a Vermont folk remedy that he had heard about in college. He hobbled out to a local apiary, Mrs. Sharp's, and procured a supply of honeybees, which he allowed to sting precise points around his injured knee. His recovery was complete (despite or because of the bee venom therapy), and he set off a year later for Sikkim and northeastern India to study Shamanism and indigenous medicine. The Explorers Club of New York financed the field study with a research grant for which United Nations ambassador Francis Kellogg, a relative and close family friend, put in a good word. Bouncing between the Himalayas, Vermont, and Britain in the mid-1980s, Baker earned a master's degree in English from Oxford, but his interest lay in the world's tallest mountains and the "scintillating chaos" of Kathmandu. The city was for him a living laboratory for studying art, Eastern mysticism, and nature, and it had the most beautiful women he had ever seen. From the day he first saw the city as a college junior, he had been bewitched.

"Kathmandu was quite a magical place during the seventies," he says. "There was no traffic, no pollution, clear views of the mountains. It felt like a medieval city ringed by green mountains and towering ice peaks. That first afternoon, walking through the streets among herds of goats and woodcutters, I said, 'This is where I'll live.' There was no question in my mind. It was a coming-home experience."

As the capital of the sixties-era "Rock 'n' Roll Raj," Kathmandu had become a crossroads for dropouts, bliss-outs, dope freaks, and dharma bums, none of which Baker was. He came to study sacred art but soon became seduced by the anything-goes lifestyle of the expatriate community and the mind-expanding rituals of Tantric yoga, in which even sex can be used to open the body's subtle energy channels and expand consciousness. When he returned to Kathmandu in 1982, he took up the pursuit of self-enlightenment through rigorous meditation and adventuring, in both the city and the Himalayan wilderness.

An anthropologist friend, Carroll Dunham, described this period as Baker's "Gauguin phase."

"To understand Ian is to understand bliss," Dunham says. "He's a bliss boy. Some people are addicted to substances, but he wants bliss, nothing else." She characterized him as "Peter Pan with a wild streak" and the "quintessential romantic," though at the same time a scholar conducting an inquiry into dimensions where others would fear to tread.

"He really believes in these [mythical hidden] realms," she explains. "He's not cynical about them. The question he asks is 'Where does myth end and reality begin?' That's the edge where Ian has lived his life."

. . .

EARLY ON AFTER moving to Nepal Baker realized that he did not have the patience to become a painter. Instead, he decided, he would pursue his twin passions for nature and art by delving into a study of landscape symbolism in visionary artworks. To grasp the imagery of Tibetan scroll paintings, with their wrathful deities, dancing skeletons, and Buddhas locked in erotic embrace with voluptuous consorts, one must consider not just the effect of the external landscape on the artist but also the influence of the artist's inner, mental landscape on the art. According to some popular theories, Tibet's endless solitude, hostile weather, and rugged mountains take shape in the artist's mind as a pantheon of terrifying spirits that must be propitiated. Understanding the interplay between the topography of Tibet and the psychology of the Tibetan provides one key to unlock the symbolism of Tibetan religious painting, sculpture, and ritual objects. But to fully appreciate a particular work, certain art historians explain, one must be familiar, too, with the mystical vision that inspired it.

Ultimately Baker became enough of a connoisseur to dabble in the art trade himself. He had a good enough eye to support himself as an art buyer for a wealthy Japanese collector visiting New York during a brief period in 1990 when Baker was pursuing a doctorate in Oriental studies at Columbia. This was a low point in his life. It made little sense to him to be studying Buddhism in New York when he could be living it in Kathmandu—and having a lot more fun, too. He fled back to his adopted home at the first chance, coauthoring a book on Tibetan culture with Carroll Dunham and her photographer husband.

Learning to distinguish authentic scroll paintings from copies, and great art from merely good, was the easy part for the cum laude graduate. It required only academic rigor to become an expert in Buddhist iconography. He learned to recognize the dizzying number of deities by name, to interpret their mythic biographies, and to understand the symbolism of their often grotesque anatomical forms—that one Buddha's sixteen legs, for example, represent "the sixteen emptinesses," and that the birds he tramples underfoot stand for "the eight magical powers."

Much more time-consuming and difficult was achieving the exalted states that the paintings depicted. Tibetan sacred art has been described as being "so obscurely encoded that access to it often seems barred to a thinking mind." Baker reckoned that the only way to fully comprehend the secret meaning embedded in the artworks was to become an initiate in the spiritual traditions that the artist had followed and which was symbolically being expressed. This was the arduous path that eventually would lead him to the great abyss of Pemakö. He had first heard of hidden lands in Sikkim, but by happenstance he picked up the trail again in 1984 when he overheard conversation in a Kathmandu art gallery about a lama who had recently returned from a *beyul* near the Tibetan border.

Baker sought out the lama, a revered meditation master named Chatral Sangye Dorje, and explained his interest in hidden lands. The *rinpoche* (*rinpoche* means "great precious one" and is a title given to highly revered lamas) told him that if he really wanted to understand what a hidden land was, he should go to one. "They are places for practice," the lama explained. "Certain kinds of experiences are possible in them that are not possible elsewhere. If you're really interested, there is no point in just going and coming back with pictures."

Chatral Rinpoche had spent much of his life wandering across Tibet and living in wild mountain hermitages, but he eventually joined the Tibetan diaspora and came to Nepal. Today, at about ninety, he still teaches meditation, and his reputation extends from Kathmandu to Hollywood. Would-be Buddhists such as action star Steven Seagal (who reportedly believes himself to be a reincarnated lama) seek him out, although the unpredictable *rinpoche* may or may not consent to an audience. He reportedly directed Seagal to go stock the Ganges with fish, and he has thrown potatoes at other disciples to awaken their self-awareness.

Some years after settling in Nepal, Chatral Rinpoche experienced a series of dreams and visions about a cave in a hidden land called Yolmo, located in the mountains north of Kathmandu. According to a treasure text written by Buddhism's patron saint, Padmasambava, and discovered in the fourteenth century, the great guru explained that he had once attained enlightenment in this cave, at whose entrance grew a species of wild rose. In time, Chatral Rinpoche moved to Yolmo and there met an ancient yak herder who knew of the cave. As a boy, the herder had gone searching for a lost yak and found it grazing beside the portal, near a bush of uniquely beautiful flowers.

The rinpoche immediately organized an expedition. According to legend, he mounted a white horse and led a group of followers to a high pass, where they became engulfed in thick fog. The old lama performed a ceremony to appease the local protector spirits, and a rainbow appeared in the distance. He directed his followers to pursue the rainbow, and off they marched, chopping their way through a primeval forest that led them to a secret valley. There was the cave. They plucked a flower from the rose bush, bore it to the rinpoche as a gift, and led him back to the cave, which he consecrated.

This is the gist of the story that Baker had heard in the art gallery. When he met the rinpoche and asked about *beyul,* the lama told him to come back the following summer prepared to spend a month meditating in one of Yolmo's subvalleys, called Pemthang, a place so charged with energy that just being there can amplify a meditating initiate's awareness. When Baker returned, the lama gave him blessings and a bag of *tsampa*, or roasted barley, and sent him off with a couple of yak herders to carry his gear.

Pemthang resembles Pemakö but on a smaller scale: a lush, wet, subtropical valley surrounded by towering cliffs and snowy peaks. To reach it, Baker had to cross several high passes, then descend through a rocky gorge to the valley. The caves—different ones for different meditation practices—looked down on a central meadow. It was the middle of the monsoon season and very wet but also spectacularly beautiful: a Tolkienesque landscape with mist reeling in and out of colossal rhododendrons festooned with moss, and streams cascading among mossy boulders.

Baker meditated in his cave twelve hours a day. He had his routine—ninety minutes of prescribed meditation upon arising; breakfast of the *rinpoche's* roasted barley, more meditation prior to a simple lunch of rice and mung beans flavored with herbs and wild mushrooms, cooked over a fire in the back of the cave; a trip to the river for water; then two more meditation sessions before and after dinner, which he made from leftovers from his lunch.

Baker will not elaborate on private visions he experienced during the retreat but says he was "very high" when he came down. "You feel the mind begin to fray," he explains. "You're excavating down to sublevels of consciousness. Unfamiliar emotions and energies are unearthed and rise to the surface. You begin to recognize that the mind is interwoven with what normally appears to be an external landscape. The unattuned traveler could walk through such a valley unaware of its transforming energy. "It's not just a question of the place but of experiencing the place," Baker says. "From a Buddhist point of view, reality is largely an issue of perception. The landscape is moving through you as much as you are moving through it. A strange, numinous encounter occurs, and that's when the journey becomes a pilgrimage, when it gains a spiritual or inward dimension. The goal is not a place but a state of mind."

Before he studied Tantric Buddhism, Baker had experienced similar states as a climber. Indeed, extreme climbing drew him to meditation as a way of focusing his concentration and overcoming fear. Once, in Boulder, Colorado, ascending a sheer rock face—alone and without a rope—he found himself in "increasingly, ridiculously unsafe conditions" that were far beyond his perceived limits. He felt his mind telescoping down to an acute state of awareness: "It was like climbing into another state of mind. The world condensed into a sphere of energy that I was moving through. Suddenly what had seemed impossible and life-threatening turned into a blissful sensation of floating through a world of rock and space and energy." He had stumbled into "a yogic level of climbing" that many other elite alpinists have described.

The risks and fears of climbing thus became Baker's "back door" into Buddhism. He was fascinated with the exalted states that came not through drugs but through putting himself in positions of extreme danger, not trying to suppress or deny fear but using it to reach other levels of consciousness.

"Rock climbing is a dance with fear, not a battle with it," he says. "When you are up on a cliff face and the holds have petered out, and the last moves you made were so extreme that you know you can't reverse them, then comes this moment of intense realism. It's a state you can't experience unless you put yourself willingly into such situations. If we give in to fear, we don't experience what's beyond it. If we try to suppress it, we experience its full potential. Only when we embrace fear does it dissolve, and something behind it begins to emerge. It's a more subtle consciousness, which is totally open and very, very aware."

After his month in Pemthang, Baker revisited Chatral Rinpoche to recount his experiences and to learn more about other *beyuls*. The *rinpoche* wrote out a list of seven place names in beautiful calligraphy. "Some of these you can reach, since they're in Nepal," the teacher told him. "But the greatest of them is one that you might never be able to get to—Pemakö."

Baker took that as a challenge and began investigating his

prospects. At that point he could find nothing written about Pemakö in English (he did not read Tibetan), and pilgrims' guidebooks to it were written in a cryptic "twilight language," as Baker calls it, that is intentionally unintelligible to the masses.

In addition, Baker faced more mundane, political problems: It was 1985, and relations between India and China over their contested border were raw. Pemakö seemed an impossible goal. So Baker returned to Pemthang for a second retreat, then traveled to another hidden land called Kyimolung, in northern Nepal. Like all *beyuls*, Kyimolung can be thought of as a mandala, a magic circle that alters everything within its perimeter. A pagoda temple occupies the spiritual center of the valley, and the encircling mountains are home to protector deities. To ensure that the *beyul*'s location remains secret, the gods administer "an elixir of forgetfulness" to deserving pilgrims who are allowed to come and go.

Certain deep Tantric practices and yogas must be performed in places such as this, where no one will observe you. One, called *Ru shen*, involves cultivating primal states by acting out in the manner of a wild dog—going barking mad, as it were. Such rituals are not written about except in a secret, coded way. When a teacher feels that the time is right, he instructs his initiates through a "whispered lineage," revealing how to attain the next level of understanding. At very advanced stages, practitioners may be introduced to the secrets of erotic mysticism, a powerful and misunderstood tool for achieving higher states of awareness.

"In the West, this aspect of Tantrism has been cheapened and misconstrued as some sort of libertine path of sexual and spiritual indulgence," Baker says. But in Tantra, every activity—from sleeping to making love to climbing a mountain—can be used to reach the ultimate goal of Buddhism: a state of unbounded empathy and awareness.

"Tantric meditations are all about the exchange and transformation of energy, and the union of opposites—of yin and yang, or in Tantrism of *yab* and *yum* [literally, father-mother]," says Baker. "The energy field of the female is a powerful support for the energy field of

the male, and vice versa." Thus, the typical Tantric deity is depicted
not as a solitary figure seated in meditative isolation but as a Buddha,
or awakened being, shown in mystical coition with his consort, who
is often seated in his lap facing him. Their union *(yabyum)* symbolizes
an "intimate, fruitful, final and perfect union between two ideas, two
psychic realities, two elements," according to Italian anthropologist
Fosco Mariani. For Baker, the conjunction between the exalted lovers
is a visual metaphor for a state of transcendent bliss. "Tantra is about
overcoming dualistic thinking that things are either sacred or profane.
Tantric art reveals that all aspects of existence can be turned into a way
toward spiritual evolution."

Chatral Rinpoche told Baker not to think of Pemakö as a paradise in the Western sense but rather in Tantric terms, as a place of un-
compromising wildness and danger. That appealed to Baker the
adventurous risk taker as much as Baker the initiate. "Only by recognizing your insecurities, when you're confronting death, do you see
the nature of life, self, and reality," he says. "In that regard Pemakö is
paradise. The misconception that it's heaven on earth is one that even
Tibetans have had. In different periods, they've gone to Pemakö
searching for an earthly paradise and found instead a terrifying place
full of tigers and wild savages. It wasn't the paradise they had in mind."

According to texts that Baker began collecting, Pemakö's energy
is essentially feminine, which also appealed to him. The gorge and surrounding mountains are physical manifestations of the goddess Dorje
Phagmo, whose supine form reclines across the landscape. Features of
the topography represent parts of her anatomy. Her heart, for example, is Padma-shel-ri, the Lotus Crystal Mountain that pilgrims and
refugees have long sought in vain. Gyala Peri, the summit on the
north side of the Tsangpo, is her head. Namche Barwa, south of the
river, is her right breast, while a peak called Zumchen Phagmo
Dong—the Radiantly Smiling Sow-Face Mountain—is her left one.
Her vagina, or *yoni,* lies across the Tibet-India border at a promontory
called Choying Gyeltsen, Victory Banner of Infinite Space, from
which issues a stream of the *dakinis'* [celestial nymphs] sexual fluids.

The Tsangpo itself is Dorje Phagmo's central meridian, her main energy channel. She is depicted dancing, and has a small sow's head emerging from her neck. The sow represents ignorance, and the goddess's dance is one of joy at having cast off the veils of ignorance. By meditating on both her form and the landscape in Pemakö, pilgrims attempt to approach her state of penetrating awareness.

"She is the key to understanding the place," Baker says. "She is the landscape but also the mind of the pilgrim traveling through the landscape." In short, she was the ideal consort for someone such as Baker, captivated as he was with the notion of the divine feminine.

According to Tibetan masters writing in the seventeenth century, Pemakö is at the center of eight hidden lands that unfold like the petals of a lotus across Tibet. The *beyul's* geography features twelve outer territories, forty inner ravines, and sixteen secret territories. Although it was first located and sealed off by Padmasambava in the eighth century, Pemakö was not opened until the Mongol invasions in the seventeenth century. Its three main pilgrimage routes relate to deeds performed by Guru Rinpoche, as the saint is also known. The pilgrim walks in a clockwise direction, stopping at various grottos, springs, and shrines to offer prayers and prostrations. One circuit around the high peaks bestows thirteen times as much merit as a circuit of the middle path around Padma-shel-ri, the heart center. And a circuit of the long, hazardous ravine path along the river is equal to thirteen circumambulations of the peak path.

Certain oral traditions also mention that the *beyul's* inner sanctum can be reached through a portal in a rock face that leads to a long tunnel. The passage eventually opens onto a magical valley—the proverbial land of milk and honey. Baker was enchanted by the idea of this other realm. "It's not a place that exists separately from the mind," he says. "Because no one has been there to see it, it's just referred to as a numinous center without designation. There are no directions to it. It's beyond conventional coordinates of longitude and latitude. It's beyond geography."

Obsessed as he was with Pemakö, Baker had to content himself with studying it from afar. By 1987, he was prepared to go, but the Chinese were still not granting travel permits to southeastern Tibet. It was still a restricted zone, and for good reason: Shots had been exchanged across the border with Indian troops only the year before. Baker would have to bide his time until 1993. In the meantime, he made another fortuitous contact when a young Iranian-American named Hamid Sardar arrived in Kathmandu to study at the School for International Training, which Baker was directing.

. . .

ABDOL-HAMID SARDAR-AFKHAMI had grown up in Iran and France under far more privileged circumstances than Baker had in New York. He was part of the Persian nobility, a descendant of the Qajar dynasty. (*Afkhami* means "the great," and *sardar* is a military title that translates as "head one.") According to family lore, his great-grandfather was killed in a Russian ambush by troops that included a young Joseph Stalin. Another distant relative, Fath' Ali Shah, had a harem of more than a hundred women and produced as many children. Sardar's parents, both architects, worked for the shah of Iran. Well-to-do, they spent idyllic summers on the Caspian Sea, where Sardar and his father, an avid hunter, went on long tramps in the lush Caspian Mountains. The family fled the Islamic fundamentalist uprising in Iran in the late 1970s and eventually settled in France's Loire Valley, where they breed Arabian horses on a wooded estate noted for its boar hunting.

Sardar and Baker grew to be fast friends. Charming, attractive, and with a wild streak of his own, Sardar had a pedigree that gave him access to the social orbit of Nepali royals, jet-setters, and club crawlers. The two also shared an eye for Nepali ingénues and became rather notorious men about town. But they were also serious scholars of Tibetan art, culture, and religion, and ultimately formed a pact to make a pilgrimage to Pemakö, legally or illegally.

Before coming to Nepal, while at Tufts, Sardar dreamt one night of a pristine landscape dominated by a perfectly shaped pyramidal mountain. A Tibetan riding a white horse galloped up and gestured at the mountain but otherwise said nothing. The dream stayed with him for days. After settling in at the school in Kathmandu, Baker suggested that he travel upcountry to see if Chatral Rinpoche would consent to interpret the dream.

"I smelled him before I saw him," Sardar recalls. "He had an incredibly musky odor, and I could hear him bellowing like a lion in his meditations. When I came into his room, we both instantly recognized each other. It was he who had been in my dream. He roared with laughter and invited me to sit at his feet."

Chatral Rinpoche agreed to be Sardar's teacher and suggested that he, too, should go to the Pemthang Valley to meditate. Baker went to the valley at the same time, but the two remained in separate caves.

During his meditations, Sardar went through a radical emotional upheaval. At first his mind chattered at him like a nervous monkey, and then he fell into a deep depression. "I saw in my own suffering everyone else's suffering," he says. "But then, suddenly, the despair gave way to complete bliss. Chopping wood or carrying water—it was all bliss."

After a month, Sardar ceremonially closed his cave and began the trek out of the valley. He became lost and ran out of food. At last he noticed a child's footprints and followed them to a nomad family's tent. Everyone inside was terrified of him, looking wild and unshaven after a month in the wilderness. When he explained that he was a student of Chatral Rinpoche's, the family welcomed him inside and the next day guided him to the path down to the nearest town.

Back at the *rinpoche*'s monastery, Sardar regaled his teacher about his experiences. "Lucky man," the *rinpoche* said. "This is the day that the Buddha began his teaching. There is no need for you to shave your head or wear robes like a monk. You can be a secret Buddhist."

Sardar spent three months in voluntary servitude to the guru. "It felt like a knight meeting his king," he says. "I felt immediately that I wanted to serve him." In time, the *rinpoche* gave Sardar his Buddhist name, Lekdrup Dorje, and a mantra to chant, and assigned to him a protector deity to focus on during his meditations. The guardian spirit was the very deity from whom Chatral Rinpoche emanates: Dorje Drolo, the wrathful emanation of Padmasambava. Like his guru, Sardar would pursue the Tantric path of Dzokchen, a further shortcut to enlightenment that can be as fraught with existential crises as a pilgrimage in Pemakö can be. Practitioners of the tradition seek a state of perfect awareness and bliss, without attachment to any thought or emotion. Once Dzokchen adepts have slipped effortlessly into a state of empty awareness, they are said to be able to recognize the space between thoughts.

After his retreats in Yolmo and studies at the feet of his guru, Sardar debated whether to renounce Western civilization altogether and commit to a monastic life. He could not bring himself to do that, and reentered the competitive academic world, where he went on to earn a doctorate in Tibetan studies at Harvard. During the long climb up the ivory tower, he learned to read and speak Tibetan and to translate centuries-old texts on hidden lands. But he also felt disconnected from the bliss and transcendent clarity he'd known at Yolmo, and wondered if he would ever achieve that sort of rapture in Pemakö.

. . .

BAKER REMAINED IN Kathmandu (except for his stint at Columbia's graduate school) and continued pursuing the dream of reaching the sacred land. He improvised a livelihood as a tour group leader, freelance writer, and lecturer, living in the "overtly modest" style of a struggling academic. To research *Tibet: Reflections from the Wheel of Life*, the book he cowrote with Carroll Dunham, he traveled to Tibetan refugee camps in India and heard stories about Pemakö that were right out of *The Lord of the Rings:* Some refugees told of seeing ants as big as dogs, birds that sang mantras and provided directions to pilgrims, and fellow pilgrims who had died in Pemakö and whose bodies had turned immediately to rainbow light. The son of a charismatic lama who had led a group of refugees to India in the 1950s told Baker that his father had found the portal to Pemakö's inner sanctum.

It was concealed behind a waterfall and led to a tunnel that opened onto a valley filled with rainbows and the singing of celestial nymphs. The lama returned to lead his retinue to the sacred vale, but the portal closed behind him and he was unable to reopen it.

In Dharamsala, India, the seat of the Tibetan government in exile, Baker had an audience with the Dalai Lama, who could not shed a great deal of light on Pemakö but directed him to his own preceptor. The lama had fled Tibet through the sacred land in 1959. With some reluctance he showed Baker a folio of hand-printed sheets wrapped in silk brocade. It was one of the pilgrims' guidebooks to Pemakö, attributed to Padmasambava and written in the arcane twilight language. Baker described it as "a Fodor's guide to the fourth dimension." He made a copy and, back in Nepal, asked a close associate of Chatral Rinpoche to translate it, which the lama did.

While he was researching Pemakö in India, Baker was smitten by a gorgeous young Tibetan schoolteacher whose grandfather had been one of the high lamas in Pemakö years earlier. She had grown up speaking the Pemakö dialect with her parents and still spoke it. Although the gorge was still not officially open, the woman agreed to try to reach Pemakö with Baker and Sardar. Yet when Baker and Sardar asked Chatral Rinpoche to perform a divination about the pilgrimage, the lama told them that the time was not right, that the two should go to Beyul Kyimolung in Nepal instead. As it turned out, the *rinpoche* was right: It was 1989, and shortly after his divination, the riots in Beijing's Tiananmen Square broke out. All travel to Tibet was suspended.

Although he continued to investigate his prospects for entering Pemakö legally, and while a few other intrepid scholars and travelers did sneak into the area, Baker resigned himself to the fact that his experience of the *beyul* might remain academic, that he might never actually visit the place. But in 1993 he received a telegram from an American outfitter named Rick Fisher inviting him to join a rafting expedition to the gorge. Fisher's Chinese contacts had persuaded police and military authorities to grant him a permit to lead a group of clients into the canyon. He had learned of Baker through a travel agency in Chengdu that both of them were using. Would Baker be interested in joining the expedition as its cultural expert and interpreter?

It was as if the gods had finally smiled on Baker. He accepted the invitation, despite harboring grave misgivings about rafting the Tsangpo, and not knowing anything about Rick Fisher.

. . .

FISHER PROMOTED HIMSELF as "perhaps North America's leading canyoneer." Compactly built, with a drooping mustache and sun-streaked hair, the forty-one-year-old Arizona wilderness guide found his niche in the adventure business leading trips into the canyons around the world. Canyoneering—a fusion of trekking, climbing, and river running—had taken him from the Grand Canyon to the *barrancas* of the Sierra Madre and beyond: to Bolivia, Greece, Peru, and Argentina. He turned his attention to the great river gorges of China in 1986, believing them to be deeper and more extensive than any canyon system in Europe or the Americas, and decided that he would prove it. In 1989, he applied for permission to visit what he thought would prove to be the grandest canyon of all, the Tsangpo Gorge.

Fisher was apparently unaware that the gorge's depth had been verified years earlier, by Bailey and Morshead and by Kingdon-Ward and Cawdor. In 1913, Bailey took a dramatic photograph of Gyala Peri rearing up icily in the background, while the Tsangpo snaked through the brooding, steep-sided chasm at its feet. He made the image near the hamlet of Gyala, where the river begins its furious plunge through the Himalayas. What he found most astonishing was that the mountain's 23,460-foot summit stood just thirteen miles away from that of Namche Barwa, at 25,445 feet, *"and between them flowed the Tsangpo, over 14,000 feet below Gyala Peri and 16,000 feet below Namche Barwa* [italics added]."

Using a boiling-point thermometer, Morshead calculated the river's elevation at the Pemaköchung monastery below Gyala to be 16,645 feet below Namche Barwa's summit—or more than three miles. His map of the area is quite detailed, showing the river's course for as far as he and Bailey could observe it, approximately ten miles past the monastery.

Kingdon-Ward and Cawdor recognized the gorge's stupendous depth, too, and so did biologists Frank Ludlow and George Sherriff in 1947. As Kingdon-Ward remarked in his 1925 Royal Geographical Society lecture about his Tsangpo expedition, "the river [tore] through a chasm 10,000 feet deep and at the bottom only 50 feet wide." He could have fixed the canyon's depth to the foot had he wanted to, instead of speaking in generalities, because he and Cawdor had taken many more elevation readings at river level and charted more of the river's course through the gap than their predecessors had. Sherriff thought it almost inconceivable that the river could "cut so low" as it surged between Gyala Peri and Namche Barwa. "I think this is the finest sight I have ever seen," he wrote about the fantastic mountainscape.

But verifying the gorge as the world's deepest and claiming that as a major discovery was not something that occurred to any of these pioneers, if only because they did not have the comparative data on canyon depths that a specialist such as Fisher had been amassing. For a professional canyoneer, establishing the gorge's world-record depth would also be a feather in his explorer's cap—and a wise career move in an era of increasingly competitive adventuring with fewer exploratory plums to pluck than had been available to earlier generations. Fisher craved recognition, and he believed he would find it in the Tsangpo Gorge.

His wasn't the first such overture the Chinese government had received. Enterprising adventure-tour operators had been jockeying to lead treks into the canyon since the 1970s, and climbers were well aware that Namche Barwa was then the highest unclimbed peak in the world. A first ascent of the mountain would guarantee a place in the record books, just as a first descent of the Tsangpo would guarantee immortality in the annals of river running, as Fisher well knew.

The Chinese response to him was nevertheless resoundingly

negative: The Tsangpo area was closed due to its military and strategic importance. The Chinese and Indian governments had been arguing over their common border running through the lower gorge ever
since the British had defined the boundary—the so-called McMahon
Line—in 1914. The long-festering dispute had erupted into all-out
war in 1962, with Mao Zedong's People's Liberation Army crushing
India's jungle brigades. Only Chinese scientists were allowed into the
canyon during the 1970s and 1980s, and their maps of it remained
classified.

But Fisher was persistent. In 1992, after three years of pressing
for a permit, his telephone rang at 2 A.M. one September night. His
Chinese travel agent had good news and bad: Fisher was welcome to
bring eight clients to the gorge, but the permit period started in just
two weeks. Unable to recruit a team on such short notice, he asked
if he could reconnoiter the gorge by himself in order to plan an expedition for the following year. The invitation held; he could come
ahead.

That first trip awakened Fisher to the scale of the gorge and to
the difficulties he would face traversing its length. It would take at least
three expeditions to survey it from top to bottom. At home in Tucson, he advertised the first two trips, one in the spring of 1993 and one
in the fall, and cabled the invitation to Ian Baker.

. . .

BAKER'S AGENDA IN the gorge had little to do with
Fisher's. Baker could have cared less about scoring a first descent of the
river or establishing a depth record for the canyon. His hope was to
follow one of the pilgrimage routes. He came to Tibet well prepared
for that, bringing notes of his interviews with refugees who had traveled through Pemakö and copies of pilgrims' guidebooks. Still, he had
signed up to go rafting, and rafting he would go.

Meeting Fisher and his team in Lhasa only heightened Baker's
misgivings. Fisher struck him as rigid and stressed-out, and some of the
clients appeared ill prepared for the physical challenge they would be

facing. Among them were a twelve-year-old boy and his mother from Minneapolis, an overweight Tucson property manager who had a prosthetic knee ligament, a land developer who had never slept in a tent before, and a sixty-seven-year-old wildlife cinematographer from Alaska who'd cashed in his life insurance policy to make a film about the gorge.

But others on the team had solid credentials. Ken Storm, a literate, adventurous forty-one-year-old Minneapolis distributor of books and hobbies, had spent a year trekking in Mexico's Sierra Madre after college, rafted big water on the Green and Colorado Rivers, and coauthored a guidebook to Ladakh. Storm had known about Fisher before being asked to join the Tsangpo team. He had read one of Fisher's guidebooks to the canyons of the Sierra Madre and phoned him to compare notes. A year later, based on that one conversation, Fisher called him back about rafting the Tsangpo. To prepare for the trip, Storm had put himself through a crash course, working out and reading everything he could about the gorge, including Bailey and Kingdon-Ward's accounts. While Baker had thought the books "prosaic," Storm found them absorbing. He was excited at the possibility of retracing some of Bailey's and Kingdon-Ward's routes, and especially about penetrating the five-mile gap that they had left unexplored.

Still more capable were two of Fisher's expedition mainstays: Eric Manthey and Jill Bielawski, Fisher's former girlfriend. Fisher considered her to be one of the top canyoneers in America and Manthey, a powerfully built plumber, to be a fearless "Daniel Boone type" and consummate outdoorsman. On rafting trips down the Colorado, the two delighted in crashing through the boiling, chocolate-colored rapids of Lava Falls, once with Bielawski at the oars and Manthey riding in the bow, chin out to the rapids, like a bearded hood ornament.

When the team reached the gorge and trekked down to Gyala, Fisher saw that rafting would be suicidal, even for the experts. Premonsoon rains had been lashing the canyon for days, and the Tsangpo was swollen and moving like a runaway locomotive—the same "foam and fury" Kingdon-Ward had described seventy years earlier. The rain had also soaked the unstable slopes above the river, raising the possibility of catastrophic landslides. Sitting on the juncture of the Asian and Indian continental plates, the gorge can be hit with quakes as violent as the magnitude 8.6 quake in 1950 that Kingdon-Ward and his wife, Jean, survived.

Fisher was under pressure to come up with a new plan fast. He called a meeting of his troops. Just then, Tibetan porters scurried up the trail from the inner canyon carrying American-made backpacks. Close behind were the owners: David Breashears, a renowned Everest climber and cinematographer, and photojournalist Gordon Wiltsie.

Wiry, supremely conditioned, and driven, Breashears had long been interested in the canyon. He was intimate with the exploratory history of the gorge and considered the pundit Kintup a hero. Moreover, the gorge was the only part of the Tsangpo-Brahmaputra watershed that he had not explored in years of Himalayan climbing. He and several friends had considered making the first ascent of Namche Barwa in the early 1980s, but the Chinese were then demanding a million dollars for that permit. Breashears dropped the idea and went on to climb Everest several times, in 1983 making the first live television broadcast from the top of the world. Wiltsie had also climbed and trekked throughout the Himalayas, and had long experience photographing in some of the world's nastiest alpine environments, from Central Asia to the Patagonian Andes to Antarctica.

Unbeknownst to Fisher, *National Geographic* had assigned the two to produce an article and photographs on the gorge. Fisher had suggested a similar article to the magazine, but the editors had politely declined. In fact, Breashears had beaten him to the punch with the idea and had managed to obtain tourist permits to retrace Kingdon-Ward's route. He and Wiltsie had reached the canyon several weeks before Fisher's team.

The two climbers had endured a miserable ordeal beyond Gyala. Cold rain had poured down without letup for eight days. Thrashing through the sodden forests, they encountered the waist-deep scrub and abrupt cliffs that had foiled Bailey and Kingdon-Ward. The two inhaled clouds of gnats with every breath, and at one rest stop Wiltsie counted sixty leeches on his boots. Six of their nine porters had quit, and the remaining three were on the brink of mutiny. The only food left in their communal larder had been a couple of rounds of Brie cheese until the porters found a dead monkey, still warm but with most of its fur licked off. Leopard tracks surrounding the body suggested a recent kill. Delighted, the porters barbecued the carcass for dinner that night, and the meat had fed everyone for the final two days of their return to Gyala.

Under pressure to produce an article and breathtaking photographs of the gorge's vistas—and now running short of time on their travel permit, and money as well—both men were in a rush but stopped to greet Fisher and his team. As they regaled Fisher's clients about the horrors of the trek ahead, Fisher walked up and said, "Hello, my name is Rick Fisher. I'd love to talk to you, but we're having an important meeting. I'll be happy to meet with you later at our camp. Please leave."

Fisher knew who Breashears was but not that he was on assignment for *National Geographic*. When he learned of the mission, in his mind pieces of an elaborate conspiracy began to fall into place. He recalled surprise encounters with other *Geographic* writers and photographers—while canyoneering in Mexico, for example—only to have "his" article appear in the magazine later. He suspected that Breashears was "a paid hit man from *National Geographic*," sent out to scoop the story he had proposed.

Breashears sat down in the middle of the group and folded his arms, as if to say, "We're here, what are you going to do about it?" Jill Bielawski thought the mountaineer was being smug and that he was baiting Fisher. And when Breashears leaned over and widened his eyes to tell her about the cliffs, the leeches, and the dead monkey on the trail, she thought, "What an asshole."

Fisher approached again. "I asked you to leave," he said firmly, "and you can leave, *now!*"

Outraged at their reception, Wiltsie and Breashears left the en-

campment. An hour later, as the two mountaineers were drinking barley brew with their porters in Gyala, Fisher and his team arrived.
Fisher was on horseback, having injured his knee training for the trip,
while the others were on foot—a picturesque image of the first
trekking group in the gorge. Wiltsie grabbed a camera, but as soon as
he raised it, Fisher jumped down and, jabbing at Wiltsie's chest, said,
"How dare you take my picture! Who gave you permission to take my
picture?" Wiltsie drew himself up and replied coolly, "I don't need
permission to take your picture. Why are you being so belligerent?
I've never met you."

The argument fizzled to a close. Darkness was falling, and Fisher
and his team faced a hike to reach the trailhead. Breashears and Wiltsie would stay the night but in the morning planned to hike back to
the Lhasa-Sichuan road near the entryway to the gorge, drive east to
the Po Tsangpo, and hike down its canyon to the confluence with the
main Tsangpo. That would put them at the apex of the Great Bend,
and from there they could mount an assault on the inner canyon from
downstream, as Kingdon-Ward had done.

What they did not know was that Fisher was planning to do the
same thing.

. . .

BAKER AND STORM had been plotting to distance themselves from Fisher since he had ruled out rafting the river. This was
their break. That night, they lobbied to complete the Kingdon-Ward
traverse that had defeated Breashears and Wiltsie. Eric Manthey and
Jill Bielawski could accompany them, while Fisher could take the
other clients around to the Great Bend via the Po Tsangpo. The plan
made sense to Fisher, and he agreed. They would divide forces and
meet at the Great Bend.

If Baker had come expecting a Tantric challenge, he found it on
the trail beyond Gyala. He and his three teammates started the trek in a
drenching downpour that persisted for thirteen days. At night their

twelve porters and Chinese liaison officer huddled among the limbs of moss-covered trees to stay as dry as they could, while the four Americans packed into one tent. It rained so hard that some nights the porters could not keep a fire going. They lost the trail after five days and wandered hopelessly—up, then down, then up again—looking for a way through the canyon. The clouds were too dense and low to allow anyone to get a bearing, and when the ceiling did lift briefly to allow a view of a distant village, no one had any idea of how to reach it.

Clambering up to eleven thousand feet, they bivouacked below a glaciated pass for an uncomfortable night. They were short of food, and although Baker asked the porters not to hunt, the men argued that they depended on bush meat for their survival. Descending to the Tsangpo, they managed to lasso three young takin, but while the meat fed everyone for several days, once it was exhausted rations grew meager. Baker began to experience a curious tingling in his arms, which he ascribed to being malnourished. Everyone was burning an enormous number of calories.

Two weeks out, still hopelessly lost, the porters were growing desperate. They had a map that a local woman in her eighties had drawn for them, recalling details of the traverse she had made as a child. Although it indicated the location of such highlights as "the place where tongues of fire emerge from a lake," the document was of little route-finding help. Nor were Baker's vaguely written guidebooks or the photocopy of a classified map of the gorge that their liaison officer had brought. The area they were traversing had turned out blank on the copy.

The journey grew into an increasingly solitary, introspective meditation for everyone, although none of them worried about getting out alive. Manthey, in particular, was made of stout stuff. Like Henry Morshead, Bailey's surveyor, he seemed oblivious to pain, insects, fear, and personal discomfort, and did the whole traverse in boating sandals.

Baker felt his mind slipping into another state, as if he were marooned in a dark Eden. He was approaching some sort of dire edge—

"a threshold where you are wavering between the world we know and can define in conventional geographical terms and the possibility of something beyond that"—but felt no fear or remorse at having come. On the contrary, he found their predicament oddly elating, a "visionary experience."

"I would awake from dreams and enter another dream state," he says. "Everything became very porous and magical, and infused with a tremendous acceptance of whatever was happening." He thought of Chatral Rinpoche's last words to him: "It may not be a paradise, but never lose faith that this is a sacred land. Don't succumb to anxiety and doubt. Just accept it. Surrender to whatever happens." If that meant dying, it was fine with Baker.

One night, to stretch his last two freeze-dried dinners, Storm divided each packet in half, then split the cooked food into four minuscule portions. The sauce packets became another meal. Finally they were reduced to several tablespoons of peanut butter and crackers—not enough to feed seventeen people. The porters hungrily eyed the four Americans taking the last, guilty finger scoops of peanut butter from the container. Afterward, Storm ceremonially sprinkled cracker crumbs on the wind. Their rations were now exhausted.

If ever there was a moment of doubt, it came when the porters spotted what seemed to be a trail—on the opposite side of a glacial river crashing down through the jungle about two miles above the Tsangpo River. The head porter took out his prayer beads and began chanting to divine the best place to cross. He and the others spent hours cutting trees and lashing the logs together into precarious catwalks, which they dropped across the torrent, only to watch the logs be swept away, one after the other. It seemed they were stranded, but after trying all morning they finally bridged the river.

The going was just as bad on the other side. Descending cliffs by clinging to vines, they finally made it down to the Tsangpo and were wading down the edge of the river when suddenly they heard dogs barking nearby. It was two hunters, who were dumbstruck that anyone would be wandering around in those parts. "You came across that pass?" they asked incredulously, gesturing back upriver. "Nobody comes across that pass."

In keeping with his pursuit of the edge, Baker felt oddly disappointed at being rescued. On the long hike to the hunters' village, he and Storm wished aloud that their ordeal could have lasted one more day, just to see what would have happened. "It was such an amazing space that our minds were in," Baker says. "There was something enveloping and wonderful about being lost and stranded. Neither of us thought, 'How are we going to get out of here? This is terrible.' We were slipping into this reverie." In the final days of the trip, exhausted and probably hypoglycemic from lack of food, Baker formed a powerful intimacy with the landscape—with everything he touched, in fact. Clinging to trees gave him a strange tactile sensation, as if, he says, he had eaten mescaline.

The hunters took them to a settlement called Lugu, downstream from the Great Bend. Fisher had trekked down to the village without his clients, hoping to find the long-overdue foursome—they had been eighteen days in the wilderness—but left a note explaining that he had gone off in search of them elsewhere.

Several porters with the four recognized relatives in Lugu who had fled down the canyon in the mid-fifties to escape Chinese troops. The village threw a huge celebration for their reunion. Tears of joy were shed, and the barley beer and food kept coming from noon until three in the morning. It was as if the four had blundered into a version of paradise—soaring mountains all around, food without end, and a sense that they had experienced a true pilgrimage, discovering their inner resources.

The same cannot be said of Breashears and Wiltsie, who rued their misfortune of having bumped into Rick Fisher.

· · ·

BREASHEARS AND WILTSIE had to find transportation to drive to the Po Tsangpo. They arrived at the trailhead village after Fisher and his clients, who had already hired most of the available porters and had moved down to a meadow that offered the only level campsite in the area. The climbers found a couple of men willing to carry double loads for double pay. They reached the meadow as evening was approaching. Fisher was hunched on a rock and refused to talk to them.

That evening, Breashears and Wiltsie's liaison officer got drunk in Fisher's camp, which was only twenty yards away in the small meadow. The "L.O." said the *Geographic* team's porters were about to quit, because Breashears had told them to prepare to walk all night. The story seemed credible; there was an unusual amount of activity in the climbers' camp. In Fisher's mind, they were now locked in a race to be the first Westerners to stand at the confluence of the Tsangpo and Po Tsangpo since Kingdon-Ward and Cawdor's day. (In fact, Ludlow and Sherriff had been there in the 1940s, and several independent travelers and scholars, beginning in 1986, had as well.)

Breashears and Wiltsie's porters were not staging a mutiny at all; they had been bustling around to prepare for a predawn departure. At five o'clock the next morning, they broke camp and set off for the confluence. All seemed quiet in Fisher's camp, but as the light improved, Breashears began noticing footprints on the muddy trail ahead of him: lug-soled Western hiking boots. "Fisher!" Breashears thought. He took off, hotfooting it down the trail.

Obsession can be a merciless taskmaster. Breashears set a manic pace, leaving Wiltsie and their two porters far behind. His pulse rose to one hundred and eighty beats a minute and stayed there for two hours. Wiltsie walked for four hours until he came across Breashears' and their liaison officer's packs, cached near the trail with a note attached: "We could not wait any longer for you. Have the porters carry these."

But the porters, already carrying double loads, could not take any more weight. Wiltsie hefted the packs onto his shoulders—in addition to his own and his camera equipment—and set off. Fuming and sweating in the sweltering midmorning heat and humidity, his temper reached the boiling point. After struggling three thousand feet uphill to a ridge top, he dumped the two packs and buried them in the forest.

Breashears thought he was racing Fisher. In fact, he was trying to catch up with twelve-year-old Ry Larrandson and Sharon Ludwig, a friend of Larrandson's mother. As the fastest hikers in Fisher's group, they had been dispatched early that morning to beat Breashears to the confluence. Under cover of darkness and carrying flashlights, they had slipped through the opposition's camp with Fisher's hung-over liaison officer and were long gone by the time Wiltsie and Breashears hit the trail. The three powered seventeen miles in eight hours and reached the confluence at noon. Weary and blistered, but feeling victorious, they posed for a self-portrait. Larrandson held a sign reading:

WE MADE IT!
12:00 NOON
4/23/93

. . .

THE "VICTORY" WAS as sweet for Fisher as it was galling for Breashears—not because the boy had outdistanced him, but because to the mountaineer the whole competition was a crock, a figment of Fisher's imagination. "What a silly day," Breashears despaired in his journal that night. "I joined the race. I made a fool of myself." Nevertheless, it had felt good to push himself, to blow off steam over an assignment going terribly wrong, although he wondered if he might have strained his heart.

Space for tents was at a premium at the evening campsite, so the two groups were again within earshot of each other. Wiltsie launched into Breashears, venting his own frustrations, to the amusement and chagrin of Fisher's clients. Fisher himself was crowing. He would later write of the competition that it "was the first known time in history that mountaineers and canyoneers went head to head in a canyon. The results clearly demonstrate that canyoneering is a sport requiring a unique set of skills, knowledge and attitudes."

The climbers left early the next day to hike below the confluence to the village of Bayu, where they divided forces. Breashears wanted to climb to a high ridge to gain a view into the gap, while Wiltsie needed to take advantage of the clear weather to photograph in the village, which is spectacularly situated a thousand feet above the Tsangpo.

Breashears hired several Monpa hunters as guides. Climbing to the ridge, the men moved like mountain goats—four thousand feet straight uphill—and Breashears stayed with them, as a point of pride and a form of penance.

Now, almost a mile above the river, which was still audible, Breashears sketched a waterfall for the hunters and indicated that he wanted to see any big ones. The next day, they moved along the ridge high above the inner canyon, dropping down for a better view of the river wherever they could. The hunters led Breashears to a point overlooking Kingdon-Ward's furthest point of progress around Rainbow Falls. Through binoculars, Breashears could see what seemed to be a bigger waterfall about a quarter of a mile downstream but could not tell how high it was, because the bottom of it was hidden from view. Judging by the height of trees near the lip of the drop, he estimated the plunge to be perhaps eighty feet high. After the river poured over the precipice, jetting and pulsing like the discharge of a gigantic fire hydrant, it hit a rock ledge halfway down and shot straight out into space. From there it seemed to crash straight into the foot of a cliff, turn ninety degrees to the right, and boil down a dark, narrow chute before disappearing from sight.

Thinking of the falls as "no big deal," Breashears wondered how many people had stood at the overlook marveling at the scene. Although the drop was no Niagara, he thought it noteworthy enough to photograph. Yet when he rejoined Wiltsie for the trek out of the gorge, Breashears was still exclaiming about the "hydraulic event" with the towering cloud of mist above it.

Back home in Boston, a sorely disappointed Breashears filed away his journals and the photographs of the intriguing waterfall. *National Geographic* had killed the story, since he and Wiltsie could not deliver the article and photographs they had promised. The trip had been a bust.

. . .

THE CONTEMPORARY AGE of exploration of the Tsangpo Gorge had dawned with mixed results: one ugly confrontation between two competing groups, an embarrassing footrace between an Everest summiteer and a schoolboy, a successful crossing of the Kingdon-Ward traverse, and, in time, bickering between Fisher and two of his valiant trekkers—Baker and Storm—over who owned the rights to photographs and videotape taken during the traverse.

Nevertheless, everyone except Breashears and Wiltsie found what they had been seeking in Pemakö. Fisher would return twice more to claim that he had discovered the deepest canyon in the world. His clients had enjoyed a grand adventure. And Baker and Storm had fallen so completely under Pemakö's spell that they would go on with Hamid Sardar to conduct an unprecedented exploration of the gorge's physical—and mystical—landscapes. While none of them thought much about probing the five-mile gap, Baker would eventually conclude that the portal to the other world and the mythical lost waterfall were inextricably linked.

Part Three

Beyond

Geography

ç

Previous page: Latter-day explorers, Tibet scholars, and Buddhist initiates Ian Baker (inset, bottom) and Hamid Sardar conducted the most thorough investigation of the gorge's physical and spiritual landscapes before discovering that the long-sought waterfall was more than a figment of the Western imagination. Baker believes that the waterfall represents one portal to the gorge's innermost secret realm. Photos by Hamid Sardar (of Baker), the author (of Sardar), and Ian Baker (of Hidden Falls).

*Hidden lands like Padma bkod [Pemakö] often appear as
landscapes of paradox—of belligerent cannibals, dangerous
beasts and violent storms, juxtaposed with gleaming glaciers,
exotic flowers and sonorous songbirds—of both purity and
danger, where the reflections of heaven and hell seem to
have perfectly merged. There is a sense that this wild,
almost wrathful mountain environment is somehow inwardly
fulfilling, providing a charged space that allows the ripening
of certain types of vision. As the poet William Blake once
said, the beauty of paradise would become banal without the
contrast of hell. Unlike the spiritual arcadias that we are so
used to in Western imagination, which have been so utterly
purified of their diabolical contamination and banished of
their serpents, the hostile elements of the hidden land play
an active role in the process of spiritual awakening.*

HAMID SARDAR, *The Buddha's Secret Gardens: End Times
and Hidden Land in Tibetan Imagination*

෴

*[T]he valley was nothing less than an enclosed paradise of
amazing fertility, in which the vertical difference of a few
thousand feet spanned the whole gulf between temperate
and tropical. Crops of unusual diversity grew in profusion
and contiguity, with not an inch of ground untended.*

JAMES HILTON, *Lost Horizon*

෴

THE ABYSS OF contradictions between novelist James Hilton's vision of paradise in *Lost Horizon* and the actual conditions in Pemakö is as deep as the Tsangpo Gorge itself. On one hand, the inhabitants of Hilton's Shangri-La are "a very successful blend of Chinese and Tibetan . . . cleaner and handsomer than the average of either race . . . good-humored and mildly inquisitive, courteous and carefree, busy at innumerable jobs but not in any apparent hurry over them." The valley of Shangri-La is a vale of beauty, peace, and security, isolated from the forces that will destroy all culture and learning.

By contrast, Pemakö is "Tibet's Heart of Darkness," according to Hamid Sardar, who made seven pilgrimages to the *beyul* in five years, usually in Ian Baker's company. Sardar's doctoral thesis traces the origins of the mythology of Tibetan hidden lands. It explains how the idea of an earthly paradise can be transformed through visualization into a real, tangible place, and how a pilgrimage to such a place can act as a "geographic support for the mind's journey to enlightenment." As supporting evidence, he cites the experiences of Tibetans past and present who traveled to hidden lands hoping to find the blissful refuge described in texts but found instead a "green hell."

Among these disillusioned immigrants were the residents of Mipi, the village in the lower gorge where Bailey and Morshead met the remnants of a group of Tibetan refugees who had come in search of the holy Padma-shel-ri, the Lotus Crystal Mountain. Instead of an elysian setting surrounded by fertile fields, they had found a steamy, disease-ridden jungle controlled by a tribe known as the Chulikatta Mishimis. After several years of peaceful coexistence, quarrels had arisen between the tribesmen and the settlers, who had begun raiding the Mishimis' granaries. The Mishimis retaliated by ambushing the Tibetans at every opportunity, setting traps on paths, showering them with poisoned arrows, and burning their huts and meager crops. Many of the Tibetans were killed, and those who weren't fell ill with tropical diseases and festering sores left by blood-sucking flies.

In 1909, most of the Tibetans gave up, convinced that they had not found Pemakö—certainly not the happy valley they had read about in pilgrimage guidebooks. Bailey and Morshead followed the refugees' trail of tears out of the gorge, toward the Tibetan Plateau, and in one isolated valley found evidence of their fatal retreat: cooking pots, a heavy millstone, and skeletons of those who had perished.

"It was a scene of the victory of nature over man," wrote Bailey.

A similar scenario occurred during the Chinese occupation of Tibet in the1950s. One group of Khampas fleeing the Communist onslaught followed a lama named Khamtrul Rinpoche into the gorge, hoping to find the crystal mountain. He sat praying before cliffs for months hoping to make them part and reveal the paradise within. Meanwhile, his disciples—attacked by natives and plagued by swarms of insects—became so hungry that they took to boiling their yak-leather shoes to make broth. The hidden land never materialized, and the pilgrims continued to India.

But the guidebooks' apparent fraud has a simple explanation: The paradise does not exist on a physical level. It is purely an ideal, a symbol of happiness and enlightenment, just as Western utopias such as Eden and Arcadia are. Paradise is a state of mind in this context, not a geographical location. "For many Tibetan yogis, the borderlands [of Pemakö and other hidden lands] were not only places to hide from armies, but also ideal places to meditate, and the physical journey to these hidden valleys became an allegory for the path to enlightenment itself," Sardar explains.

Without an abiding faith that the *beyul* does, in fact, hold the keys to higher realms of consciousness, the lay pilgrim is doomed to suffering. But for the spiritually enlightened, the heavenly and hellish aspects of Pemakö's physical landscape provide access to the deepest levels of meditative vision. Pemakö becomes a pure land for these adepts, in which cobras exist to encourage mindfulness and leeches to draw away one's bad karma. Every step of their pilgrimage route is a step closer to self-enlightenment.

This is the sort of odyssey that Sardar and Baker began in Nepal when they retreated to the hidden lands recommended by their guru, Chatral Rinpoche, during the late eighties. Their later journeys through Pemakö revealed many secrets about the *beyul*'s physical and sacred geography, and culminated in late 1998 when Monpa hunters agreed to guide them into the gorge's unknown inner sanctum: the gap that had eluded all previous western explorers.

. . .

SARDAR'S FIRST TRIP to Pemakö took place in the spring of 1994. During the same period, Rick Fisher, Eric Manthey (the fearless plumber on the 1993 Kingdon-Ward traverse), and two adventurous land developers from Scottsdale, Arizona, Gil and Troy Gillenwater, were attempting to raft the Tsangpo, although not in the gorge. They launched about a hundred miles upstream from the Great Bend, in the Yarlung Valley, paddling a four-person raft. From the start, the river's force was so overwhelming, and its course so tortuous and rapid-filled, that they abandoned the effort after only three miles, stashed the raft, and hiked down the canyon to join Fisher's trekking clients.

At about the same time, far down the river below the Great Bend, Sardar, Baker, and Ken Storm, Baker's teammate on the Kingdon-Ward traverse, entered the gorge from the northeast, retracing an old trade and pilgrimage route. Their trek took them across the snowbound Gawalung pass from the Lhasa-Sichuan road and then south along the Tsangpo to Medog, a garrison town near the Indian border. Surrounded by an orchid-festooned nature reserve inhabited by tigers, the town is populated by a mix of natives, soldiers, and prostitutes. At its center rests an incongruous monument to man's triumph over nature: a rusting two-ton truck buried up to its fenders. The truck had succeeded in navigating the only road in the lower gorge, one constantly raked by landslides and usually closed, but found its final resting place amid the squalor of Medog's concrete blockhouses and karaoke bars.

Baker and Sardar wanted to reach the nearby Marpung and Rinchenpung monasteries to study scriptures about Pemakö's secrets and to collect oral histories from the lamas. In reading Tibetan texts about Rinchenpung, Sardar had learned that three eighteenth-century yogins spread among the gorge's tribes a kind of gospel known as "The Seven Profound Teachings of the Luminous Web Opening the Gate of the Hidden Land." One of the three visionaries reported having a dream in which a woman dressed in rags commanded him to build a temple shaped like a heap of rice in a sequested valley in the lower gorge. This was the Rinchenpung monastery, and it was still standing two centuries later. The gold-roofed temple remained a vital center of Pemakö's religious life. According to the pilgrims' guidebook based on the "Luminous Web," the site corresponds to Dorge Phagmo's navel. The guide also referred to various edible and medicinal plants that grow in the surrounding jungle, including a hallucinogenic species said to produce ecstatic visions.

There was one snag: Rinchenpung was not a specified destination on the team's travel permit, and their Chinese liaison officer refused to let them go there. Not to be denied, Baker and Sardar concocted an excuse that the team needed a rest day and wanted to find a waterfall near town in which to bathe. Then they ran off with their daypacks.

Baker had started an adventure-travel outfit called Red Panda Expeditions, after the elusive creature that inhabits the lower gorge. Jokingly, the outfit's secret motto, "Confuse and elude," described tactics that were often necessary to visit pilgrimage sites that the Public Security Bureau considered off-limits to outsiders.

The truants had only a vague idea of where the monastery was located, based on their ambiguously written guidebook, but didn't want to ask directions of anyone, as the gendarmes in Medog would surely hear of their plans. They simply plunged into the jungle and followed their instincts—straight up the side of a mountain. Gnats and biting flies devoured them (Bailey and Morshead had been similarly plagued on their visit to Rinchenpung), and the daylight began to wane on the long climb.

"We reached the top of the ridge in this very, very dark jungle and had no idea which way to go," Baker says. "At that moment,

Hamid saw a huge raptor with a snake in its talons swooping off toward our left. It was such a strange apparition that we said, 'Okay, we'll go in that direction.'"

Thirty minutes later they reached a clearing and could see the gleaming temple roof—with a double rainbow over it. One end of the rainbow seemed to emanate from the temple door. "We noticed a monk holding a large brass bowl coming across the fields to meet us," Baker continues. "It was *chang* [fermented barley beer]. We asked him how he knew we were coming, and he said, 'Oh, the rainbow only appears if someone is coming.'"

Everyone had a sense that they were not in an ordinary place, that they had been led to the monastery by auspicious means. It was classic Pemakö, says Baker. "Signs and portents occur this way in Pemakö if you're there with the right intentions or simply lucky. This is just one example. There have been quite a few other dramatic events like it. You pay attention to animals or birdcalls, and the place opens up. You have to suspend your rational mind and allow a more mythic consciousness to guide you, rather than relying on satellite maps or compasses. You have to let the oral traditions of a mystical land be your guide."

The pilgrims spent the night at the monastery as guests of the head lama. He wore his hair long, like Chatral Rinpoche, indicating that he, too, was a practitioner of secret tantras. The holy man and his female consort held the audience seated beneath a giant statue of Sardar's wrathful protective deity, Dorje Drolo, a terrifying three-eyed figure wearing a garland of freshly severed heads and sitting on the back of a tigress.

In the morning, returning to Medog, the group encountered the local police chief. Their liaison officer had assumed the worst when he discovered them missing: that they were spies for India who had fled across the border with intelligence about troop strength. The chief had rounded up a platoon of native trackers and set out in hot pursuit. When they found the team coming down to Medog, he drew his revolver, cocked it, and told them they would have to come to police headquarters to sign confessions.

"At the station, we kept writing, 'Thank you for the rescue mission; we are paying you a thousand yuan [about $120] for your kindness,'" Sardar laughs. "The chief tore up the paper and screamed, 'No confession!' So we wrote 'rescue mission' again and again, until he finally threw us out—after collecting the fine. They could not deal with us, or understand why anyone living in the material paradise of America would want to be in their leech-infested jungle."

From Medog, the team crossed to the west bank of the Tsangpo via a hanging bridge of woven bamboo and trekked to the Marpung monastery, where the pundit Kintup had lived in indentured servitude more than a century earlier. The resplendently dressed abbot welcomed them to spend the night inside the little monastery. Lying awake in the temple's still darkness, all of them noticed strange lights dancing on the ceiling—only the local protector spirits checking them out, the abbot explained the next morning. He said it was an auspicious sign.

Rather than retracing trails north of Medog to the Lhasa road, the team decided to complete a circuit of the southern gorge and exit via the Doshong La, the rhododendron fairyland Kingdon-Ward had described. The pass would lead them to the village of Pe at the northwestern entry to the gorge, where the Tsangpo begins its plunge toward the twin peaks of Gyala Peri and Namche Barwa. From Pe they could easily reach the main road to Lhasa.

On the way out, their porters warned them against accepting food or drink from anyone they met. The southern gorge is home to a poisoning cult whose practitioners—all women—believe that they gain merit by doing away with unsuspecting victims, which may include pilgrims, monks, their own husbands or children, or even themselves. Called *dugmas,* the women make the poison by first burying an egg. When a mushroom sprouts at the spot, they paint half of their faces black and braid one side of their hair. Under the light of a full moon, they say a vow to use the poisonous mushroom. If their in-

tended victim is suspicious, they may ask him or her to try the prof-
fered food or drink first, then add the poison afterward by concealing
it under a fingernail, or administering it in the night by scratching the
person.

Worried about falling prey to a *dugma,* the porters refused to
sleep indoors in villages along the way, and always posted sentries at
night. A year earlier, according to Baker, the wife of Tenzing Norgay,
the Sherpa who climbed Mount Everest with Sir Edmund Hillary, was
on a pilgrimage to Pemakö when she was poisoned. "She dictated a
final letter to her lama from her death bed at a hospital in Silugiri,
India," wrote Baker in an article about their trek. "'I have made it to
Pemakö. My life is complete.'"

The moon was in fact full on the night before the group began
their ascent of the Doshong La, the eve of a holy day commemorating
the birth of the Buddha. The porters cut boughs of juniper and heaped
them onto a smoldering fire, sending clouds of fragrant smoke into the
sky as an offering. At dawn, already under way, the team trudged up
through the mists with avalanches crashing down all around them.
Cresting the pass, they turned back for a final view of Pemakö.

It was a transporting moment for Baker. "We look back toward
the fluted snow peaks guarding this primeval land that for explorers
and pilgrims alike is a place of infinite possibility," he wrote. "Already,
the ridge we have just crossed—the snowy hips of [Dorje Phagmo]—
is veiled again in impenetrable mist."

His and Sardar's first pilgrimage together had succeeded beyond
their expectations. But they had not reached the key pilgrimage site of
Kundu Dorsempotrang, the mountain that is the northern gateway to
Dorge Phagmo's *yoni*—her secret sexual center. During their night at
the gold-roofed Rinchenpung monastery, the lama had told them that
the pass leading to the holy site was still snowed in. Even during the
summer, he said, one must cut steps in the snow, and by October early
snow would close the pass again.

Thus, by the time they left Pemakö, Baker and Sardar were already laying plans for their second pilgrimage. The trek to Dorsem-

potrang would require stealth and cunning—a trip in the "confuse and elude" mode—because Dorje Phagmo's sexual center was across the closed border, in the dark, lubriciously moist jungles of northern India's state of Arunachal Pradesh. Anyone caught crossing the border would be arrested.

. . .

AFTER THEIR FIRST pilgrimage together, Baker and Sardar became the Bailey and Morshead of the *beyul*'s sacred geography, while Ken Storm inherited the mantle of Kingdon-Ward, at least in Sardar's mind. Before making the 1993 Kingdon-Ward traverse, Storm had all but dismissed the idea that the gap might contain a major waterfall. But on subsequent expeditions, he underwent a profound spiritual transformation and came to believe that Bailey and Kingdon-Ward had given up their quests out of a "failure of vision."

"A trip to Pemakö is not single-faceted," Storm says, declining to elaborate on his private epiphanies. "Aspects of it come out only upon reflection—as Wordsworth said, 'Thoughts recollected in tranquility.' It's a deepening process. Seldom a day passes that I don't think about the Tsangpo Gorge."

Thoreau, Emerson, and other Transcendentalist writers became sounding boards for Storm after each journey, reshaping his ideas about the interrelatedness of landscape and perception, and the nature of exploration. Prior to his first trip, he had viewed exploration as "a going out and seizing of something, a selfish gesture." Afterward, he adopted a humbler attitude that opened his mind. "You merge into your surroundings and become more attentive to the world around you," he explains. "For me, it evoked a sense of enchantment and wonder that I felt as a child hiking with my father in the Sierra Nevada."

The same is true of Baker and Sardar, who described their pilgrimages as a process of "creative regression"—a return to the spirit of adventurousness and wonderment they tasted on their first wilderness outings as youngsters.

Although none of the three believed that the Falls of the

Brahmaputra was anything more than a Western fantasy, in the back of their minds each of them was aware that no one had gone through the gap. They did not believe that Fisher had, despite his claims of covering the gorge from top to bottom without spotting any drops that would qualify as the mythical lost falls. (Fisher's theory, and that of some Chinese geologists, was that if any major drops had existed in the heart of the gorge, cataclysmic earthquakes had so rearranged the landscape that the falls had been demolished.) Whatever the case, neither Baker, Storm, nor Sardar felt any urgency to forge through the gap and claim a first. They had a sense of the gorge as their private wilderness playground. Pemakö was for them a realm where petty ambitions and competitiveness had no place. Those were ego-driven impulses that a devout pilgrim would attempt to overcome.

. . .

OF THE THREE, Sardar was least interested in the mythical waterfall. "Who cares about the damn falls?" he would say when the subject arose. In searching the texts and guidebooks, he could find no reference to a huge waterfall in the unexplored section of the gorge, and the hunters and lamas he interviewed said they knew nothing about one. No one ever goes into the gap, they told him.

Instead, Sardar's chief interest has been to retrace Pemakö's classical pilgrimage routes and to experience the gorge on the hunters' terms. He loved nothing more than going feral with the Monpa hunters of the upper gorge, the Bhutanese descendants whose stamina and bravery had so impressed Kingdon-Ward. Traveling fast and light with them, eating game that they shot, and sleeping on the ground under their plastic tarps, Sardar never became sick. He credited that to maintaining "pure vision." At times he left Baker, Storm, and Baker's clients to explore the gorge's sacred geography by himself and to film the Monpas for a documentary he was producing for Harvard's film center.

During these journeys, Sardar abandoned himself to Pemakö and formed a "deep conspiracy" with the land. Despite the Monpas' grueling pace and the risks they took, he felt utterly secure with them chasing after bear or takin or crossing forty-five-degree scree slopes where one slip would prove fatal. The experience took him back to his boyhood, when his father would take him hunting in the Caspian Mountains, whose forests resemble Pemakö's in some respects. They are nourished by warm, humid air moving across the Caspian Sea but on the mountains' lee side give way to high desert. The same sort of transition takes place in the Tsangpo Gorge: tropical forests on the south side of the Himalayas, desert on the north where the Tibetan Plateau begins. "There were bear in those forests," recalls Sardar of his childhood expeditions, "and the last of the Caspian tigers." Similarly, the last of Tibet's tigers roam the jungles of the lower gorge, around Medog.

Sardar's father always hunted with a guide named Nader Gholi Khan, or "bear killer," who was renowned for his bravery. One day, coming back from cutting wood, Nader Khan had spotted a bear about to attack a village child. Reacting instinctively and without fear, he grabbed a log, brained the beast, and decapitated it with his ax.

One memory stands out from those idyllic summers. Sardar was nine at the time. He was walking in the woods ahead of his father and Nader Khan when a bear came charging through the trees straight at him. "I wasn't afraid," Sardar says. "There wasn't time to be. The bear was just a blur. Suddenly I heard a pinging sound over my head. The bear fell and skidded up to my feet. My father had aimed over my head and brought him down with one shot."

In perilous circumstances, a Buddhist prescription for overcoming fear or doubt is to envision a place of ultimate security—a primeval forest on the Caspian Sea, for example, safe in the knowledge that your father and a great hunter will safeguard you. Thus protected, one can surrender to the wilderness without worry. The images and sensations that Sardar conjured up from his Caspian summers—hunting with his father and Nader Khan, skinny-dipping with his older cousin and seeing her bare bottom for the first time—provided just such a sanctuary. They were comforting, sensual, almost sexual memories for him. But so were those of being enveloped by the all-embracing jungles of

Pemakö and meditating on Dorje Phagmo, the divine feminine. Those experiences, at least when recollected in tranquility, have been for Sardar like blissful unions with a consort.

"All the horrors of Eden we forget," he says. "A month goes by [after a pilgrimage] and I'm dying to get back. I literally feel as if I'm in a different order of space and time when I'm there."

. . .

MOUNT DORSEMPOTRANG lies east and south of Medog, the main outpost in the lower gorge. For their second attempt to reach it, in 1995, Baker and Sardar chose August, when the snow on the pass to the sacred mountain would be at its lowest. Storm chose not to join them, but the Gillenwater brothers, Gil and Troy, the Arizona land developers who had tried rafting the Tsangpo with Rick Fisher in 1994, signed up for the trip. After their rafting ordeal, the Gillenwaters had bumped into Baker in the lobby of their hotel in Lhasa. Freshly arrived from his pilgrimage to the Rinchenpung and Marpung monasteries, Baker had impressed the brothers, particularly Gil, who is a student of Buddhism. Thickly muscled and clean-cut, the elder Gillenwater rides Harley-Davidson motorcycles, operates a charity for abandoned Mexican children, holds a black belt in martial arts, and, like his quieter, more introspective younger brother, Troy, is a keen and accomplished outdoorsman. The two once hiked eight hundred miles across Arizona, and every year they try to make a rough adventure trip together. For the Dorsempotrang pilgrimage, they persuaded their younger brother, Todd, to join them and discover what a Buddhist pilgrimage is all about.

Sardar had invited a beautiful Thai princess, Oy Kanjananavit, whom he had met at a party in Kathmandu. Holding a doctorate in ecology, Kanjananavit had been charmed by Sardar and intrigued by his descriptions of the gorge's subtropical jungle. She intended to collect plant samples and hoped to find a new species or two.

Finally, there was the team's speedy lama-guide, Kaba Tulku. He was the only one who knew the route, but nearly every day he would vanish into the jungle, leaving the group to wallow through what Baker describes as "a jungle from hell," full of leeches and vipers, and blanketed by waist-deep ferns that blocked the view of the muddy ground. The terrain was very steep, and as expected, it was pouring rain. On the first day, the group became separated from their porters but kept pressing ahead. Finally, one of the coolies caught up with them. "Why are you going forward?" he asked. "The camp is an hour and a half behind us."

That night, huddled together with the others under a dripping plastic tarp, trying to stay warm, Sardar awoke to find a blood-engorged leech attached to the inside of his lip. In the morning, the lama pulled his vanishing act once more. A tiger began stalking the party and left huge pawprints in the mud around their camps. But for Sardar, being with the porters was a novel experience. They were Lopas, the short, sturdy tribesmen whom Kingdon-Ward had derided as "simian-looking."

"They had a much different vibe than the Monpa tribesmen of the upper gorge," Sardar says, "and they thrived in a rain forest where no one else could. They could catch fish by hand just by moving their fingers like weeds in a stream."

Kanjananavit, who was a tough field scientist, was similarly astonished by the diversity of plant species. Many she could not identify, but she did recognize one as a species new to science: a bat lily, with delicate white petals and long, gracefully drooping purple tendrils.

One day, crossing the snowbound pass to the sacred mountain, the porters found a frozen, partly decomposed bear carcass. They cooked it, and everyone ate some. Five days later, then in the midst of the jungle, the three Gillenwaters started feeling nauseous. At first they thought that they had fallen prey to the *dugma* cult and been poisoned. The lama and porters had a different explanation. They had come across the Gillenwaters bathing in a spring one evening. The lama was horrified. "I cannot believe they are swimming in that water," he told Baker and Sardar. "Those are sacred springs; they're ruled over by malevolent spirits." Whatever the case—spoiled bear meat, poison, or a spiritual faux pas—the brothers succumbed to a kind of Tibetan Montezuma's revenge, purging from both ends and feeling tremendously sapped.

Conditions deteriorated at higher altitude. Wading through a swamp at ten thousand feet, in driving rain and with mud up to their knees, the pilgrims lost their porters again. They separated to hunt for footprints but then could not find one another again in the dense forest. Eventually Baker, Kanjananavit, and Sardar regrouped and found the porters' camp by following the smell of the campfire. As darkness fell and temperatures plummeted, two of the Gillenwater brothers began displaying signs of hypothermia. Todd, the youngest, offered to push on for help. Later that evening, he staggered into camp and immediately dispatched men with dry clothing, a thermos of tea, and a tent to rescue his older brothers. An hour later, in complete darkness, Gil and Troy struggled into camp, "totally terrified and exhausted," said Baker.

The brothers reached Dorspempotrang but were too ill to attempt the circumambulation. The others did, however, completing the pilgrimage circuit at twelve thousand feet in a drizzling mist, with the lama nowhere to be seen. The return trip to Medog was as horrific as the outbound journey. "Shangri-La it was not," says Troy Gillenwater, "unless your idea of paradise is puking your guts out, leeches from head to toe, inbred natives with deformities, and four hundred inches of rain a year."

In Medog, the Gillenwaters took a room in a dingy hotel and went out to buy some beers. Gil made the mistake of taking several pictures, and that evening four soldiers barged into their room accusing them of photographing a militarily sensitive installation. "The captain and his four shirtless flunkies were all armed, and he was waving his pistol around screaming at us," Gil says. "They reeked of alcohol. It was obvious that the captain was putting on a show for his subordinates."

Worried that the situation was getting out of control, the brothers summoned their liaison officer and through him explained that they had permits to be in Medog and every right to take pictures there. The captain would not relent and demanded all of their film. (They had about sixty exposed rolls in their packs.) "Put the damn guns down and get out of our room," Gil barked. At that, the captain flew into a rage.

"I thought he was going to shoot one of us on the spot," Gillenwater says. "Troy, Todd, and I exchanged rapid glances, and we all knew what had to be done—a kind of brotherly telecommunication. Troy opened a camera containing a new roll, exposed the film and two other new rolls, and handed them to the captain with our apologies. The officer was swaying back and forth, still clutching his pistol with his finger on the trigger. After our liaison officer translated our apology, the captain looked around smugly at his men and marched out into the night."

· · ·

W HILE THE GILLENWATER brothers usually finished their days on the Dorsempotrang pilgrimage by bathing, Baker and Sardar meditated. Reflecting on the day's events was as fundamental to their pilgrimage as stopping to pray and chant at power places was for their fast-paced lama. "It is not enough to be a sympathetic Westerner in Pemakö," Sardar says. "You must follow a practice."

But faith was the key to their experience. Without faith in the transforming power of a hidden land, a pilgrimage to Pemakö is just a tough journey. If the landscape seems paradoxical—like heaven and hell at once, beautiful yet threatening—the same sorts of paradoxes and extremes are part of our own nature. "The point of an existential pilgrimage is not to overcome these contradictions but to use them as a kind of creative tension," Sardar says. "The forest becomes a mirror of the inner paradoxes if we approach it in the right frame of mind. You have to embrace the unknown and unexpected. A pilgrimage is all about surrendering yourself to the land to achieve self-awareness."

Exhaustion, thirst, and discomfort are the pilgrim's allies, he adds, because in a depleted state one's fears and neuroses rise to the surface. But there are also Tantric techniques and practices that can be performed to rise above anxieties, to avoid focusing on them. Such crippling thoughts should be observed and let go, like leaves floating past on a brook.

On such miserable treks as the one to Rinchenpung or Dorsempotrang, Sardar meditated on the essence of his protector deity, Dorje Drolo, the wrathful, taming emanation of Padmasambava. He chanted his mantra, "*Om ah hung vajra guru padma siddhi hung*." He concentrated on "entering the moment, without attachment of the past, present or future," to achieve a state of psychic emptiness. The rain, mud, and leeches became provocations to open the mind and reach a clear, penetrating awareness of the physical, spiritual, and mental landscapes, which for the initiated pilgrim are inseparable.

The most successful pilgrimages for Sardar were yet to come after Dorsempotrang, when he was traveling with Monpa hunters. Sleeping in caves, climbing mile-high slopes to the point of utter exhaustion, and facing repeated crises of confidence, he gained "a sense of empowerment in an overwhelming wilderness.

"All we can hope for in these moments is a glimpse into a state of total peace and simplicity," Sardar says. "You endure tremendous hardship in Pemakö to come to basic realizations about yourself. It's all about shedding neurotic baggage. It is the greatest feeling to be completely at peace and at home with these wild people."

Baker, on the other hand, compared his pilgrimages to encounters with a femme fatale. Pemakö's primordial jungles radiate a mythic feminine energy, whereas the energy of Kailas, the holy peak in the dry, cold, dusty reaches of western Tibet, represents "the mythic male principle," he says. "The two are almost in opposition yet complementary. Circumambulating Kailas [at up to eighteen thousand feet and higher] is very different from losing yourself in the jungles of Pemakö. The orientation of the mind is different. You don't set out to conquer the land, which is what I found so troubling in the language of Pemakö's past explorers. It is a place you must surrender to. If you try to conquer it, you lose it and have no encounter with its hidden dimensions. If you surrender to it, the place opens before you, in the same way that a woman does. If you try to conquer her, you will never know her. It's a land you cannot seduce; it seduces you."

Baker likens the landscape to a muse who reorients one's relationship to the world and who inspires "a mystical, enraptured perception." The rain, mud, toxic nettles, and other hardships are not a penance for him, or a price to pay for a divine vision. Indeed, he does not think of them as hardships.

"Being there takes us back to our first experiences as a species," Baker says. "Wading through swamps, clinging to trees, feeling as if you are about to be washed away—there is an incomprehensible elation attending that, whether one attributes it to the divine feminine— rivers and streams as the fluids of Dorje Phagmo—or to an encounter with nature in its primal state. You gain a sense not of conquering but of deep participation in a world, that is infinitely larger than ourselves. Experiencing this dimension of the natural world, our own boundaries and sense of who we are is enlarged. We begin to see through different eyes."

That ability to feel the landscape's inherent, compelling power is not strictly a matter of believing in esoteric Tibetan mythology. Eric Bailey and especially Kingdon-Ward felt it, as evidenced by their writings. Even so, those who follow the Tantric path have an advantage, because the ideals and goals of Tantrism are symbolized by features of the physical landscape—the shape and color of a cliff, for example, or of a copse of trees. They are associated with "moments and places in time by which these ideals are actualized," Baker says.

While Tibetans may be predisposed to see eruptions of rainbows from sacred boulders, Baker never has witnessed such a display in Pe-makö, to his regret. "I wish I could," he says. Still, he has felt energy radiating from rocks and sacred springs because he understands their mythic associations—that such-and-such a diety trimphed over an evil force at particular spots, as the guidebooks explain.

"The landscape is enriched by knowledge of sacred geography as the Tibetans understand it. I can go into temples where I have no connection to that particular faith and I don't feel much. In a mosque, I can appreciate the vaulted space and the devotions being performed, but I can't relate to the specific configuration of energy those around me feel. I can appreciate their devotion but can't participate in it.

"It's the same with Pemakö. Some people can go there and the place just doesn't do it for them. There's no resonance."

. . .

GIL AND TROY Gillenwater were hooked on Pemakö after the Dorsempotrang pilgrimage. As after any trying experience, the memory tends to filter out the sour notes and amplify the sweet ones. It was as Sardar had told them one evening: "Memory is simply the storehouse of the imagination. Your memory of this trip will be different tomorrow than a year from now, and it's already different from my memory of what has occurred. Time, like all else that we perceive, is in a constant state of flux. The past, present, and future are dynamic. They are what you make of them."

Months after the mud-soaked trek, while scripting a slide lecture, Gil Gillenwater recalled an illuminating incident at one of his low points. The rain had been pounding down that day when he and his younger brother, Todd, came upon a log that had fallen chest-high across the trail. There was no way under or around the obstacle, so Gil jumped at it stomach first and slid over the top. Smeared with mud, he cursed "the log and the goddamned rain."

At that point, the team's lama, Kaba Tulku, was behind the Gillenwaters. To lighten the moment, Todd suggested that they hide in the bushes to see how the lama would handle the hurdle. Sloshing up the trail, Kaba Tulku took a running jump at the downed tree, smacked into it with his generous belly, and slid back into a puddle. "Shaking his head, he burst into spasms of laughter," wrote Gil. "He tried three more times and each time, his laughter grew louder. On the fourth try he made it but slid headlong into the puddle. Continuing to chuckle, he wiped himself off and lovingly patted the log as if it were a dear friend, and proceeded up the trail smiling.

"At that moment it became obvious to me that it wasn't the external world that was my problem but how I chose to perceive it. . . . The choice was mine. I could experience life as a helpless victim, with my happiness contingent on shifting external circumstances, or as a positive creator-conductor of my own experience. With this awareness came a tremendous sense of control and freedom."

. . .

IT DID NOT take long for the world to beat a path to Pemakö. By 1995, three years after the Chinese government had opened the gorge to tourism, a line was forming at the heavenly gates. A number of elite American kayakers and rafters were investigating a first descent of the Tsangpo through the inner canyon, and trekking clients signed up for trips that Baker and Rick Fisher had announced.

After Fisher had verified the canyon's enormous depth, he issued a flurry of press releases about his "discovery." His announcements received faint fanfare, but news of the record was obviously read in China. A few months after articles on Fisher appeared in *Asia Week* and various newspapers, mainly in Arizona, the Chinese Academy of Sciences announced that its teams had documented the canyon's depth, and claimed the record as its own.

In interviews about the canyon, Fisher inevitably faulted *National Geographic* for naming Peru's Colca Canyon as the world's deepest canyon and Nepal's Kali Gandaki Gorge as the world's deepest valley. *The Guinness Book of Records* had accepted his data, he pointed out. He invited the magazine to send a reporter and experts to the gorge, but the editors brushed him off. They were sorely peeved about his public criticisms, although they did agree to reconsider their published depth record listings.

While the publicity had put the gorge in the spotlight, public awareness was limited to its physical geography. Nothing in the articles mentioned a Buddhist paradise or sacred geography. But new travel guidebooks did, notably Victor Chan's 1994 *Tibet Handbook,* a magnificently researched doorstop of a book that called the gorge "a botanist's paradise" and "one of the most sacred and mystical regions in Tibet." Chan, a particle physicist by training, had visited the gorge in 1986. He was not able to trek the gap through the inner canyon due to rotten weather, but he conducted extensive interviews with local people and knew of Bailey and Kingdon-Ward's attempts. Chan's detailed map of the gorge and twenty-page text about its mythology emphasize that the trek is "treacherous."

That sort of cautionary language appealed to those who looked for elements of risk, exotic culture, and esoteric Buddhist mythology in their travels. It was the mid-nineties, and adventurers with three weeks and ten thousand dollars to spare could find themselves on a "journey of discovery" in Tibet—doing the Kingdon-Ward traverse, for instance, or trekking to the Rongbuk monastery at Everest base camp, just as George Mallory and Andrew Irvine had done when they started their fatal climb in 1924. At a more advanced skill level, hardcore adrenaline junkies were contemplating challenges that once even elite athletes might not have considered, thanks largely to technological advances in clothing and equipment, but also to the celebration of extreme sports in the popular culture.

White-water kayaking is a case in point. The sport did not exist when the Chinese occupied Tibet. Kayaks then were native vessels for hunting and transportation or, in the case of European folding kayaks, for touring coastal waters and flat-water rivers. In 1950, if you wanted to run a white-water river, you made do in a canoe, river dory, or military-surplus survival raft. Just twenty-one years later, in 1971, an Idaho physician named Walt Blackadar redefined the limits of expeditionary kayaking when he successfully navigated the perilous rapids of Turnback Canyon on British Columbia's Alsek River, paddling alone at the age of forty-nine in a hard-shelled fiberglass kayak. By the early 1980s, Olympic-level slalom racers such as Wick Walker, Tom McEwan, and McEwan's younger brother, Jamie, a bronze medalist at the 1972 Munich Games, were making first descents of rivers in the Bhutanese Himalayas in high-performance polyethylene kayaks stuffed with supplies and flotation bladders. Inspired by their Himalayan kayak descent, Walker and the elder McEwan applied to run the Tsangpo in

1983, and although the Chinese embassy in Washington, D.C., snubbed them, they never forgot about paddling what Walker described as "the riverine equivalent of Mount Everest."

Although Walker and his paddling pals were among the first to recognize the Tsangpo as the ne plus ultra of white-water rivers, a group of well-financed Japanese scored the first permit to run it. The China-Japan Yarlung Tsangpo Scientific Expedition was launched in August 1993, some months after a Sino-Japanese team made the first ascent of Namche Barwa. The alpinists' celebrated success was still fresh in the minds of the kayakers as they flew to Tibet.

The team consisted of a film crew backed by NHK-TV, several Japanese and Chinese scientists, and three paddlers, among them a twenty-four-year-old slalom racer named Yoshitaka Takei. The expedition reached Lhasa in late August and by September 6 had trekked down the Po Tsangpo to the confluence with the Tsangpo near the apex of the Great Bend. Both rivers were raging and bitterly cold, and at the confluence a standing wave as big as a Greyhound bus pulsed evilly up and down like a geyser. Takei and his teammate Yasushi Tadano decided to take a practice run on the last few hundred yards of the Po Tsangpo above the junction, and slipped into their kayaks while the film crew prepared to record their run.

Immediately after Tadano pushed into the current he was in grave straits. His boat was sucked into a deceptively powerful rapid and capsized. Seeing his friend in trouble, Takei launched at once. He, too, was bowled over in the rapids but immediately rolled upright in a maneuver called an Eskimo roll. Standing on the shore, their teammates were too far away to throw a rescue line, which neither boater could have caught anyway because of their predicament.

With the confluence rapidly approaching, Tadano bailed out of his boat. Miraculously, he avoided the giant standing wave at the junction of the two rivers and washed across the Tsangpo. From the shelter of a boulder on the Tsangpo's south bank, he turned to look for his friend and saw Takei's inverted boat shooting past in the roller-coaster waves, but riding low in the water, as if weighed down by a body.

The team conducted thorough searches up and down the river, and Takei's parents also mounted a later rescue mission. Eventually, the family resigned itself to their son's death. In May 1994, on a beautiful springtime Sunday in Pemakö, with the rhododendrons in full bloom, Takei's friends and his father, Heihachi, held a simple ceremony on the banks of the Po Tsangpo. After planting a peach tree seedling and cosmos seeds brought from the family home on Shikoku Island, the team offered a toast of Havana Gold Cuban rum, Takei's favorite drink, and mounted a plaque on a boulder near the confluence. The simple monument reads in Chinese and Japanese:

Yoshitaka Takei

September 10, 1993

Attempting a first descent

Given by his father of Takamatsu, Japan

May 20, 1994

According to local beliefs in Pemakö, Takei did not suffer. Indeed, it was an honor and a blessing to die in the sacred land. At the moment of his death, according to legend, he had been instantly transported to Bodhgaya, the site of the Buddha's enlightenment.

· · ·

VILLAGERS IN THE upper gorge could not comprehend why anyone would want to challenge the river in a kayak. The only reason to come to Pemakö, in their minds, was to perform a pilgrimage, which required staying on land and being properly reverent and humble. Those were Baker and Sardar's sentiments as well. There were plenty of adrenaline rushes along the gorge's precipitous pilgrimage routes, and much to be accomplished there for the two spiritual geographers. Thus the reason for their repeated returns to Pemakö. It would have been impossible in one or two trips to visit every holy site mentioned in their pilgrimage guidebooks, and the texts were vague about the location of certain shrines. Directions to some of them were exclusively oral traditions. Information that Baker and Sardar gathered on one pilgrimage would lead to another, and so on. Their hope was to eventually experience every site they could locate.

The year after the Dorsempotrang pilgrimage, in 1996, Baker turned his attention to the upper gorge, around the inner canyon. He wanted to reach areas of the inner canyon that had been blocked by landslides on the 1993 Kingdon-Ward traverse, in order to look down on stretches of the Tsangpo that he and Storm had been unable to see. His plan was to hike upriver from the Great Bend, following the Tsangpo's north side (the Gyala Peri side), ascending or descending where necessary to keep the river in sight. For that, he brought ropes, hardware, and lightweight spelunking ladders.

Sadar and Storm joined this expedition, as well as a German couple Baker had recruited to help spread the cost of the expedition, and Baker's half brother. Leaving the Lhasa-Sichuan road, the team hiked down the Po Tsangpo to its meeting with the Tsangpo. That is a relatively easy three-day trek, but by the time the Germans reached the confluence, they were terrified by the steep trails, the leeches, and the weather. (As Baker explains, Pemakö inspires in some people rapture and mystical visions, in others morbid fear.) He helped the couple pitch a tent on a leech-free rock promontory overlooking the Great Bend and told them to sit tight until he and the others returned in about a week. At the end of the trip, the husband was so grateful that he gave Baker the Rolex watch off his wrist. "Thank you for saving my life," he said.

Sardar decided not to make the trip up into the gap. Uninterested in the route as a pilgrimage, he wanted instead to find a way to reach Pemakö's secret inner sanctuary, the *yangsang ney,* the ultimate refuge in the prophesied Armageddon to come. Specific directions to the magic valley were not in any of the texts that he had translated, but some clerics in the gorge might have been given oral teachings about it, Sardar thought. He left the team to ferret them out on his own.

While the main team turned west into the gap, Sardar headed south toward Bayu, a Monpa village downstream from the confluence.

A hunter there invited Sardar to spend the night in his simple log cabin. In the course of the evening, Sardar learned that the hunter's brother was the village lama. The holy man had recently been initiated into the same Tantric lineage to which Sardar had been introduced by his guru, Chatral Rinpoche. The following day, the lama was surprised and pleased to hear a foreigner recite the prayers and mantras of the lineage. Sardar, who was using his Buddhist name, Lekdrup Dorje, had gained the lama's trust.

"He brought out his pilgrimage guidebooks and let me read and photograph them," Sardar says. There had once been a text about the *yangsang ney* in the monstery's collection, the lama explained, but the Chinese Red Guard had either burned it or thrown it into the Tsangpo during the Cultural Revolution. All that the lama could recall about the secret valley were the stories about refugees searching for the place in vain. He thought that the portal to it was nowhere near the inner canyon, but south of Namche Barwa in the jungle, where the refugees of the 1950s had searched for it.

Sardar came away from Bayu with little new information, but he had formed a bond with the Monpa brothers that would later prove invaluable. Baker and Storm had also had mixed luck in trying to survey the river from spurs of Gyala Peri that plunged down into the gap. Their view of the river had often been obscured by these steeply descending ridges, but at least they could see that the only possible route into the gap from downstream was on the opposite side of the river. Future probes of the inner canyon would have to start in Bayu and proceed west over the spurs dropping down from Namche Barwa's icy heights.

. . .

THE MONPA HUNTERS believe that the weather in Pemakö indicates who will or will not have a successful journey. Fair weather is auspicious, while clouds signify trouble ahead. The Chinese, they say, are invariably greeted by abominable weather.

So it was for Baker and Sardar's 1997 pilgrimage—rain sheeting down, the gorge sealed off by low-lying clouds, trails slick with sloppy mud. Storm had come along, and so had two of the Gillenwater brothers, Gil and Troy, along with several trekking clients. The Gillen-waters had discovered that Sardar had been right about the transience of black memories and mutability of the past. Time had erased their darkest memories of the 1995 Dorsempotrang death march, and they were eager to experience another pilgrimage with Baker and Sardar as spiritual guides.

Sardar's conversations with the lama of Bayu about the location of Pemakö's secret center prompted them to head south again. He and Baker wanted to record oral histories in villages along the lower Tsangpo. They intended to leave the gorge again via the Doshong La, a pass Sardar had come to loathe. Since Kingdon-Ward's day it had gone from a rhododendron fairyland to a trash dump, littered by the heavy traffic of traders, coolies, and military units heading to and from the garrisons of Medog. Nevertheless, it was the shortest, most logical way to exit the lower gorge.

The group planned to enter the gorge from the northeast, over the Su La, one of only two passes in southeastern Tibet where the dwarf red lily, *Lilium paradoxium,* can be found. During his expedition with George Sherriff in 1947, botanist Frank Ludlow was swept away by the diversity of plants on the Su La. He intended to spend the bet-ter part of a field season there collecting seed and specimens, but his plan came to naught when the Chinese invaded Tibet two years later. During the ensuing guerilla war in the gorge, Poba tribesmen slaugh-tered more than a hundred Chinese soldiers on the Su La in one en-gagement, repeating the bloodbath that occurred there during China's 1911 campaign against Tibet.

Now, as the team ascended through sacred forests to the pass under a monsoon rain, they witnessed effects of China's Maoist-era policies to conquer nature and exploit every inch of unused ground. Claire Scobie, a British journalist who had joined the team in hopes of finding the red lily, described the scene as a "battlefield" littered with enormous trees "like fallen soldiers."

The ascent to the top of the fourteen-thousand-foot pass took all day—twelve hours in the rain. The trail went from being a "marsh" to a "boulder-strewn scramble," but as they neared the summit, Storm cried out, "Found it!" It was Scobie's lily, though unfortunately not in seed. Collecting the whole specimen of such a rare plant would be bad form, so Scobie had to content herself with appreciating it in situ.

On the opposite side of the pass lay Pemakö—what could be seen of it beneath the low clouds. As they descended from the snowy heights into the heat, humidity, and driving rain of the lower gorge, the Gillenwaters despaired over having returned to such abysmal conditions. Apart from the weather, mud, and insects, a lustful German woman on the team was making uncomfortably frank overtures to Baker. Group dynamics were strained. The brothers, Baker thought, were having a "crisis of confidence."

Indeed they were, and lasted only several days before announcing that they wanted to leave the group and walk north, toward the cooler high country of the central canyon. The group's itinerary did not include points north, however, and villages there were not listed on their permit. Were the brothers to be stopped, they would risk arrest. Yet Baker could see they were adamant, so he sent them off with two of his most trusted Nepali Sherpas. Watching the Gillenwaters pack up and leave, Ken Storm was torn. He decided to stay with the main group but changed his mind the next day, reversed direction, and caught up with the brothers in a village near the Tsangpo. The three and their retinue passed a "magical" night in the village, according to Gil Gillenwater. "Fireflies danced like *dakinis* in the electrically charged air," he wrote in his journal, "and a lightning storm filled the gorge with flashes of colored brilliance."

The weather was breaking. It was an auspicious sign signaling good fortune ahead.

In the village of Gande, situated high above the Tsangpo, Storm and the Gillenwaters received another favorable sign when they ran into a hunter the brothers had met in 1995. It had been raining hard that afternoon, and they were sloshing down a muddy track under the gloom of the jungle canopy when the hunter, named Matuk, and his young son appeared. Looming out of the darkness and wearing clothes that he had never seen before, the Gillenwaters presented a curious sight—like beings from another world. As a gesture of friendship, Gil had presented the startled hunter with a laminated photograph of the Dalai Lama posing serenely in front of a saguaro cactus in the Arizona desert. Awestruck at his good fortune, the Monpa had touched the image to his forehead over and over, thanking Gillenwater profusely.

Now Matuk wanted to show his gratitude. He gave the brothers and Storm a plump, ripe squash and offered to be their guide. The next day, they left the village and began descending a steep trail to a swinging bridge across the Tsangpo. On the way down, the hunter paused to point out a promontory on the skyline miles to the west, near a pass called Tsebum La. He said he could get them that far, but the territory beyond was foreign to him.

Three days later, after climbing more than eight thousand feet from the river through thickets of wet rhododendrons, the team crested the Tsebum La. It was four-thirty in the afternoon and the weather was closing in, with bruised, evil-looking clouds blotting out the sky and the vistas from the pass.

A grinning Matuk gestured that the Gillenwaters and Storm should follow him: He had a surprise. Though they were spent from the long climb, the three followed the hunter down a steep ridge that ended at a sheer precipice. As they inched across a ledge at the top of the cliff, the storm burst into full fury, presenting an extravaganza of crashing thunder, shrieking wind, and bolts of lightning that exploded all around them.

It took an hour and a half of difficult hiking to reach Matuk's surprise: the outcrop that he had pointed out from near his village. It was a famous and powerful pilgrimage destination. Tradition held that pilgrims must make three clockwise circumambulations of the seventy-foot-tall granite pillar, which leaned out into space over the canyon below. The ledge above the abyss was no wider than a boot sole. Inching around the base of the boulder, the four men passed yak skulls and prayer flags that pilgrims had left as offerings, and coins pressed into cracks in the rock. At one point, Matuk pointed out a shallow hand-shaped depression in the stone. "Padmasambava!" he yelled above the wind and rain—the handprint of the master himself, as if it had been burned into solid granite.

On the third circuit, Matuk led Storm and the Gillenwaters through a cleft in the stone that they had overlooked on their previous circumambulations. The passage opened onto a small clearing, like a hidden chamber, and against one wall stood a stack of notched sticks. Matuk explained through gestures that each notch represented a year in the life of the pilgrim who had carved it. He handed out fresh sticks and indicated that the three should start carving.

The ritual forced Gil to relive each year of his life. "Forty-three years!" he later wrote in a travelog about the expedition. "Vivid memories of the first days of school, friends long forgotten, brothers being born, first job, first girlfriend, first kiss, driver's license, leaving home, football games, graduations, hopes, dreams, trips, business deals, lovers—all of it crystal clear in my mind. . . . The simple exercise brought sharply into focus the Buddhist principles of impermanence, transience and the fact that the present moment is the only true time."

The next phase of the circuit involved crawling through a muddy tunnel that represented a birth canal. Pilgrims who had just re-lived their lives carving "long life" sticks symbolically left those years of ignorance behind by worming through the tunnel, to be reborn at the other end as enlightened beings. Squeezing through the passage, the four pilgrims emerged into the blazing light of the setting sun. The storm's miraculous passing gave them a panoramic view of Pemakö and its encircling snow-covered peaks. Far below them was the sinuous inner canyon, flanked by the gleaming peaks of Namche Barwa and Gyala Peri.

Now they had their bearings. Storm and the Gillenwaters thought they could see a way to traverse a series of spurs that plunged down the flanks of Namche Barwa and an adjacent peak named Sanglung, "like dark furry arms," as Kingdon-Ward had written. Some of these ridges dropped straight into the tumultuous Tsangpo, forcing it to abruptly change course. From where they were, the three adventurers could see that they had to strike a chord across the inverted loop of the Great Bend, heading west over a pass called Senchen La, then clamber over the corrugated terrain high above the river to a point where they might be able to look down on Rainbow Falls and perhaps even into the five-mile gap. This was essentially what Kingdon-Ward and Cawdor did in 1924, only in reverse.

The porters were having none of it, however. There was no trail to the Senchen La, they protested, and no one ever traveled that way. Only by sweetening each porter's wages to twelve dollars a day from seven did Storm and the Gillenwaters prevail.

Above the timberline, the party entered a sea of rhododendrons so tangled that walking through them was impossible. Instead, they followed the thickets' margins, picking along crumbling knife-edged ridges that fell away thousands of feet into the gorge. A bank of clouds moved in, and no one could tell which way to go. Porters became separated from one another and called out in the pea-soup fog. Suddenly the mist parted to reveal a silhouetted figure about a quarter of a mile away, watching them intently. Gil called out to the man, who bounded downhill "effortlessly, like a cross between a mountain goat and a gazelle."

He was a Monpa hunting for takin. Short and stocky, he explained to the porters that he could lead them forward along an old and seldom-traveled pilgrimage route that they would never find by themselves. The porters were leery. Ahead was the sacred peak representing a wrathful protector deity of the inner gorge. Again, they refused to proceed for fear of offending the spirit.

That night, the hunter had a dream in which Storm and the Gillenwaters appeared. They were seated at a dining table in a spotlessly clean room when a goddess entered to serve tea, followed by a male deity sounding a musical instrument made from a sacred conch shell. In the morning, the hunter interpreted the vision as a clear sign that the three must be led over the holy peak and into the hidden inner gorge. The porters concurred, and they were off again.

The clouds moved in to obscure the way. At a point where the first hunter became lost, yet another hunter appeared from the mists. Tall and wiry, with more chisled features than his fellow Monpa, he cut a noble figure posing with his emaciated hunting dogs. The hunter explained that he knew a secret trail into the gap that led to a "big waterfall." Storm and the Gillenwaters looked at each other in disbelief. Could it be the lost waterfall?

Visibility was down to a yard as the column began its descent into the inner gorge. But as if by divine intent, the mists began to lift. A burst of sunlight broke through the clouds, illuminating "the jaws of the deepest gorge in the world," as Gil wrote. Rainbow Falls was directly below them but still out of sight because of the pitch of the slope.

Their newfound guide led the group downhill through brush so thick that the only way they could advance was to throw themselves on top of it and "swim" over the surface. As soon as Storm saw Rainbow Falls, he recognized it from Jack Cawdor's 1924 photograph in *The Riddle of the Tsangpo Gorges*. But that is not what transfixed the three trekkers. About a quarter mile downstream was the top of what appeared to be a much bigger drop.

"We found them!" Storm cried out. "We've found the Falls of the Brahmaputra!"

"I was trembling," says Storm. "Something that had been such a vital force in the Western imagination had been lost, because the explorers had lost faith in the falls. They'd lost their vision." Part of his spiritual transformation in Pemakö involved recapturing this vision after first having accepted "the seal of Western exploration" that dismissed the big drop as a figment. Now, looking down on the cascade, he understood the value of faith.

Storm could barely contain himself but knew he must. From the angle they had on the drop—above and upstream—they could not see the bottom of the cascade. "The process of discovery," as he told the Gillenwaters, would be incomplete until they could rappel down to the base of the waterfall and measure it from top to bottom. Only if it met Kingdon-Ward's standard of being about a hundred feet high would it qualify as the Falls of the Brahmaputra. If it didn't, it would be just another waterfall of many in the gorge—dramatic but not the cascade of legend.

Without climbing ropes or measuring devices, Storm proposed that they come back with Baker and Sardar the following year properly equipped. First, though, they needed to photographically document the waterfall. At dawn the next morning, they started inching downhill behind the porters, who hacked a path through the scrub with machetes. The further they dropped, the less they could see of the cascade. That explained why Kingdon-Ward and Cawdor had missed it. In 1924, the botanist and his surveyor had been standing at river level upstream from Rainbow Falls. From such a low angle, their view downstream would have been blocked by rock spurs jutting into the river from both sides. These obstructions forced the river into an S-turn, jogging left, then right before it hurtled over the lip of the hidden drop.

From their point of furthest progress, about a quarter of a mile from the falls, Gil Gillenwater estimated the height of the drop at about a hundred feet. "We discover Rainbow Falls and Hidden Rainbow Falls," he wrote in his journal. "AMAZING! THE MISSING LINK." He called the sighting a "historic discovery."

. . .

I N *The Myth of Shangri-La,* author Peter Bishop refers to Tibet as a place caught "between the world of fantasy and romance and that of science and so-called reality." Reality, after all, is simply a matter of perception, and landscapes are what we make of them. Where one person sees only rock and ice, another perceives a crystal palace. Likewise, one explorer's Falls of the Brahmaputra can be another's run-of-the-mill waterfall.

"No big deal" was the way David Breashears had described the presumed waterfall he saw in 1993, and he was as steeped in Kingdon-

Ward lore as Ken Storm. But later, meeting Baker in New York City, Breashears showed off his picture of the drop, wondering what Baker made of it. Baker thought it interesting but not worth pursuing at the expense of his inquiry into Pemakö's sacred geography.

Peter Bishop's point that landscape is shaped by the eye of the beholder is well made when one compares Breashears' 1993 photograph to one that Gil Gillenwater made four years later. The two are almost identical. Breashears and Gillenwater had stood on virtually the same piece of ground to take their photographs. For one observer it was a divinely ordained discovery of a lifetime; for the other, just a curious "hydrologic event," as Breashears dryly characterized it.

. . .

IN 1924, WHEN Frank Kingdon-Ward and Jack Cawdor arrived at the Pemaköchung monastery, they were at the beginning of the Tsangpo's steepest section—thirty or more miles of gradient that averages eight times that of the Colorado River's through the Grand Canyon, and in places is up to thirty times as steep. Below the dilapidated temple, the river bored into the chasm as if spilling from the roof of the world. Pemaköchung sits at an elevation of about eighty-five hundred feet. By the time the river thundered over Rainbow Falls, some fifteen miles downstream and to the east, it had lost about fifteen hundred feet of elevation, according to Cawdor's boiling-point reading. Another twenty miles brought it halfway around the Great Bend, to the holy site of Gompo Ne at the confluence with the Po Tsangpo. By then, the Tsangpo had dropped another eighteen hundred feet.

The loss of more than three thousand feet in thirty miles initially excited Kingdon-Ward and Cawdor. "For a river of this size to descend 112 feet a mile was amazing," Kingdon-Ward wrote about the stretch between Rainbow Falls and Gompo Ne. "[T]here was plenty of room for a big waterfall of 100 feet or so" in the portion of the canyon below Rainbow Falls.

However, when they realized that the gap was impregnable, Kingdon-Ward recalled having heard a legend that from the Pemaköchung monastery to Gompo Ne, the Tsangpo contained seventy-five waterfalls, each with its own guardian spirit. If that was true, he calculated, and if each fall was only twenty feet high, it would very nearly account for the river's loss of elevation and thus rule out the probability of a Niagara-sized drop in the gap. This is the point where logic obscured vision, and he and Cawdor gave up the search.

For a certain class of white-water athlete, however, a river with seventy-five waterfalls in fifteen miles would constitute a kind of paradise. That was the way one such boater saw it, a waterfall specialist and former Olympic racer named Wickliffe "Wick" Walker.

Walker learned about the Tsangpo when he first read Kingdon-Ward's book as a young man. He was among the paddlers representing the United States at the 1972 Munich Olympic Games, where he finished eleventh paddling an enclosed, or decked, canoe. Three years later, he and several friends made the first descent of the Great Falls of the Potomac near Washington, D.C. They went on to become pioneers in the emerging sport of expeditionary kayaking, running rivers from the Appalachians to Canada and Mexico. One technique they perfected was to lower their boats by rope into an isolated canyon, rappel down, and paddle away. They practiced loading their boats to the limit with food and supplies to see how they would handle in big water on a long, self-contained expedition. Walker and several cronies pioneered the rivers of Bhutan in 1981 and afterward set their sights on the Tsangpo. But while Chinese authorities rejected their application in 1985, Walker and his friends were destined to realize their hope of running the canyon of seventy-five waterfalls.

By the mid-1990s, publicity about the Tsangpo being "the last great first" in expeditionary river running had attracted a number of other contenders. Steve Currey, a Provo, Utah, outfitter, had designs on the river. He had rafted the Brahmaputra River in India in 1992 and hoped to "close the circle" by running the Tibetan part of the river right across the border—a double first: first to raft the Tsangpo Gorge, first to cross the contested boundary. Such a coup would be good for business as well, and Currey planned to offer commercial white-water trips on the river below the hazardous inner canyon. In his view, the lower gorge held great promise as an adventure destination for boaters and trekkers.

Scuttlebutt in the tightly knit white-water community also had it that a number of other expeditionary kayakers from the United States and Germany had designs on the Tsangpo. There was also pressure from the East. In the spring of 1998, *China Daily* previewed a rafting expedition that was to run the length of the Tsangpo the following September, starting at the river's headwaters in western Tibet and ending at the Sino-Indian border in the lower gorge. A geology professor named Yang Yong was to lead the twenty-person team. A minor hero in China, he had been among the chauvinistic boaters who ran the Yangtze River in 1986 hoping to beat an American team attempting a first descent from the river's Tibetan source. Pummeled by massive rapids and plagued by the death of one team member from cerebral and pulmonary edema, the Americans aborted their expedition, and Yang and his colleagues saved face for China.

In soliciting members for Yang's Tsangpo expedition, the *China Daily* article pointed out that American teams would be on the river at the same time as the Chinese. The idea of losing the first descent to foreigners again prompted a number of Chinese rafters to apply for the team, motivated by what one member called "somewhat narrow-minded pride for our deeply loved motherland."

Unlike Yang's 1986 Yangtze expedition, the Chinese team did not have the government's blessing. Beijing was instead supporting an expedition of forty scientists from the Chinese Academy of Sciences, who were to go to the canyon in October 1998 along with thirty-five television and newspaper reporters. The academy conducted a scouting expedition in April to investigate routes through the canyon and study the fauna and flora of the Great Bend. The nineteen-member probe was led by geologist and geographer Yang Yichou, considered to be the godfather of the Great Canyon, as it is known in China. Since 1973, he had led six other expeditions to the gorge, and in 1994 he was officially recognized in China for determining its record depth, not Rick Fisher.

Fueled by fact and rumor, the competition to run the river through the gorge grew to the point that one inspired magazine editor headlined a news item about the race "Leggo My Tsangpo." Baker cared nothing about the river runners' aspirations, but word of the Chinese scientists' plans got his competitive juices flowing. He, Sardar, Storm, and the Gillenwaters had made a pact to measure the hidden waterfall in November 1998, about the same time as the massive scientific team and three dozen Chinese journalists would be laying siege to the inner canyon.

Baker and Sardar returned to the gorge in May 1998, ostensibly to film the Monpa hunters for Sardar's documentary film. Harvard's Film Studies Center had awarded Sardar a small grant to complete his film, with the help of Ned Johnston, an award-winning cinematographer who lectured at the center.

The three arrived at Pelong near the Po Tsangpo trailhead to find the town in delirious and boozy celebration of a religious festival. Sardar recognized one of the tipsy celebrants: Tsering Dondrup, the Monpa hunter from Bayu he had met in 1996 while researching traditions about Pemakö's secret center. Dondrup and his lama brother had told him then that they knew nothing about a big waterfall and that no one ever went to the inner canyon.

Now, well into his cups, Dondrup rushed up to embrace Sardar. In reminiscing about Sardar's stay at his house, the hunter blurted out that he had misled his friend. In fact, Dondrup did know a way into the inner gap. His son had just been hunting takin there and found the area rich with game. The boy had also seen the huge, hidden waterfall.

"Hey, listen to this," Sardar called to Baker and Johnston. As the story unfolded, Sardar suggested that they shift their focus away from the area where he had intended to film to the gap. If takin were to be found there, he and Johnston could film the hunt and the waterfall that Storm and the Gillenwaters had spotted. Dondrup consented to guide them down a route that would put them right at the top of the falls rather than upstream from it.

Liquor had loosened Dondrup's tongue, but so had his admiration for Sardar and Baker's inquiry into Pemakö's sacred geography. "By then the legend of Lekdrup and our daring *ney kor* [pilgrimage] to Dorsempotrang in 1995 had spread far and wide among the inhabitants of the upper gorge," Sardar says. "They now perceived us as pilgrims and insiders with a knowledge of Tibetan ritual and sacred guidebooks."

The four trekked down to Bayu and, after engaging porters, ascended the humpbacked mountain that the Tsangpo loops around, forming the Great Bend. It was raining hard, and the slick trail uphill was lined with sliced-off bamboo stubs as sharp as punji sticks. "Every time we slipped, we risked being impaled," Sardar says.

From the snowy backbone of the mountain, they could see the river far below as it emerged from the gap and flowed northeast toward the apex of the big bend. At their backs, it flowed southwest, careening down toward the lower gorge. As they began dropping off the ridge toward the gap, the sound of the river behind them faded as the rumbling before them grew, like an ominous echo.

The concept for Sardar's film, as Johnston understood it, was to evoke the Monpas' relationship to the land and animals of the gorge, specifically the takin. Buddha's first principle—that all life is sacred and inviolate—would seem to rule out hunting altogether. In the hidden land of Tsari, which lies immediately to the east of Pemakö, hunting, butchering, and even plowing or burning for agricultural cultivation are forbidden. Tsari is revered as a kind of holy national park, and those who violate its environmental proscriptions have been beaten so severely in public that they have died from their injuries.

But in Pemakö, the Monpas have a convenient rationale for hunting takin: Padmasambava created the beasts for their consumption. As residents of the hidden land, they believe that they will suffer no karmic consequences for killing and butchering the sacramental animals. When they shoot a takin, the hunters explain, its spirit immediately emerges from tiny holes at the tips of its horns (or a nubbin in the center of its forehead) and enters the Buddha fields. Monpas also say that when future emanations of Padmasambava return to Pemakö to open the innermost hidden land, his incarnations will materialize as takin and lead the faithful to everlasting paradise. There the takin will graze on magic grass that will permit them to leave footprints in solid rock.

Takin were not in evidence on this trip. Dondrup found spoor and fresh dung at one point and sent his dogs charging off after their scent, but the prey had evidently departed. Johnston was exasperated. He had come to film a sacred hunt, not to trek to a waterfall. It was still raining dismally, and the hunters were crossing slopes so steep and loose with scree that filming was out of the question.

As promised, Dondrup led them to a ledge about two thousand feet directly above the waterfall. From their precarious vantage point, they could see the falls from top to bottom, but because they were looking straight down on it, no one had a sense of its height.

"We were pretty much convinced that it wasn't going to turn out to be anything," Baker says, "although we still were committed to coming back in November, when the hunters felt we could get down to it more easily [because the vegetation would be lower and thinner]." They had not brought measuring devices, and despite the temptation, Baker suggested that they not descend any further. They had made a commitment to Storm and the Gillenwaters, he reminded Sardar. Sardar was in agreement about turning back, although for different reasons: He had still not found a reference to the waterfall in Buddhist guidebooks, and oral traditions held that a waterfall somewhere in the lower gorge was the gateway to Pemakö's Eden. The hunters simply referred to this one as "the big waterfall."

Looking down the "wild display of hydraulics," Sardar had a provocative thought. What if the titanic 1950 earthquake that rocked the gorge had reconfigured the inner canyon? Could the waterfall have been created then, not destroyed, as Rick Fisher believed? The sharp edges of surrounding cliffs suggested to him a recent geological event. That would be ironic: The dream of Western explorers and geographers might have materialized long after they had abandoned their hope of finding it.

. . .

MEETING DONDRUP WAS not the only serendipity on the expedition. Before setting out for the falls, Baker and Sardar had also run into Steve Currey, the Utah rafting outfitter who was in the gorge scouting white water that would be suitable for experienced clients. His "grand design" was to lead an exploratory expedition in which Chinese military helicopters would shuttle trekkers and boaters into every part of the canyon, culminating with a "historic crossing of the India/China border." For sponsorship, Currey planned to approach *National Geographic*.

Baker and Sardar impressed him as ideal leaders for his land-based teams. After returning home, he included their names in a prospectus that he intended to present to the *Geographic*'s Expeditions Council that summer. Baker was going to be in New York then and agreed to come to Washington to show his slides during Currey's presentation. Minutes before the meeting, Currey asked him to lead the treks. Baker said yes, he would.

The pitch went badly for Currey. Apart from his projected cost for the expedition (four hundred dollars for the helicopters alone), the council did not want to underwrite what some of its members considered an adventure boondoggle. Baker's addition to the team as cultural expert, they thought, was mere window dressing.

Baker, on the other hand, impressed the council. He was low-key, serious, and well versed. The editors pulled him aside afterward and encouraged him to submit his own grant application. The society's magazine and television divisions were planning special coverage of the gorge in 1999, and the expedition to measure the hidden waterfall would be a valuable addition to the package. If the council approved the application, Baker would join a "dream team" of writers, photographers, and experts. David Breashears was on the team. So was George Schaller, the distinguished wildlife biologist, conservationist, and author. And, as it turned out, so were Wick Walker and his paddling cronies. They, not Steve Currey, would be covering the whitewater adventure angle.

A month later, in September 1998, Baker submitted an application to the council asking for forty-two thousand dollars to "document conclusively the topography of the Tsangpo Gorge between Rainbow Falls and the Po Tsangpo confluence." The gap was "a blank spot on the map of world exploration," Baker wrote, and because of the Monpas' historic unwillingness to take anyone there, it was also "one of the world's best kept geographical secrets." He did not mention that he, Sardar, Storm, the Gillenwaters and Breashears had already seen the hidden waterfall, because, as he explains, he feared that it could become "a red herring"—no more than one of many hydrologic events on the Tsangpo. His stated objective was simply to probe the gap and measure whatever waterfalls they found. Yet in a separate proposal to the television division, he did specify that the team had already seen, but not measured, a spectacular waterfall that might qualify as the Falls of the Brahmaputra. The proposed documentary would "reveal how this 'lost vision' interfaces with the Tibetans' quest to discover an earthly paradise in these remote gorges."

The council approved the proposal in late October, granting Baker thirty-eight thousand dollars. The television division also wanted the documentary and assigned a videographer to the team. And thus began what Hamid Sardar referred to as "Ian's minuet with *National Geographic.*"

. . .

EVERY ERA OF explorers has relied on patronage and sponsorship. The bargain has always been a trade-off: the explorers got to fulfill their dreams, and the sponsoring institution or individual got to brag about them. It was no different in 1998 than it was in 1888. In exchange for granting book, magazine, and photo rights to the *Geographic,* Baker and Walker's teams could travel to Tibet without having to worry about money and with the society's seal of approval. Indeed, had the Expeditions Council rejected Walker's grant application instead of approving a sixty-thousand-dollar contribution, he and his team intended to postpone their expedition for a year.

In Baker's case, working with the *Geographic* was a dream come true. As a freelance magazine journalist and author of several books about Tibet, he had always aspired to write for "the revered institution," as he thought of it. The society was one of the few reliable sources for expedition funding, and it compensated its correspondents handsomely. In addition to covering expenses, the magazine paid some writers five dollars a word for articles. Two pieces a year could earn him forty thousand dollars, as much as an advance on a book that might take him two or more years of travel, research, and writing.

There was also a good deal of respectability to be gained by working for the *Geographic*. Baker may have moved to Kathmandu to escape the air-conditioned nightmare of living in America, but he was also seeking "freedom from conventional expectations that contract and limit the lives of many people I know who live in the U.S. They've felt compelled into certain careers or marriages just because that's what is expected."

Living in Nepal was a way of not being defined by the expectations of family and friends, of being free to explore a "larger kind of identity or orientation to life." Friends say that Baker never really escaped parental expectations, even if the pressure he felt was self-imposed and imagined. He was forty, without a family, and making a precarious living as a writer and spiritual adventurer, in spite of appearances when he came home to be feted at lavish book parties attended by celebrity Buddhists, film stars, and fashion models.

The *Geographic* took a gamble on Baker, trusting that he would provide an exclusive, in-depth look at a unique region. But there was more to the quid pro quo than that. The society labors under the weight of a hundred-and-ten-year-old tradition of supporting great explorers engaged in "the increase and diffusion of geographic knowledge." A successful probe of the gap would burnish the institution's image and help to restore some of the luster that it enjoyed when it was underwriting landmark expeditions to the far and unknown corners of the globe—Robert Peary to the North Pole, Hiram Bingham to Machu Picchu, Louis and Mary Leakey to Olduvai Gorge. Baker was not in their league, but after his presentation to the Expeditions Council, everyone agreed that he seemed to be made of the right stuff.

While he was in Washington waiting for a verdict on his grant application, Baker met with Wick Walker and several members of the white-water team at the suggestion of *National Geographic* editors. There were to be four boaters on Walker's river team, Baker learned, but Walker was not among them. Past his boating prime and out of paddling condition, the retired army intelligence officer planned to lead one of two ground support crews that would resupply the boaters at prearranged locations and respond to any emergencies. The other ground crew would be composed of Harry and Doris Wetherbee, a Foreign Service couple whom Walker had met in Pakistan and who were hosting the meeting at their suburban home.

The expedition would be launched at Pe, the village at the head of the gorge, and continue down to Medog in the lower gorge. No one on the boating team expected to paddle the entire hundred and forty miles; they would have to portage around unrunnable rapids and waterfalls. But if they could pass beneath the theoretical line joining the summits of Namche Barwa and Gyala Peri, they would become the first boaters to run the world's deepest canyon.

Tom McEwan was the nominal leader of the river team. McEwan was fifty-three and ran an outdoor youth camp in Maryland that his parents had founded. He had known Walker since age fifteen. The two had made the pioneering 1975 run over the Great Falls of the Potomac and went to Bhutan together. McEwan's younger brother, Jamie, had been on the Bhutan expedition as well and had joined the Tsangpo team. He had been Walker's roommate at the 1972 Olympics and earned a bronze medal in the canoe slalom event. Twenty years later in Barcelona, at almost forty, McEwan competed in the same event and narrowly missed winning another medal. He was strong, highly skilled, and very determined.

The third pillar of the river team was Doug Gordon, a research chemist who had earned a silver medal in the 1982 national kayaking championships and a bronze in 1985, and had joined Walker on numerous expeditions. Analytical by nature but gutsy, Gordon would often take the lead running dangerous rapids. He had a gift for reading a river's current and executing split-second moves, and his Eskimo roll was said to be bombproof. Everyone on the Tsangpo team considered him to be first among equals.

Finally, there was Roger Zbel, an alternate who joined the team in August after four other candidates got cold feet and declined Walker's and Tom McEwan's invitations to go to Tibet. Zbel, a bearish man of forty-two with a bushy blond beard, was not an Ivy League college graduate like Walker (Dartmouth), the McEwans (both Yale), and Gordon (Harvard). He had never gone to college, raced in the Olympics, or been on an expedition. But he dominated the wildwater racing circuit on mountain rivers in West Virginia and western Maryland, where he owned a rafting outfit, and he had been paddling five days a week for more than twenty years.

Until the night of the meeting with Baker, Walker had been so circumspect about the expedition that even prospective team members had to agree to total secrecy. He approached the expedition like a covert mission in his army days in Southeast Asia. He did not want to be scooped by other kayakers rumored to be considering the Tsangpo.

While Baker shared his impressions of the river, Walker and the Wetherbees brought out maps, aerial photos, and satellite images of the canyon, some of which they had obtained through contacts at the State Department. "All of this interested me considerably," Baker says, "as my own 'maps' to the area had been primarily ancient Buddhist texts describing a kind of parallel landscape." Privately, he believed that the sophisticated satellite imagery was of little use compared to the "mythic consciousness" and oral traditions that he relied on to navigate the mystical land.

A year earlier, in September 1997, Walker, the Wetherbees, and Tom McEwan had made a month-long reconnaissance of the gorge, and they showed slides of that trip to Baker. Their scouting mission had taken them down the Po Tsangpo trail to the confluence. There they divided forces. The Wetherbees had turned downstream toward Bayu, while Walker and McEwan had gone up into the gap on the north side of the gorge. From the flanks of Gyala Peri, they had seen perhaps five miles of the inner canyon and noticed that the big drops seemed to be interspersed with boatable stretches of white water. Although their survey was cursory, Walker felt that they had seen "enough to make some informed judgments."

Baker was impressed by the team's experience, exacting preparations, and "spirit of humility," but he had misgivings about their prospects. "It was a funny scouting trip," he says, calling it "irrelevant to the section they wanted to boat." They never saw the upper canyon, and none of them put a paddle in the river.

Baker described what the Tsangpo had looked like during his 1993 traverse of the upper canyon and told the team that, personally, he would never think of attempting to boat such a river. He also mentioned a possible "escape route" out of the gorge below Rainbow Falls, along game trails that he had spotted in 1996 while attempting to forge upriver from the Great Bend on the flanks of Gyala Peri. Beyond that, he revealed nothing about the hidden waterfall or network of hunters' trails on the other side of the river that he and his team expected to follow down to the big drop.

"It was not in our expedition's interest to reveal at this time the extent of the hunters' knowledge [of the unexplored regions] of the gorge," Baker explains. "It didn't seem essential to their safety nor to their mission." After sharing with the team everything that he considered relevant to their success, he bid them goodnight, and wished them well.

· · ·

BEGINNING IN EARLY August 1998, the *New York Times* initiated coverage of disastrous flooding in China. Monsoon rains had caused the Yangtze and other rivers to reach record levels. Fourteen million people had reportedly been left homeless and fifty million acres damaged, and the flood season was not yet over. In Tibet, record floods and mud slides along the Tsangpo had killed fifty people and more than four thousand yaks and sheep. A quarter of Tibet's population was engaged in fighting the floods—so many that celebrations commemorating the thirty-third anniversary of the founding of the Tibetan Autonomous Region were canceled.

Despite their concerns, Walker and his teammates decided that the only way to tell if the river was unsafe was to go to Tibet and see it for themselves. The monsoon season would have ended by then and, they hoped, floodwaters in the gorge would be receding. Even if they decided not to run the canyon, they could still trek alongside the river and gather data for a subsequent attempt. In their opinion, every undocumented river mile they could scout would represent progress.

The team flew to Kathmandu and checked into a hotel surrounded by neatly tended gardens. Working outside, they spread out a mountain of equipment and food on the lawn and began repacking for the expedition. Porters would carry most of the supplies to designated stops in the canyon, but some of those were a week or more apart. The boats would be loaded with freeze-dried meals, water filters, communications equipment, camping gear, medical supplies, clothing, ropes, and climbing hardware, plus the men themselves. "It's going to make for some heavy boats," Zbel observed, looking around at the tons of equipage.

Assembled around an outdoor breakfast table, the team discussed strategy. "What happens if things go badly wrong?" Walker asked. "I've never been on a river trip where there was a death, but suppose that were to happen? I hate to raise this, but what are your thoughts?"

"You mean would we keep going?" asked Jamie McEwan.

Walker's own philosophy was to have his teammates "carve my name on a tree and go on." Others weighed in with different views. "That's easy for me," said Doug Gordon. "If I die, leave me there. If someone else does, get to the next access point and take off."

"You mean abort the expedition?" Walker asked.

"I do," said Gordon, fiddling with the strap on his river sandal, looking contemplative. "I don't think I could go on. I feel like I ought to be home talking to that person's family or doing something other than paddling white water and having fun."

"You still think this is going to be fun?" Walker shot back to lighten the mood.

The group laughed nervously.

With a nod to Kingdon-Ward, the so-called Riddle of the Tsangpo Gorges Expedition rolled out of Lhasa on September 29, 1998, bound for Pe in three Land Cruisers. Four days later, they stood on the banks of the river. Although it was receding, it still carried thirty thousand to forty thousand cubic feet per second, double the flow of the Colorado at high water. "All of us were intimidated," says Tom Mc-Ewan. "We knew that once you lost control, you would never stop."

Doug Gordon and Jamie McEwan were eager to begin paddling; Zbel urged them to wait to allow the river to subside further while they scouted a few miles downstream. A well-used trail led down to the village of Gyala, and though the footpath was about a thousand feet above the river, they could still see the first rapids they would be facing. In the end, he prevailed.

From the trail, the Tsangpo looked no more treacherous than big white-water rivers in Europe or the Americas. But the scale of the gorge can be deceptive. Against a backdrop of twenty-three-thousand-foot mountains, rapids that appear to be three feet high are ten feet or more. As soon as the paddlers put on the river, they realized what they were in for.

To run the first rapid of the trip, Jamie McEwan initially chose a line down the center of the river but suddenly changed his mind. The colossus of standing waves in midchannel was far bigger than he had expected. McEwan veered off and sprinted for calmer water along the shore, while behind him Gordon stuck to the "action line" of mid-channel, where the current was strongest. Powering into the first wave, Gordon's loaded kayak cartwheeled as if it weighed nothing. He was shaken loose from his seat and did not roll up for air for about twenty seconds. It was not like him to miss a roll.

The next day, as Jamie McEwan was wriggling into his decked canoe to launch, the boat slipped off a shoreline boulder and plunged into white water. McEwan had had no time to fasten his spray skirt around the cockpit, which began filling with water. He made a quick exit, but the canoe—containing all of his gear—was swept away. While the rest of the team continued on the river, McEwan hiked the trail to Gyala. Remarkably, two pilgrims found the boat below the village, floating in a pool beneath a fifty-foot drop—a ghost boat that had gone eighteen miles before stopping. They returned it for a reward, and the river team was back to full strength.

Gyala marks the beginning of the steep, narrow inner canyon. The team had no aerial photos of the river for about ten miles below Gyala, which made scouting ahead imperative. The current in mid-channel was becoming so unmanageable that they could not ferry across from one bank to the other. Were they to hug one side of the channel running blind, they might encounter one of the many spurs that drop into the river from Namche Bawra and Gyala Peri. In boating parlance, they would then be "cliffed out," with no way to proceed downstream, no way to paddle across the action line to the opposite shore, and possibly no way to walk back upstream.

The next resupply point below Gyala was Rainbow Falls. Because of the distance to the falls, each man had to pack fifteen days of meals rather than the normal eight. That would carry them through should they be forced to stop short of the waterfall and return to Gyala on foot or to hike down to meet Walker. The extra food added thirty cumbersome pounds to each of their already heavy boats.

The team paddled away from Gyala on a stretch of flat water—a "lake," as Tom McEwan describes it—but soon met with rapids and cliffs that put them ashore. To retrace the miles they had gained paddling the river, they had to walk back upstream though the jungle. Cutting a path through the vegetation and dragging heavy boats behind them took a full day. They were making "negative progress," says Tom McEwan, and were discouraged and exhausted.

After boating across to the other side of the river and sneaking down the shoreline, they again became cliffed out. It took four days of portaging to reach a spot where they felt comfortable launching again. The third day found them clambering over jagged, wet boulders until they were forced to rope the boats over a hundred-and-fifty-foot-high spur jutting into the river.

The weather was miserable for most of the portage, and they were working hard at an altitude of about nine thousand feet. By that point, everyone on the team was somewhat numbed to the constant risk they were facing, though not to the point of cowboying into the terrific power of the main channel. Their system was to scout well ahead on foot, spend the night in a forward base camp, and retrieve the boats in the morning to paddle as far as they could. They were making steady progress, but only about three miles a day.

The eleventh day of the expedition, October 16, dawned fresh and clear. It was a glorious, sunny morning, and as the team paddled downstream they shot glances over their shoulders at the shimmering white massif of Gyala Peri. Hanging glaciers spilled down from the heights, plowing through the forest almost to the river's edge—a magnificent backdrop for video footage.

At about eleven o'clock, the four men stopped to investigate a difficult section ahead. Mid channel was a series of gigantic haystack waves interspersed by deep troughs, where the river poured over submerged obstacles and rolled back on itself. Becoming trapped in one of these reversals would be a fatal mistake, because it could be impossible to break free. The backwash was powerful enough to force a boat to the bottom, where it could become wedged under a rock.

Gordon and the McEwan brothers picked out four possible routes along the river's edge, but Zbel rejected all of them. A tiny mistake might put him in harm's way, and in any case, another set of rapids a hundred yards downstream would force another portage. What was to be gained?

Gordon volunteered to go first. He intended to take a chute well away from the main channel but changed his mind at the last minute. Accelerating his heavy kayak, he shot over an eight-foot drop nearest to the action line and crashed into a cauldron of recirculating white-water below. Backwash flipped his boat bow over stern. For a sickening moment the kayak stood vertical, wobbling in the tremendous current, then tumbled back into the maelstrom.

Everyone was horrified, but Gordon had pulled out of worse scrapes. His kayak washed out of the cauldron, but he was unable to right the craft. Gordon tried again to roll in a long, agonizing, laborious attempt. Once more he failed. The boat was being drawn toward the haystackers. Standing ashore, the other three expected him to pop up at any moment. They prayed for him to roll. But in the middle of his third try, halfway up, time ran out for Douglas Gordon.

"He was swept right into this huge crashing thing," says Jamie McEwan. "I turned to run for shore. When I looked back, he was gone. I never saw him again."

"The whole river went over a drop of about sixty to seventy feet, and then it was one huge hole after another," Tom McEwan recalls. "Running downstream, I wanted to hear Doug's voice calling, 'Here I am!' Realistically, I never thought he had a chance." As Zbel and Tom McEwan dashed along the rocky shoreline, Jamie McEwan paddled and portaged along the edge of the river. He did not get far before another certain-death rapid put him ashore for good.

For the next three days, the team searched downstream for any trace of Gordon or his equipment, while Walker (who had been notified by satellite phone) worked upriver. Neither team found anything. "We were sick at heart," says Tom McEwan. "It was like a *via doloroso* walking down the river. All the happiness of the expedition was gone."

. . .

WALKER AND HIS teammates left the gorge a week after giving up the search for Gordon. They had held a funeral for him along the banks of the Tsangpo, near the Pemaköchung monastery, on a cold, drizzling day. Tom McEwan, who is devoutly Christian, led the service. He had inscribed Gordon's name on a rock and placed it near the river, while the porters chanted prayers and sang a song about the

Tsangpo. Their belief that Gordon's body had gone to the Buddha fields was scant comfort.

On the drive to Lhasa, the bereaved team met Baker's group coming in. A landslide had blocked the road, and both teams had to pitch in with shovels to clear the way for convoys of trucks stuck in frozen mud on opposite ends of the slide. Baker had already received word of Gordon's death from the *Geographic*. The kayaking team told him where they had looked for Gordon's body, and Baker promised that he would continue to search in the gap and to ask downstream villagers if they had seen or heard anything.

As usual, Baker had recruited a number of Nepali Sherpas for the expedition. They had driven overland to Lhasa with the expedition supplies, while Baker, Storm, Sardar, and *Geographic* videographer Bryan Harvey flew to the capital city to begin the tedious three-day drive to the gorge. The Gillenwaters had decided not to come along because of pressing business at home.

After hiring porters, the group again made the trek down the Po Tsangpo to Bayu, where they would pick up Tsering Dondrup and the other Monpa hunters. Sardar was irked that Harvey appeared to be focusing his video camera mostly on Baker and Storm, but he said nothing. It was already clear to him that the documentary was going to have a "great white explorer" storyline and that he would play an accessory role to Baker and Storm or none at all. Mulling over his options, Sardar decided to skip the trek to the falls altogether. Instead, he would enter the gap from the downstream end, taking Dondrup with him. Let the others dance for their supper, he thought. He had already seen the falls from above and was not inclined to see them again or to compete with Storm, who he felt was hamming it up for the camera.

"When Hamid chose to separate from the main expedition, Ken and I were both a bit envious," Baker says. "It wasn't much fun having a video camera continually intruding on one's experience, particularly when we had all shared a vision of a film [for Harvard] quite distinct from what was emerging."

Sardar had brought his own video camera, and he intended to use it. Marching into the gorge with the full expedition of perhaps twenty porters, Sherpas, and sahibs would spoil any chances of filming a traditional takin hunt, if only because the takin would be spooked away by such a huge caravan.

When Kingdon-Ward had entered the gorge in 1924, he had one object in mind: "to explore that part of the gorge which had been hidden from us, between the rainbow falls and the Po Tsangpo confluence . . . Here, if anywhere were the Falls of the Brahmaputra, which had been a geographical mystery for half a century; and the final solution—falls? Or no falls?—was now within our grasp."

That same passage could have been Baker and Storm's mission statement. They knew a waterfall was there, but was it the hundred-footer that Kingdon-Ward had sought? They would not know until they were in a position to measure it.

En route to the gorge, Baker and his teammates were aware of the impending arrival of the enormous Chinese Academy of Sciences expedition. News of the CAS team's progress was featured on Chinese television nightly, and the BBC World Service radio network was carrying reports from time to time. The other Chinese team that was rafting the length of the river had reached Pe the day after Doug Gordon disappeared. They had abandoned the idea of rafting the canyon and were walking through the gorge even as Baker and his team was trekking down the Po Tsangpo.

In Bayu, Sardar told Tsering Dondrup of his plan. The hunter did not want to return to the falls any more than Sardar did; he wanted to go hunting with his pal Lekdrup and to explore the lower end of the gap. The two dispatched Dondrup's capable nephew Buluk to lead the measuring team back along trails to the falls overlook.

Until then the weather had been crisp and clear, but after the two teams left Bayu, clouds started massing over the inner gorge. There would be snow up high, rain down low. By November 6, Baker, Storm, and Harvey had moved upriver into the gap and were poised to begin their final descent to the waterfall. That morning, one of their men, a lama, performed the ceremony to propitiate the local spirits. As if by magic, the clouds concealing Namche Barwa parted, and sunlight streamed down into the gorge, illuminating the slopes of Mount Dorje Phagmo opposite their camp.

After rigging prayer flags at the campsite for good luck, the hunters started downhill on forty-five-degree slopes streaked by landslide chutes. Chopping steps in the loose rubble with a crude adze, they sent a hail of stones over cliffs below and into the abyss. Here the river was still two thousand feet below them and out of sight, but they could clearly hear its thunderous descent toward the falls.

Finally, Buluk motioned for the team to stop. They needed to turn straight down to reach the ridge directly above the hidden waterfall. "We slipped, floated, and clambered though a dense, hanging forest of rhododendron, hemlock, magnolia and other unidentifiable trees," Baker later recorded in his journal. "Large ferns hid the ground itself, and at several points we fell though layers of moss, getting caught between the roots and limbs of trees, our feet dangling in the shadowed space below."

At last they reached the overlook where Baker and Sardar had stood the preceding May. They could look down on Rainbow and Hidden Falls from that point, but they were too far away to get readings on Storm's digital rangefinder or clinometer. There was no discernible route down to the river, but the hunters began cutting through the underbrush with a sense of dead reckoning, dropping rapidly downhill toward the roaring below.

Two hours later, the group reached a ledge about three hundred yards above the river. Storm took out his instruments and aimed them at the pools at the top and bottom of Rainbow Falls. The cascade was captivatingly beautiful, with plumes of mist dancing above and delicate ribbons of water streaming down the adjacent cliffs.

Kingdon-Ward and Cawdor had estimated the height of Rainbow Falls to be around forty feet, but Storm's readings showed they had been off by nearly half: Rainbow Falls measured seventy-two feet high according to his range finder. Here was very nearly the hundred-foot waterfall that Kingdon-Ward had hoped to find. If the hidden drop a quarter of a mile downstream was higher still, as the hunters promised, the mystery of the Falls of the Brahmaputra would be solved at last.

Aiming his instruments toward the lower falls, Storm took several readings on the cliffs girding the big drop. Each time the range finder indicated that, yes, this might be a drop that exceeded a hundred feet, and if so it would qualify as the waterfall that Kingdon-Ward had hoped to find. After traveling thousands of miles to the gorge, he and Cawdor had given up a little more than a thousand feet from their goal.

Continuing downhill at an angle that would put them right at the lip of the falls, the team came to an apparently impassible cliff at about half past five in the afternoon. The sun had dropped behind the mile-high walls of Dorje Phagmo opposite the falls, and darkness was gathering quickly. The hunters made camp in a grove of weeping pines, built a fire of rhododendron logs, and bedded down with their feet to the embers. Everyone passed the night in restless anticipation, but at dawn one of the hunters appeared at Baker's tent door to announce that there would be a delay: The Monpas had spotted a small herd of goral, the goatlike antelope whose hides they still sew into reversible capes, just as they did in Kingdon-Ward's day.

The hunters hit a large male with their first shot, but it slid downhill and plunged over a cliff into the river. The men nearly slipped to their deaths over the same precipice, but succeeded in downing one female and carried her back to camp. After performing rites to liberate the animal's life force and speed it to the Buddha fields, they butchered the carcass and roasted some of its organs. Buluk presented Baker with a piece of liver, cooked very rare, and Baker ate it, his hands streaming with blood.

Then came the final push to the falls. The Monpas found a way to avoid the cliff that had blocked them the previous evening and led the party to a clearing just above the hidden drop. They were now less than a hundred yards from their grail, but Harvey had Baker and Storm stop to narrate the moment of discovery.

"We're not sure what we'll find," said Baker awkwardly.

"Let's go," Storm broke in. "We have a waterfall to find."

The Monpas had gathered at the lip of the falls and were mesmerized by the spectacle. A torrent of silted water slid into space in a brown arc, then exploded into a spray of dazzling white as it hit the ledge midway to the bottom.

"Amazing!" cried Baker, whooping jubilantly. "Oh, my goodness," Storm exclaimed. "All that water! The whole of the Tsangpo flowing from Mount Kailas, past Everest . . . All that energy!"

"As much as I'd prepared myself for that moment," said Storm later, "it was not adequate. Standing there, I was awed."

Now came the moment of truth. To take the conclusive measurements, Storm and Baker would have to descend to the base of the waterfall. They put on their climbing harnesses and fixed two ropes to a pine tree near the brink. "See you in paradise," Baker said impishly as he backed away from Harvey's camera lens and began rappelling into the void. At a ledge fifty feet down, he paused to take photos. Clinging to the rope and buffeted by spray from the waterfall, he gazed into the face of the cascade, hypnotized by its power. For a second, he felt a strange urge to surrender himself to the river.

Storm rappelled down to the ledge next. He took more rangefinder readings, which corroborated the previous day's measurements. The Hidden Falls of Dorje Phagmo, as they named it, was slightly more than a hundred feet high and fifty feet wide. It did not compete with Niagara's one-hundred-eighty-two-foot-high horseshoe-shaped drop, or Victoria Falls' three-hundred-and-forty-three-foot plunge into the gorge of the Zambezi. Still, it ranked among the highest waterfalls in the Himalayas, and more important, it met Kingdon-Ward's standard.

"Our measurements clearly established that after more than a hundred years of searching, the Great Falls of the Brahmaputra was not a myth but reality," Baker wrote in his journal. "Today, this lost vision was resurrected."

He and Storm used mechanical ascenders (called jumars) to scale the fixed ropes back to the top. Now they wanted to see the base of the falls. Harvey was not interested. "The film is over," he told Baker. "We don't need to film the whole falls."

While Harvey waited at the top, Baker, Storm, and three Monpas scrambled down scree gullies and tilting cliffs to a slippery rock shelf at the bottom of the falls. Looking up, Storm could not see the lip of the falls, so he took readings off the soaring wall on the far side of the river. The rangefinder's readout kept displaying one hundred and eight, a sacred number in Tibetan Buddhism (rosaries contain that number of beads).

The Monpas were less impressed with figures than the clouds of mist rising out of the cauldron at the foot of the drop, which to them resembled sacred smoke. They studied the unreachable cliff face that Storm was measuring and saw several fissures in the glistening black rock. One was an oval slit shaped like a vaginal opening. The hunters kept pointing at it. The opening led to a tunnel, but only the mouth of the passage was visible. And there was no way to cross the river to see how far back the cave extended or, as Baker fantasized, what might lie on the other side. Was this the portal to paradise?

"As the Tibetans recited magical formulas and scouted below the falls for secret passageways, we felt ourselves to be standing at a place where anything could happen," wrote Baker. "Here was a place of confluence, a place where the Victorian dream of a Great Falls converged with a Tibetan search for a lost Eden. Standing beneath the falls, encircled by towering cliffs, the implacable drone of the Tsangpo filling our heads, we shared with our Tibetan friends a rare moment where, each in our own way, we penetrated beyond geography itself."

. . .

N OW THE REAL object of the expedition—to close the gap and search for other waterfalls—commenced. For the next several days, the group moved downstream across extreme terrain. "We were just bushwhacking all day, without any top of a mountain to reach, no objective," says Harvey. "To go out on each little ridge just to see if there were any more falls . . . well, I saw no point in it."

When they met Sardar and Dondrup coming upriver, everyone took a step back. Sardar's face was inflamed with insect bites—scores of them, inflicted by red gnats. His hair was disheveled, his clothes were a mess from "rhododendron swimming," and he had slept rough in caves or under tarps with the hunters. In short, he had visited his version of paradise.

There had been no sign of takin in the gap, but the hunters had shot an Assamese macaque out of the trees. Their dogs had set upon the wounded monkey, which fought for its life at Sardar's feet and badly mauled the hounds before dying. The river had not been visible the whole way through the gap, Sardar reported, but he did not believe there were any more big waterfalls to be found.

The original plan had been for Sardar to continue upstream to the falls with Dondrup and his men, while Baker, Storm, and Harvey retraced Sardar's steps to the lower end of the gap. Instead, the teams turned around together and struck out on the direct route to Bayu. The film, after all, was over. It was too late to alter the storyline to include Sardar, even though he alone succeeded in "closing the gap." It would not be reported that Sardar was the only outsider to have explored a blank on the map that had been tantalizing the West for more than a century.

. . .

B EFORE LEAVING H IDDEN Falls, Baker strung a line of prayer flags between two pines near the top of the falls, partly out of respect for the area's protector deities but also to literally plant the flag, as mountaineers often do on a summit. If the Chinese scientific team did find the waterfall, Baker reasoned, the prayer flags would show them that they had been beaten, much as Roald Amundsen's banner demonstrated to Robert Falcon Scott that he and his men had lost the race to the South Pole.

Back at Bayu, villagers reported that the Chinese team was still in the upper canyon, around Pemaköchung. The scientists had radioed ahead that they needed food and that fresh porters should await them in Bayu for the trek into the gap.

It was a minor victory for the American team but worth reporting, Baker thought. Harvey had a satellite phone with him, and after the team trekked back up the Po Tsangpo to the trailhead, he placed a call to his boss at the *Geographic,* Maryanne Culpepper, half a world away.

"Congratulations," Culpepper said to Baker. "You found the falls. Why do you think you succeeded while others did not?"

Baker had a sudden premonition. He felt the story slipping away from him. "I could see that, because of the way her questions were being posed, the focus was not on Pemakö and its spirit but on a kind of one-upmanship—who got where first," he says. "Here we were in a place where you can be blissfully cut off from the rest of the world, talking on a Magellan satellite phone to an institution in Washington, D.C. I was beginning to feel, 'Hmmm, I'm not so sure this is a good idea.' "

Of course, Baker could have set Culpepper straight about the difference between "discovering" and "documenting" Hidden Falls. He might have explained that they were merely the first to have measured the drop, but he did not. "I liked the fact that we got there before the Chinese, with their huge media-driven expedition," Baker says, overlooking his own sponsor's agenda. "If the Chinese team hadn't been in the gorge, things might have turned out differently. But I must admit that there was a real satisfaction in being able to present the first documentation of Hidden Falls. And that's all I want to call it. The word *discovery* has such ambiguity. Is it the first person to see something that gets credit for discovering it? Or is it the first person to know what he saw?"

Those questions were beside the point now. Ian Baker was about

to become a celebrity explorer, and to discover that this destiny, like
Dr. Faust's bargain with the devil, had aspects of both heaven and hell.

. . .

"LOST WATERFALL DISCOVERED in Remote Ti-
betan Gorge," read the headline over the *Geographic*'s press release. "It's
very exciting to find the waterfall of myth to be real," Baker was
quoted as saying. "People assumed the story of a great falls on the
Tsangpo was just romance. But it's here and larger than we imagined."

Storm was also cited in the release. "I didn't believe in the waterfall," he said. "I thought reports from the past were right—that it
probably didn't exist. It shows that even if you're told something isn't
there, you have to keep looking."

The press release was only a page of copy that a publicist had
drafted. Storm had sent her a detailed chronology of when people had
seen the falls, including his own and the Gillenwaters' sighting, and
Baker and Sardar's. But the publicist had to distill the story to essen-
tials: that the National Geographic Society had sponsored a team that
had made a major discovery.

She did a good job. Anchor Peter Jennings showed a photo of
the falls on the ABC-TV news that evening. Jim Lehrer of PBS interviewed Storm. In Kathmandu, Baker spoke to *Newsweek,* explaining
that the references James Hilton had consulted before writing *Lost
Horizon* came "very clearly from reports made by explorers in the
Tsangpo Gorge."

Worldwide, the Internet picked up the story, too. A Web site that
touted books on the lost continent of Atlantis ran an item announcing
that Shangri-La was a real place. Although Shangri-La had not been
mentioned in the *Geographic*'s press release, a Chicago *Tribune* reporter
led his article on the discovery with "Explorers have finally found
Shangri-La." He had interviewed Expeditions Council director Rebecca Martin and misquoted her: "If there is a Shangri-La, this is it.
This is a pretty startling discovery—especially at a time when many
people are saying, 'What's left to discover?' "

The *Tribune*'s syndicated article was picked up by wire services and appeared around the world. The Gillenwater brothers and Rick Fisher read it in the Arizona *Republic.* Among other errors, the reporter credited Baker and his teammates with proving that the Tsangpo and the Brahmaputra are connected. "There is no record of any human visiting, or even seeing, the [gap] before," the story read, ignoring the Monpa hunters.

The Gillenwaters were dumbstruck. Where were they in the article? They phoned Storm, who assured them that he had included them in his chronology but that they had been cut out of the final press release.

Feeling betrayed, mostly by Baker, the brothers wrote a letter of protest to the *Geographic,* including photographs they had taken of the waterfall and a fourteen-page report distilled from Gil Gillenwater's 1997 field notes.

"Troy and I have intentionally held off releasing our story and photographs until such time as a joint announcement could be made to your publication," Gil wrote. He demanded that the record be set straight and threatened legal action if the society did not issue a correction. They had been approached by several magazines and a book publisher, he pointed out, and they needed to protect these "secondary opportunities" to tell the true and fair story of the falls' discovery.

The brothers did not wait for a response before setting the record straight themselves. The following day, the Arizona *Daily Star* carried a front-page article under the headline "Explorers Dispute 'Discovery' of Waterfall in Shangri-La." In it, Storm confirmed the Gillenwaters' charges and said the *Geographic* had "inadvertently" omitted their names in the press release. The *Star*'s reporter also talked to Fisher, who called the discovery "ludicrous."

Several days later, in a self-serving letter to the *Geographic,* Storm distanced himself from the Gillenwaters. He explained that had it not been for him, the brothers would not have known the significance of what they had seen in the gorge. "The Gillenwaters give the impression in their account that I was following 'their' expedition [in 1997],"

Storm wrote. "This was simply not the case." The brothers' failure to credit him for explaining the history of the search for the lost falls was "a serious oversight," he complained, adding that the three of them had never discussed the idea of a joint announcement.

Gil Gillenwater received a copy of Storm's letter and could only shake his head. All the commiserating Storm had done with him over the phone—that the *Geographic* had had all the facts, including their names, but that reporters had heard only what they wanted to hear—rang hollow, Gillenwater's bitter conclusion was that the revered institution had reported the facts selectively—only those that supported the expedition it had financed.

. . .

T HE *GEOGRAPHIC* PRODUCED two *Explorer* segments, one on the kayaking expedition and the other on the falls. Both shows were entered in the juried Mountainfilm Festival, held in Telluride, Colorado. David Breashears and Gordon Wiltsie had been invited to speak at the festival. The Gillenwaters came as well, and although Rick Fisher had wanted to attend, the festival's director told him that he was not welcome. The festival would not become a forum for Fisher to vent his bitterness toward Baker and the *Geographic*.

Fisher had accused the *Geographic* of faking the photograph of the falls. In letters to the society, he charged that Baker had beaten a baby takin to death in 1993, "tore hunks of still quivering raw meat from the body and stuffed them into his blood-spattered face" before driving the remaining adult herd into the river to be drowned. "He proceeded to eat it as 500 pounds of American food sat near by," Fisher wrote. Villagers in the gorge regarded Baker as a "reincarnated blood-spattered devil," Fisher claimed, and Sardar was an Indian spy—a *sirdar,* or headman, Fisher thought—whom Baker used to procure a gang of Nepali wildlife poachers "for his dirty work."

The *Geographic* asked Baker about Fisher's allegations. In his written rebuttal, wickedly titled "Confessions of a Blood Spattered Devil: A Response to My Inspired Detractors," he called the charges "entirely fanciful." During the 1993 Kingdon-Ward traverse, he conceded, their guides did kill three takin to supplement dwindling food supplies. "I had absolutely no involvement with this at all," Baker wrote. "The hunters shared some of the meat with us, as we were also very low on food. We ate it well cooked. Fisher's extraordinary claim that my feeding frenzy was witnessed by [my three traveling companions] is easily refuted."

Fisher's screeds arrived at the society's Washington headquarters every other week—to retired chairman Gilbert Grosvenor, the publisher, the director of public affairs, the senior vice president, the editor in chief. He criticized the *Geographic* for its "hoax" about the waterfall and for sponsoring Walker's expedition. Walker, a Vietnam veteran, was nothing but "an old man sending young Americans to their deaths in the jungle where there is *no real chance for* success," Fisher wrote. "Conventional warfare could not win in Vietnam, conventional boating cannot succeed in this Tibet Canyon." He called Walter a coward for not attempting the river himself.

The staff was alarmed at Fisher's belligerence, and when he started labeling his attacks "news release," they notified their lawyers. Ultimately, the lawyers decided that suing him for libel would be a no-win battle. The *Geographic* dismissed Fisher as "a longtime pest who unsuccessfully tried to peddle his pictures to *National Geographic* years ago."

Privately, the canyoneer confessed to feeling slighted. He thought his "major" accomplishments in the gorge had been overlooked. Baker tried to mend fences with him, telephoning from Kathmandu, but ended up with an earful of venom. "I'm going to get you," Fisher screamed into the phone. "You have been exposed!"

"Who's been exposed?" Baker asked. "Rick, I don't know what you're after."

Baker never received a satisfactory answer. "I really would like to know what Rick wants," Baker says. "I find it revealing and at the same time troubling that a person who feels so zealously about the gorge is destroying his reputation by making such ludicrous accusations. But that is what the texts say about Pemakö: People who approach the area with skewed motivations will not perceive the blessings of the landscape. Quite the opposite. The protector spirits will destroy them."

. . .

IN TELLURIDE, BREASHEARS, the Gillenwaters, Wiltsie, and Bryan Harvey, the videographer on the falls expedition, appeared at a panel discussion on the nature of discovery at the end of the millennium. Breashears showed off the photograph of the top of Hidden Falls that he had taken in 1993, and compared it to the one the Gillenwaters had made in 1997. So who had discovered the drop? Should the credit go to him? Or should the glory be Storm's and Baker's, because they went the extra distance to document the height of the waterfall?

The issue was never resolved, but Wiltsie had the final word. "I am the person with the least interest in this," he began. "What has happened here is symptomatic of exploration today. The world of exploration is no longer about putting names on a map. It's about looking within ourselves. What I find distressing about the Tsangpo is the acrimony, the threatened court cases, when in the grand scheme of discoveries, this one is quite insignificant."

His point was well made the next day when mountaineer Conrad Anker arrived in town, fresh from Mount Everest. Anker had found George Mallory's frozen body, with its skin as pale as ivory, lying below the summit.

Finding Mallory, after all these years! Everyone at the festival had the same thought: Now *that* was a discovery.

. . .

TO THE SELF-PROCLAIMED victors go the laurels. Just as Kingdon-Ward and Bailey were honored for their explorations of the gorge—both received medals from the Royal Geographical Society—so, too, was Baker. The premier issue of *National Geographic Adventure* named Baker one of seven "explorers for the millennium," crediting him with having "the creative vision and the audacious curiosity" to ignore the notion that the Age of Exploration is over." The magazine's studio photographer had Baker pose for a portrait dangling upside down from a climbing rope, regarding the camera with serene expression.

As the articles about the waterfall expedition proliferated, Baker sought the help of a literary agent. In New York, editors of one publishing house offered Baker a reported half million dollars for his story, which he accepted. After the whirlwind schedule of interviews, meetings, and receptions, Baker flew back to Kathmandu. "My God, it is good to be back," he told a friend.

Time and sudden fame had improved his circumstances considerably. Baker had moved into the two top floors of a gated cottage near the royal palace, a flat owned by an eccentric art collector whose tastes in home decor ran to the baroque—red walls, ornate carvings, stained-glass windows, and marble floors. Among its warren of rooms, Baker had a library, office, meditation room, black marble bathroom with spa tub, several sitting rooms, and a modern kitchen with a sophisticated water filtration system. From the living room, a spiral staircase led to an upstairs salon and rooftop patio, and from there one could climb to an observation deck for a panoramic view of the city.

Baker's maid and cook kept the flat fastidiously clean, and it was sumptuously decorated with his collection of antiques, rugs, and artwork. His friend and coauthor Carroll Dunham joked that it resembled "a cross between a bordello and an antique shop, without much room for female energy." Yet the rent was less than five hundred dollars a month.

Baker's fitness routine involved three days of working out at the Yak and Yeti Hotel's health club, alternating with two days of yoga and meditation. He was acutely careful about his diet and consumed various potions and indigenous tonics, some of which he had brought back from Tibet. His telephone never went long without ringing: invitations to dinners, parties, picnics, or outings into the nearby mountains. One of his friends joked that souvenir shops in Kathmandu's backpackers' ghetto were carrying T-shirts that read, "I came all the way to Kathmandu and didn't meet Ian Baker."

Sardar, meanwhile, was still living like an impecunious graduate student. Like Baker during his early days in Kathmandu, Sardar had accepted a position as director of the School for International Training. He would earn two thousand dollars a month and live rent free in a dark little cottage in the school's walled compound.

A certain amount of friction had developed between the two. Sadar felt that Baker had not given him due credit for his contributions, appropriating parts of his persona in constructing the story of the falls' discovery—a tale that he says amounted to a "masquerade of half-truths and baseless lies." He especially resented playing second fiddle in Baker's version of events; it was he, after all, who could read the ancient texts, not Baker. It had been he who first met Tsering Dondrup, the hunter who confessed drunkenly that the gap was a secret hunting ground.

Sardar was not embittered, just disappointed in Baker. "It's all part of his unfolding destiny," he says philosophically. Having sown the seeds of ambition, his friend would now reap the karmic rewards. "Ian always aspired to write for *National Geographic* and to be famous," says Sardar. "But there's a tragic human quality about him. He makes mistakes, too. That's why he is so lovable."

. . .

THE NIGHT BEFORE Sardar was to greet his first students as director of the School for International Training, Baker hosted a dinner for him, appropriately enough at Kathmandu's exclusive Shangri-La Hotel. Sardar had just arrived from France, with a long delay in Bangkok, and was happy to be back. Whatever differences existed between him and Baker had been put aside. Sardar was escorting two sisters from Nepal's former ruling family, one of them his former girlfriend, a flighty socialite who carried a chic Prada handbag and spoke of shopping and parties in London. The hotel lobby was decorated with period photographs, several of her father and grandfather posing majestically with their retinues on tiger hunts. Bailey had been the British emissary to their court.

Later, at home, Baker reflected on his fortunes as a poster boy for the *Geographic:* "Reaching this waterfall was the culmination of all my earlier trips. It completed a cycle for me. But at the same time, almost inadvertently on my part, it put me in a position of supposedly making great claims and discoveries. That's the trouble with the way the story was presented. It was as if the media and the Western mind, the public, could only conceive of the importance of the trips in some conventional way, which meant, 'Oh, well, why else would you go to those places if you didn't have a concrete goal in mind? Obviously you didn't report anything earlier because you hadn't found the waterfall yet.'

"They missed the whole point. It wasn't about a waterfall. But the waterfall was important as a symbol, because it gave me this tremendous insight into the Western mind, the world that I left behind when I moved here. I hadn't realized that I had traveled so far in my departure from these conventional orientations of Western explorers. It made me see how much of an inner journey and a pilgrimage the trips had been.

"The last trip to the falls had none of the aspects of inner discovery that the previous ones did. I felt we were being made players in a film that had its own agenda. Bryan Harvey said he wanted to make a film that would be like looking at the gorge through my eyes. They weren't my eyes; they were *his* eyes looking at my eyes. I saw the film as an American home video gone mainstream. The show does what it does well, given its mandate. But it misrepresents my feeling about and relationship to the land and the people. I'm hesitant to show it to anyone."

His had been a lesson in human nature, he said. He was bemused by how the story had polarized people. Either they applauded him and projected Shangri-La on the gorge, or as Rick Fisher had done, condemned him as a charlatan and hoaxer.

For him the trip to the waterfall was just part of an ongoing exploration of Pemakö's cultural and spiritual landscape. His next pilgrimage there would be one of "expiation," he said.

"The waterfall is a doorway into further journeys. It's not a final ground; it's nothing to lay claim to; nothing to attach one's name to. It's just another landmark within a geography not just of the environment but also of the mind, the consciousness. The Western model cannot seem to appreciate a landscape without seeing it through the lens of the individual ego. That's what I discovered."

. . .

SOON AFTER RETURNING home from Washington and New York, Baker flew to Tibet with Sardar on an assignment for the *Geographic*. The editors had asked Baker to organize an expedition to survey the gorge's natural history, and they had enlisted wildlife biologist George Schaller to conduct the study and write about it. Schaller has long worked in Tibet to establish protected areas and national parks, and he maintains close relations with the Tibet Forestry Department, which is overseeing the creation of the so-called Great Valley Nature Reserve in the gorge. But when the team convened in Lhasa, officials rescinded their permits and told them the gorge was off limits. There would be no article.

The *Geographic*'s grandstanding had infuriated officials in Beijing and caused China to lose face. In an attempt to rewrite history, *China Daily* ran an item headlined "Chinese Explorers Get to Falls First." "Although Chinese scientists are surely not short on bravery, rigour and a desire for perfection," the article read, "they sometimes may be slow to communicate their findings." Geologist Yang Yichou, a coleader of the Chinese Academy of Sciences expedition, reported that he had known about the hidden waterfall for years. In 1986, a People's Liberation Army photographer had brought him several aerial pictures of Rainbow and Hidden Falls, taken from a helicopter. The geologist had named them Number One and Number Two Zangbo Badong Falls.

In a separate interview published in Chinese on the Internet,

Yang said, "It is illegal for Americans to peek into our canyon." He accused profiteering tour operators in China of catering to foreigners, "who have robbed our treasures" of the gorge.

The upshot was that the gorge was again closed to outsiders. Chinese scientists said the closure would allow them time to develop conservation and development plans for a national park and wildlife sanctuary in the gorge, which greatly pleased Schaller. The only way the gorge would be spared, he said, was as a protected reserve. But it took more than a year of fence-mending for him to be able to return to the canyon and continue his work there.

To Sardar, the announcement of a national park had the sound of a death knell. Certain Chinese are obsessed with taming Pemakö's wilderness, he says, and no project seems too daunting. There has been talk of building a cable car to the falls, so tourists can view it in comfort. Engineers have proposed blasting a flume under the Doshong La to divert part of the Tsangpo to a generating plant in the lower gorge, and constructing a network of roads that would link Pemakö to the motherland.

"There are two ways to open the gorge: under the Chinese ax or by imposing environmental protections on the sacred pilgrimage areas," Sardar says. Either way leads him to the same conclusion: that his days of going feral with the Monpa hunters are numbered. "We will witness the end of wildness in Pemakö within our lifetimes."

But, before that occurred, Sardar wanted to make one more pilgrimage, to locate Pemakö's paradisical *yangsang ney,* the mythical inner sanctum of bliss and sanctuary. The last unexplored, uninhabited subvalley in the gorge was his best hope. Known locally as Bodlunga Valley, it is located on the southern flanks of Namche Barwa. He and Baker had wanted to explore the valley in 1997, after the Gillenwaters and Storm had turned north to explore the inner gorge. But villagers explained that the journey would be impossible. It was August, and the grass would be too high to find the way, they said; better to try in spring or winter.

At several hunters' cabins along the lower Tsangpo, Sardar had noticed the skins of a curious white-haired primate. The hunters had shot them in the Bodlunga Valley. Sardar was unable to recognize the species, but he thought it too large for a monkey. It was more like an ape, a white ape. Thus his name for the isolated valley: The Valley of the White Ape. Based on his textual research and oral histories, he was certain that it held the *yangsang ney.*

While Baker was busy writing his memoir, Sardar agreed to return to Pemakö, at my request. His first stop would be Bayu, to deliver copies of guidebooks he had found that contained obscure directions to the *yangsang ney.* They would replace copies at the Bayu Monastery that the Red Guard had destroyed. Along with Tsering Dondrup and his lama brother, Sardar then wanted to go to Hidden Falls to have the lama perform a purifying ceremony, in order to clear the negative energy that had accumulated at the spot in the preceding months. From there, they would climb a spur of Namche Barwa and drop into the Valley of the White Ape. The lama had never been there, but Sardar felt that it might provide the Monpas with a refuge during the coming Armageddon of chainsaws, bulldozers, guest houses, park rangers, and ecotourists. They would be sealed off from the twentieth century, just as the scriptures had promised.

. . .

INITIALLY SCHEDULED FOR November 1999, the pilgrimage had to be postponed until the following May because Sardar could not get away. The grass in the valley would still be low then, he thought, although the monsoon could cause trouble. Another potential problem was that the gorge was still officially closed, but Steve Currey, the Utah rafting outfitter who had been turned down by the *Geographic,* thought that his sources in Chengdu would be able to obtain restricted-area travel permits by spreading a little money around among their military contacts.

Currey was still eager to exploit the gorge's potential as an adventure travel paradise and thought that treks to the Valley of the White Ape could be enormously popular. He wanted to join Sardar, bringing a videographer and a telecommunications expert to beam daily progress reports to a Web site via satellite uplink. Such a "virtual expedition" would help attract sponsors and promote his business. Currey proposed an expedition of ten to defray costs, including the Gillenwaters, who were interested. A team of ten would require perhaps thirty porters, swelling the size of the caravan to colonial-era proportions.

Sardar was uncomfortable. The trip was to be a pilgrimage, after all, not a siege-style assault and media feast. As usual, he asked his guru, Chatral Rinpoche, to perform a divination about the expedition.

Afterward, Sardar sent the following message to Currey: "The result of the divination for the trip to the Valley of the White Ape was negative. Negative for the place and also negative for the people going. The lama reiterated that the innermost reaches of the hidden land are yet to be opened, and that they are meant to be visited only by people who have a connection to the spiritual lineage of the place. The idea of taking journalists, professional video-makers, photographers and INMARSAT equipment does not conform to the idea of a Buddhist pilgrimage."

The Valley of the White Ape Expedition would not take place.

But the pilgrimage would. After withdrawing from the expedition, Sardar went back to Chatral Rinpoche and asked for another divination. Without the Gillenwaters, Currey, or his entourage, there would be only three on the pilgrimage: Sardar, me, and a Canadian mountain guide named Jeff Boyd, who had been in the gorge twice before and who was chief of emergency medicine at the Banff hospital.

The *rinpoche* emerged from his visions and pronounced, "All shall go in freedom." But he also warned that we must maintain a very low profile, to avoid arrest. "The tiger is your ally," he advised. "Move silently through the forest like him, with stealth and cunning."

Bad news awaited us in Lhasa: a major landslide had blocked the

Lhasa-Sichuan road and dammed a tributary to the Po Tsangpo River called the Yigrong. This was a notoriously unstable area. In 1901, another landslide had come down across the Yigrong, causing a lake to back up behind the rubble. After rising for a month, the impounded water burst through the dam and roared into the Po Tsangpo Canyon. Bailey and Morshead saw the aftermath twelve years later.

"A great avalanche of water, earth and rocks" had hurtled down the Yigrong Valley, Bailey wrote, piling up a fan of debris two miles wide and three hundred and fifty feet thick. Three villages on the Yigrong were buried. The wall of debris (called a GLOF, for glacial lake outburst flow) scoured down the Po Tsangpo and, when it met the confluence with the Tsangpo, continued down to India. Tribesmen in the lower gorge had told Bailey of finding the "bodies of strange people," that is, Tibetans from upriver. He and Morshead followed the Yigrong to its juncture with the Po Tsangpo and found the remains of a demolished village. They calculated that the wall of debris had been one hundred and seventy feet higher than the previous year's high watermark.

Nearly a century after this flood, the Yigrong had become blocked by two slides, one touching off the other. Heavy snow in the upper Yigrong drainage had melted rapidly as winter gave way to spring, saturating the slopes above the river. The first slide—a relatively minor one—triggered a release of three and a half billion cubic feet of debris. Researchers estimated that the debris hurtled downhill at one hundred and sixty feet per second. The grinding slurry gouged out another three and a half billion cubic feet of rubble in its path, and when the combined flow slid across the river (in the same spot as during the 1901 slide) it formed a dam four hundred feet thick and almost two miles wide. The event took less than ten minutes, according to witnesses, and left a gash in the earth that was clearly visible on satellite images. A Chinese hydrologist estimated the slide to be the largest ever in Asia, and the world's third largest.

A lake was again backing up in the Yigrong Valley. Worried

about a repeat of the 1901 flood, authorities had halted all traffic in the area and were evacuating people from threatened villages along the Po Tsangpo and Tsangpo. Were the earthen dam to burst, the backed-up water and debris would prove fatal to anyone in the way—including three Western pilgrims trekking down the Po Tsangpo canyon to the village of Bayu.

Sardar thought of a way to avoid this fate and the roadblocks: stop short of the landslide and hike into the head of the gorge over the sixteen-thousand-foot Nyima La. Bailey and Morshead had crossed the pass in 1913, and not far away Bailey had spotted the showy sky-blue poppies that bear his name, *Meconopsis baileyi*. The poppies would be buried under knee-deep snow at this season, Sardar thought, but if we could make it across, the trek down the canyon to Bayu would still be possible, without risk of being trapped in a GLOF.

Chancing that the Public Security Bureau would approve the plan and grant the permits, we left Lhasa to drive west to Bayi, the last main town before the landslide. Sardar was friendly with a powerful police captain there. Without the captain's consent, the expedition would be doomed.

In Bayi, the captain, a Khampa Tibetan, was pleased to see Sardar again but apologetic. He did not have the authority to approve a travel permit. Tibet's vice chairman was personally overseeing the effort to drain the glacial lake, and traffic beyond Bayi was limited to police, military, and consulting geologists from Chengdu. Still, he would phone his superiors in Lhasa that night to plead on our behalf.

That night, we checked into a government guest house called the Welcome Hotel, a three-story concrete barracks with a desultory staff and flooded communal bathrooms. Strolling the nearly deserted streets of Bayi after dinner, Sardar grew depressed. In the middle of town, an open sewer littered with plastic shopping bags and bald tires flowed past a new shopping mall shaped like a pyramid and flanked by two towers that resembled giant mushrooms.

"This is what Tibet is becoming," Sardar said. "Nomads come to town and see this and hear the karaoke bars that drown out the sounds of nature, and they think, 'Yes, this is it!' "

Back in his hotel room, amid the echo of loud voices from down the hall and a miasma of cigarette smoke that seeped under his door, Sardar said, "To get to paradise, you must first go through the inferno, and Bayi is the inferno. I am going to bed."

There was little sleep to be had that night. From one o'clock in the morning until three-thirty, the hotel courtyard indeed sounded like Dante's inferno. A stock truck packed with pigs bound for slaughter had parked beneath our windows. Their squealing was bloodcurdling and nonstop, like a chorus of the damned. At times one could almost make out words—desperate, guttural pig words of terror.

Reveille was at six-thirty, when loudspeakers around the courtyard started blaring martial tunes and soggy pop ballads. It was a cold, gray morning, and threatening rain. At breakfast, Sardar remarked about the pigs.

"Hellish noise," he said. "I think it was the voice of Vajravahini [the name of the sow goddess, Dorje Phagmo, in Sanskrit]. Maybe it was an omen."

. . .

A CCORDING TO BUDDHIST scriptures, those who are not meant to go to Pemakö will meet with storms, floods, landslides, and possibly death. Omitted from the list are bureaucrats and police.

At the police station that morning, the captain broke the ice by showing off his new edition of Rick Fisher's *Earth's Mystical Grand Canyons*. Fisher had stopped on his way to Lhasa from the gorge a month earlier, while the impounded lake was still low, and had presented the officer with the book. Ironically, its cover photograph had been taken in Bayu, where Sardar wanted to deliver copies of the Valley of the White Ape texts.

Sardar could tell the news was bad. He argued peremptorily that the captain should seize the moment and join him on the pilgrimage, to see the gorge and investigate sites for ecotourism lodges. Many other agencies had an eye on the gorge's resources, he said, and they would challenge the captain's authority in the region. Now was the time to consolidate his power.

"Mr. Hamid, you are my friend," the captain said. "I would like to help you. But a whole mountain came down across the river. Very dangerous. My bosses say you cannot go forward. You must return to Lhasa. Why not come again someday, and we will go to Pemakö together?"

On the drive back to Lhasa, Sardar said, "It's the earth rebelling. It's seizing up for a major cleansing. Dorge Phagmo wants to purge the canyon of energies that have surrounded the place since 1993. It's been all about ego since then—first to do this, first to reach that—and some human craving for fame."

To a Buddhist, the message was as clear as the screaming of pigs in the night: The *beyul's* inner sanctum was not to be opened—either via a waterfall portal or via a valley inhabited by white apes—until the time was auspicious. And that time had not yet arrived.

Epilogue

After
the Flood

∽

Previous page: A cataclysmic flash flood ripped through the gorge in June 2000, scouring the canyon walls down to bare rock up to six hundred feet above the normal high-water mark. Buddhist texts warn that those who are not meant to reach the sacred hidden land will meet with floods, landslides, and perhaps even death. Photo by Gary McCue.

At about midnight on June 10, 2000, nine days after the sow-goddess's warning to us, the impounded water in the Yigrong Valley burst through the landslide. Chinese engineers had been trying to drain the lake through a ditch, but the water got away from them. Within minutes, it tore a gash through the rock rubble. As the lake drained, the breach widened until finally the dam collapsed. A wall of water, mud, and debris swept downstream and burst into the Po Tsangpo canyon. When the flood reached the Great Bend, a surge of water backed up into the Tsangpo's inner canyon, but most of the flow continued down toward the Indian border. As in the 1901 flood, the glacial outburst scoured the canyon walls bare—right down to bedrock—hundreds of feet above the normal high water mark. Footbridges and cable crossings were swept away.

No Tibetan or Chinese lives were lost, however. In early May, villagers along the Po Tsangpo were evacuated and those in the lower Tsangpo canyon took to the hills, where the Chinese air force dropped food and supplies to them. But no such warning was issued to India. Across the border, some thirty people drowned and fifty thousand were left homeless. Indian journalists demanded an explanation of China's Water Resources Department. A spokesman told them, "Tibet is a very sensitive issue with Beijing," and refused to elaborate.

Biologist George Schaller had been in the lower gorge around Medog with a five-person team for the month preceding the flood. (They left on June 8, two days before the catastrophe.) During that time, they walked about two hundred fifty miles, collecting data and interviewing villagers about livestock losses to tigers.

Schaller discovered that tiger predation was rare before 1990, but it increased sharply in 1992, coincidentally the year the gorge was re-opened to the outside world. At its peak in 1995, he documented that tigers had claimed one hundred forty yaks and other livestock and twenty-seven horses around Medog and adjacent Chimdro River Valley—a remarkable tally considering that perhaps only twenty tigers were then stalking the forests. The loss of even one yak or horse is a heavy blow to the impoverished villagers, and they have reacted by killing tigers despite a ban on hunting them. Since 1996 four tigers are known to have been slain, and the loss of cattle and horses in the villages surveyed has declined by more than half.

After leaving the gorge, Schaller and his team of Chinese colleagues produced a report urging "a thorough economic appraisal of the potential value of tourism [there]." Officials have predicted that more than seven hundred thousand Chinese and foreign tourists will visit the gorge before the year 2005, notwithstanding the difficulty and cost of reaching it, and the fact that it was still officially closed when Schaller's report was issued. To accommodate the expected visitors, a resort of "holiday villas" for a thousand guests was being planned for Nyingchi, near the upper end of the gorge, as well as a luxury hotel that will cater to the wealthy and powerful. Anticipating the tourist boom, business owners in Nyingchi prefecture formed a club dedicated to investigating reports that a "legendary wild man," presumably a yeti, inhabits the gorge.

Under the Tibet Forestry Department's conservation plans, the Great Valley Nature Reserve is to receive the highest priority for development in the next ten years. The world's deepest gorge is envisioned as a mainstay of Tibet's tourist economy, one of three world-class scenic spots in the country. In one trip, a ten-year master plan pointed out, visitors will be able to see the world's highest peak, the deepest river valley, and Lhasa, "the mysterious culture at the third pole of the world."

Hunting, logging, mining, and permanent dwellings would be banned in five core areas within the three-thousand-five-hundred-square-mile reserve. The Monpa village of Bayu would become an education and culture center, where villagers could sell handicrafts, mushrooms, cooking oils, natural dyes, and medicinal plants, much as Africa's once pastoral Maasi people peddle beadwork and leather goods to tourists.

Schaller was skeptical about the predicted flood of tourists and the value of ecotourism as a conservation tool. "Tourism is unlikely to repay government for money invested, contribute much to the cost of managing the reserve, or even benefit the local people," he wrote, pointing out that Nepal's long-established Annapurna Conservation Area generates just 60 percent of its annual budget from tourism, the rest coming from donor agencies. Only 7 percent of the money that tourists spent in the conservation area reached local people. "Promises of benefits are worse than no promises at all," Schaller wrote.

"The Chinese plans for tourism are completely unrealistic," he told me, explaining that other parts of Tibet are culturally richer than the gorge, not so remote and inhospitable, and open to foreign tourists. Nevertheless, China has such a vast population and a growing middle class that the new park might not have to rely on wealthy Europeans and Americans. New resorts in Yunnan and Sichuan's mountains are attracting Chinese tourists eager to see the beauty of the alpine wilderness and its Tibetan culture.

Around the turn of the nineteenth century, Sir Thomas Holdich, the president of the Royal Geographical Society, envisioned a smart new hotel for sightseers and sportsmen overlooking the Falls of the Brahmaputra. Holdich did not mention particulars of design, but one imagines him thinking of a gracious wooden structure with wide verandas, in the style of the hill-station resorts in Darjeeling or Simla. Bailey and Morshead's 1914 report to the RGS about the gorge's forbidding topography put a quick end to that folly, and it all but ruled out the likelihood that a great waterfall even existed.

Now, almost a hundred years later, it turns out that Holdich's vision was not completely off the mark. There is a dramatic waterfall in the gorge, and lodges for adventurous sightseers will be built in the canyon, although not overlooking the falls. What sort and how many of them there will be, along with hundreds of other questions that will affect the future of the canyon's physical and spiritual landscapes, remain to be answered.

. . .

AFTER RETURNING FROM Tibet, Hamid Sardar decided to leave Kathmandu to start a branch of the School for International Training in Ulan Bator, Mongolia. As its academic director, he spends a good deal of the year exploring the wilds of the Mongolian outback with his students, living with nomadic herders and exploring the great open spaces of the steppe.

Jeff Boyd plunged back into emergency medicine in Banff, but a year later he traveled to western Tibet with George Schaller to trace migration patterns of the endangered chiru, or Tibetan antelope, from the Chang Tang region to their unknown birthing grounds north of the Taklamakan Desert, in the western Kunlun Mountains. Having studied the graceful, lyre-horned animals since 1988, Schaller helped the Tibetans establish a reserve for them in 1993 and hopes to do the same for threatened species in the Tsangpo Gorge.

The Gillenwaters constructed a Web site about their adventures in Pemakö, illustrating the text with some two dozen photographs, and they wrote a similar account for an expedition clothing catalog. Neither forum had the prestige of an acknowledgment in *National Geographic*, but at least the brothers set the record straight as they saw it.

Ken Storm collaborated with Baker and others in publishing a new edition of Kingdon-Ward's *The Riddle of the Tsangpo Gorges* in 2001. In January 2002, Storm joined a large expedition that successfully kayaked parts of the upper gorge and claimed the first descent that had eluded Walker and his teammates. Storm was not boating himself, but he was billed as the team's historical and geographical expert— "one of the great explorers of the Tsangpo Gorge [whose] name will be forever linked with [its] waterfalls," according to a television documentary about the attempt.

Led by veteran Himalayan kayaker and filmmaker Scott Lindgren, and sponsored by *Outside* magazine and Chevrolet (which supplied three forty-thousand-dollar sport utility vehicles to transport the team in Tibet), the team was composed of six other paddlers from the U.S., Britain, New Zealand, and South Africa, and a support crew of about eighty, including porters. Lindgren chose the depths of winter for the attempt, when the Tsangpo was flowing at its lowest volume. Even so, the river nearly swallowed several paddlers as they worked downriver from Pe to a point just above Rainbow Falls. From there, they humped over the snowbound Senchen La, a treacherous ascent on which each kayaker backpacked his own boat to the summit. On the opposite side, at the village of Lugu, where Baker and Storm had been so warmly feted in 1993, the porters mutinied, demanding to be paid an extra ten thousand dollars—about $200 per porter, hardly an unreasonable sum considering the dangers of the portage. After a three-day standoff, Lindgren grudgingly paid the money and hired new porters, but he might as well have given up. The flash flood had so altered the Tsangpo below the Great Bend that satellite maps were useless. Facing blind runs, river-wide rapids that could not be portaged, and a dwindling budget, Lindgren chose to pull the plug and return home.

By paddling at low water and in boats that were only lightly loaded, the team had managed to navigate sections of the canyon that had killed Doug Gordon and Yoshitaka Takei. In scripting his documentary for NBC, Lindgren called it "one of the most accomplished expeditions of our time." Yet for all of its sensitivity toward the culture and spiritual mythology of the gorge, it was just the sort of venture that Sardar's guru, Chatral Rinpoche, had categorically rejected: a siege-style, media-driven assault that posted daily progress reports, photos, and sound bites on the World Wide Web. Reading them and the magazine article, and watching Lindgren's exciting and beautifully filmed documentary, I imagined that the lama would have taken much delight in explaining that Dorje Phagmo had defeated another Western dream team, just as it had foiled Wick Walker's and my own.

After Boyd, Sardar and I left Tibet, I began to look into the Yi-grong landslide that had sabotaged our attempted adventure in paradise. Had we been told about it earlier, we might have delayed our expedition by several months. In fact, mountain guide and Tibet expert Gary McCue, who led the Lhasa portion of my first trip to Tibet in 1988, did take four clients into the gorge four months after the flash flood and reached Hidden Falls. McCue and his partner, Kathy Butler, said the trek was among the most difficult they have ever made, yet also one of the most rewarding.

The scale of the landslide across the Yigrong—and the danger posed by the impounded water—became clear to me on a colorized satellite image produced by the European consortium SPOT. The gash in the mountains above the river showed up on the image as hot pink and the rising lake as sapphire blue. Another satellite photo that Boyd e-mailed to me displayed the entire Tsangpo Gorge. The digital image, taken months before the flood, was so sharp and realistic that I imagined being in the spacecraft that photographed it. Any part of the photo could be greatly enlarged to show features of the landscape in uncanny detail. All it took was the click of a computer mouse.

At the optimum magnification, I could clearly see Rainbow and Hidden Falls, even the spray rising above them. I was able to make out the cliffs that prevented Bailey and Morshead, and Kingdon-Ward and Cawdor, from penetrating the gap. The spots where Doug Gordon and Yoshitaka Takei disappeared were visible, and so was the arduous route that we were to have taken from Hidden Falls to the Valley of the White Ape.

To be honest, I was never eager to make that trek. Apart from the general anxiety that always precedes a difficult expedition, I felt a deeper foreboding about this one. About a week before leaving for Tibet, I decided to photocopy several maps of the gorge, including a satellite photo of the falls section. The copy of the latter came out entirely black except for the white ribbon of the Tsangpo and three blank spots that resembled skeletal fingers. The bony appendages were pointing straight at Hidden Falls.

I am not a superstitious person. *Just a toner problem*, I thought.

When I checked the machine's toner cartridge, however, it was full. The next copy came out perfectly.

Sardar and Baker say that you must heed such signs, listen to your intuition, and suspend rationality in order to safely navigate the hidden land. Maybe nothing would have happened on the expedition. But if there is one aspect of mountaineering that frightens me, it is traversing steep slopes without being belayed. A more irrational fear—of becoming lost and perishing alone in the wilderness—dates to a childhood experience of being ditched by my playmates in a forest and wandering for hours, terrified that I would never find a way home. In a jungle as thick and disorienting as Pemakö's, where hunters and pilgrims sometimes slip to their deaths, and tourists become separated from their teammates just by stepping off the trail to urinate, both of those scenarios would have been more than passing worries.

So it was with a mixture of relief and regret that I left Tibet. At home, I would often study my maps and satellite images to better understand routes the gorge's pioneers had followed. Inevitably, my attention would fall on that enlarged satellite view of the gap, and I would get down on my hands and knees to study the waterfalls through a magnifying glass, wishing that I could have seen them at close range.

One day, it dawned on me that the river in that section traces the profile of a takin's head. The Tsangpo curves around a gradual ninety-degree bend to form the animal's muzzle, then enters a straight chute that resembles a takin's flat face. Where its eye would be, the river divides around a large midstream boulder, and then plunges over Rainbow Falls on the beast's brow. Hidden Falls is located at the nubbin between the takin's horns, where the Monpas say the animals' spirits are instantaneously released at death. The long, straight flume downstream from Hidden Falls resembles part of a takin horn.

The Monpas believe that when the apocalypse is nigh, the gods will return as takin and lead the way to Pemakö's sacred center. Could the allegory hold a clue about the timing of Armageddon? Did it mean that the ultimate siege would be at hand when outsiders invaded the Monpas' secret hunting grounds and drove the takin away?

Maybe Baker was right about the mysterious cave at the bottom of Hidden Falls. Perhaps it is the portal to paradise. Sardar cynically suggested that Baker might be a *terton,* a treasure finder, whose real discovery in Pemakö was in finding a story of compelling power and hope. As a Buddhist treasure text, it might read something like this: When men can fly like gods and look down on Pemakö from the heavens, they will possess the power to destroy the Monpa way of life. That will be the time to follow the takin and seek the *yangsang ney,* the secret refuge.

There could even be a happy ending: A lost waterfall captures the world's imagination and prompts conservationists to protect Pemakö as a treasure house of biological, cultural, and spiritual resources. The Monpa way of life is preserved.

The reality of the situation is that barbarians are poised at the gates of Shangri-La. Forces of greed and corruption in China are pitted against forces of enlightenment with a more optimistic vision of Pemakö's future. In the legend of Shambhala, the forces of good rise up to defeat the forces of ego and selfish desire. Yet in the realpolitik of China today, the outcome of the struggle is uncertain. The future is plastic, and the Monpas may yet have to seek the *yangsang ney.* At the moment, all they know is that when the final siege is nigh, only the faithful and deserving will find their way to paradise.

Notes

PROLOGUE: THE RIDDLE OF THE TSANGPO

3   *"the font of authority"*: Meyer and Brysac, *Tournament of Shadows*, p. 310.

4   *"an allegory for the path to enlightenment itself"*: Sardar, *The Buddha's Secret Gardens*, p. 6.

PART ONE: THE LOST WATERFALL

15   *"where no white man has ever trod"*: Kingdon-Ward, *Riddle*, p. 5.

16   *his best work*: Lyte, *Frank Kingdon-Ward*, p. 29.

17   *"villages clustered in the cultivated valleys at their feet"*: Kingdon-Ward, *Riddle*, p. 6.

18   *"impenetrable mountain defence which rings Tibet like a wall"*: Kingdon-Ward, *Riddle*, p. 8.

19   *"where no white man has ever been . . ."*: Lyte, *Frank Kingdon-Ward*, p. 6.

20   *"the great romance of geography"*: Kingdon-Ward, *Riddle*, p. 205.

22   *the scoundrel had sold him into slavery:* Or perhaps the lama's problem was simply that he was lousy at covering his tracks—both as an adulterer and as a surveyor-spy. As Vanderbilt scholar Derek Waller astutely notes in *The Pundits*, p. 242, Bailey and Morshead revisited the area around Tongkyuk Dzong in 1913, when they came up into the lower gorge from Assam. They met a minister of the Poba people who told of "a Chinaman" who some years earlier had come from the west "counting his paces and writing numbers down in a book." The lama was promptly banished from the region, the minister explained. Indeed, Waller proposes that the lama may well have had to flee for his life. Whether he actually did sell Kintup into slavery to raise road money or whether the crafty *dzonpon* seized the opportunity and duped Kintup is unclear.

25   *"he used to give them large presents of opium and other things"*: Bailey, *China-Tibet-Assam*, p. 141.

25   *"I had to proceed with great caution"*: Bailey, *No Passport*, p. 27.

26 " 'Yes,' said the letter carrier. 'Great anger.' ": Bailey, *No Passport,* p. 30.

26 *"the events which precipitate most wars"*: Bailey, *No Passport,* p. 30.

27 *three hundred the next*: Lyte, *Frank Kingdon-Ward*, pp. 33–34; Bailey, *China-Tibet-Assam,* p. 65.

27 *"There was something comic in their terror"*: Bailey, *China-Tibet-Assam,* p. 81.

28 *he did not see another white face*: Bailey, *No Passport,* p. 89.

28 *"they were in the habit of killing all strangers"*: Bailey, *No Passport,* p. 109.

28 *"My disappointment . . . reluctantly started on my return"*: Bailey, *No Passport,* p. 110.

29 *"three dull, morose men . . . with long hair tied in a topknot on their heads"*: Bailey, *No Passport,* p. 127.

30 *"must have astonished and dismayed her"*: Bailey, *China-Tibet-Assam,* p. 167.

31 *"calculated to put the fear of God into all who heard it"*: Allen, *A Mountain in Tibet*, pp. 165–66. Allen's history is among the most comprehensive and readable sources on British difficulties with the Abors and other hill tribes.

31 *trek into the gorge and find Kintup's waterfall*: Swinson, *Frontiers,* p. 80.

31 *"not a man to fail"*: Lyte, Frank Kingdon-Ward, p. 48.

32 *"I had to be responsible for Morshead's tropical hygiene"*: Bailey, *No Passport,* pp. 53–55.

33 *"we might well have flinched"*: Bailey, *No Passport,* p. 103.

33 *"It was getting worse and worse"*: Bailey, *No Passport,* p. 125.

34 *"the pain and throbbing of the cuts in my knees"*: Bailey, *No Passport,* p. 131.

34 *"an exaggerated rapid of 30 feet"*: Bailey, "Exploration on the Tsangpo," p. 361.

34 *ten-mile-long gap*: At the point where he was forced to give up, Bailey figured that he and Morshead had left the river on their inbound journey forty-five miles downstream, leaving that as an unexplored "gap." However, he was unaware that a military survey party coming upstream had forged further upstream than he had, and the untrod part of the canyon was in fact only ten miles long. Source: Bailey, "Exploration," p. 351; Waller, *The Pundits,* p. 243.

36 *"marry me when you came home"*: Lyte, *Frank Kingdon-Ward,* p. 66.

37 *a letter to India took but seventeen days*: James Morris, *Pax Britannica,* pp. 59–60. Morris, a foreign correspondent for the London *Times* in the 1950s (who later in his illustrious career underwent a sex change and became Jan Morris), sent his dispatches from the Nepali Himalayas to the British mission in Kathmandu by runner. In a marvelous account about the imperial mail, he evokes the proud heyday of the Indian runner service by citing Kipling:

> In the name of the Empress of India, make way,
> O Lords of the Jungle, wherever you roam,
> The woods are astir at the close of the day—
> We exiles are waiting for letters from Home.

Let the rivers retreat—let the tiger turn tail—
In the name of the Empress, the Overland Mail!

37   *in war-torn Sudan, from which Britain was withdrawing:* Thos. Cook & Son
archives. The rescue mission was an enormous undertaking, involving eighteen
thousand troops, four thousand tons of supplies, and twenty-eight steamships to
transport the men and gear. Cook's handled all the arrangements, and fulfilled
their part of the bargain in delivering everything to Khartoum. Alas, the city
fell to Sudanese rebels—the followers of a mystic known as the Mahdi—in January 1885, and Gordon famously went to his death at their hands.

38   *"tear this last secret from its heart":* Kingdon-Ward, *Riddle,* p. 205.

39   *"picturesque but monotonous":* Kingdon-Ward, *Riddle,* p. 15.

39   *"showed symptoms of intelligence":* Kingdon-Ward, *Riddle,* p. 183.

39   *"The local coons made a beastly wailing noise":* Lyte, *Frank Kingdon-Ward,* p. 70.

40   *"I lived chiefly on milk":* Kingdon-Ward, "Botanical and Geographical Explorations in Tibet, 1935," p. 412.

40   *stopped in at Fortnum & Mason:* In a tribute to British efficiency, Fortnum &
Mason was able to find the original order form for "Captain Ward's hamper,"
according to Lyte, who lists the provisions right down to Wrigley's chewing
gum and HP sauce.

40   *"antics of certain English travelers":* Kingdon-Ward, *Riddle,* p. 18.

41   *lodged a diplomatic complaint:* Swinson, *Frontiers,* p. 207.

41   *They had helped orchestrate his narrow escape:* This was the second time in a decade
that the Dalai Lama had fled Lhasa. In 1904, he'd slipped into Mongolia when
Younghusband's troops marched through the city's West Gate, at the foot of the
Potala, His Holiness's winter palace.

41   *disguising His Holiness as a* dak wallah, *a postal runner:* Years later, Cawdor related this excellent story to James Morris, cracking that it was the "only time
on record when His Majesty's mails were carried by an Incarnate God." See
Morris, *Trumpets,* p. 416.

42   *"to investigate and explore and enjoy":* Kingdon-Ward, *Riddle,* p. 22.

42   *"First pony wouldn't gallop, second wouldn't go near the ball":* Lyte, *Frank Kingdon-
Ward,* p. 91.

43   "off the map": Kingdon-Ward, *Riddle,* p. 25. Yamdrok Lake is the site of
Samding monastery, whose abbess, the Dorge Phagmo, is a living Buddha. Like
the Dalai Lama, she ranks as a *khutuktu,* or phantom body. Though Kingdon-
Ward seems not to have been aware of her significance when he passed Samding, the Dorge Phagmo is the emanation of the protector deity of Pemakö, the
sacred hidden land located within the Tsangpo Gorge. In Buddhist iconography, she is represented by Vajravarahi, a goddess whose name means "adaman-
tine [or 'diamond'] sow." Typically shown in a dancing pose, with her right leg
bent, dagger held high, and a human skull-cup held over her heart, she has a

small sow's head emerging above her right ear. The pig is said to represent ignorance, and her dance, to signify the triumph over ignorance.

44 *an "imaginable complexity,":* Bishop, *Myth,* p. viii.

44 *"but also with their creation":* Bishop, *Myth,* p. 3.

44 *"a mere rumor in the mid-eighteenth century . . . to this day.":* Bishop, *Myth,* p. 2.

44 *"I felt deliciously comfortable":* David-Neel, *My Journey,* p. 133.

46 *"We could only turn back and continue our journey":* David-Neel, *With Mystics,* pp. 199–204.

46 *"an idealized Eastern never-never land":* Schell, *Virtual Tibet,* p. 237.

46 *"We approached the matter":* Kingdon-Ward, *Riddle,* p. 206.

47 *"felt the atmosphere lift immediately":* Lyte, *Kingdon-Ward,* p. 71.

47 *"God never intended him to be a companion to anyone":* Lyte, *Kingdon-Ward,* p. 72.

47 *"He was . . . a very, very difficult man":* Lyte, *Kingdon-Ward,* p. 110; personal communication with Charles Lyte.

48 *"He was never satisfied":* Lyte, *Kingdon-Ward,* p. 114.

48 *"It was one of the only times I saw him laugh":* Lyte, *Kingdon-Ward,* p. 113.

48 *"I could do justice to a damned slice of Figgy Duff . . . tonight":* Lyte, *Kingdon-Ward,* p. 74. Figgy duff, or figgy 'obbin, is a traditional Cornish baked desert that actually contains no figs but rather raisins, which are what the Cornish call "figs."

48 *"Could anything be more charming and peaceful . . . ?":* Kingdon-Ward, *Riddle,* p. 27.

49 *"Good Samaritan and Pioneer Sergeant":* Lyte, *Kingdon-Ward,* p. 79.

52 *"What a pedestrian way to record one's assignation":* Bailey, *No Passport,* pp. 113–114.

54 *"rain-wind":* Kingdon-Ward, *Riddle,* p. 98.

54 *"filled with dwarf rhododendron in astonishing variety":* Kingdon-Ward, *Riddle,* p. 104.

56 *"what the traveller has to contend with":* Kingdon-Ward, *Riddle,* p. 110.

56 *"Every cell and fibre in one's body seems worn out":* Kingdon-Ward, *Riddle,* pp. 70–71.

57 *the "sting of winter":* Kingdon-Ward, *Riddle,* p. 179.

57 *"The great river was plunging down":* Kingdon-Ward, *Riddle,* p. 204.

58 *The Colorado River . . . loses about eight feet per mile:* From the launch site at Lee's Ferry to the takeout at Diamond Creek, 225 miles downstream, the river's drop averages 7.8 feet per mile.

58 *"to scale the cliff seemed·equally impossible":* Kingdon-Ward, *Riddle,* p. 220.

62 *"narrowest and most profound depths":* Kingdon-Ward, *Riddle,* p. 245.

62 *"They were a most remarkable body of men . . .":* Kingdon-Ward, *Riddle,* p. 250.

63   *a Tibetan branch of the Assam railway*: Holdich, *Mysterious,* p. 219, cited in Swinson, *Frontiers,* p. 299, note 128.

63   *one of the Raj's most trusted frontier officers*: Waddell, "The Falls," pp. 258–60, cited in Swinson, *Frontiers,* p. 314. The article contains the sketch made for the survey officer Dr. L. A. Waddell. Also from Bailey, *No Passport,* p. 276.

63   *"with the strength of a lion he is a host in himself"*: Allen, *Mountain,* p. 154.

64   *carved or painted on a rock behind the cascade*: Bailey, "Exploration on the Tsangpo," p. 351. According to another report, the shrine was a statue chained to the rocks behind the waterfall. Pilgrims came there to worship in winter, when only a small amount of water spilled in front of the icon.

64   *"I am afraid we must give up"*: Bailey, "Exploration on the Tsangpo," p. 362.

64   *"the whole [natural] history of the Tsangpo"*: Kingdon-Ward, "Explorations," p. 121.

65   *"one cannot live by exploration alone"*: Lyte, *Frank Kingdon-Ward,* p. 44.

65   *four of their fourteen years*: Lyte, *Frank Kingdon-Ward,* p. 115.

66   *"a worthwhile discovery in Asia, truly finished"*: Kingdon-Ward, *Himalayan Enchantment,* p. 207, (excerpted from *Assam Adventure*).

66   *"I am . . . perhaps too wise"*: Lyte, *Frank Kingdon-Ward,* p. 128.

66   *the Tsangpo diaries were not among them*: Lyte, personal communication. Florinda was renting out rooms at this point. A tenant discovered the diaries in the attic and said, "Do you realize what you have here?" The next thing he saw was the gardener wheeling them out in a cart to be incinerated.

66   *"a rather small, shrunken, shriveled little man"*: Lyte, *Frank Kingdon-Ward,* p. 144.

68   *"He was tough, really tough, and a great man"*: Lyte, *Frank Kingdon-Ward,* p. 114.

68   *the magnificent blue poppy*: Lyte, *Frank Kingdon-Ward,* p. 81. The *Times* obituary is cited in Swinson, *Frontiers,* p. 232.

68   *"he had been physically Tibetanized by his experiences"*: Morris, *Trumpets,* p. 417.

69   *"he was murdered" by unknown assailants*: Bailey, *No Passport,* p. 282; Allen, *Mountain,* p. 171.

69   *"The Dead Hand of China"*: Bailey, "Exploration," p. 360.

70   *"tomatoes, lettuce, turnips and radishes"*: Fletcher, ed., *A Quest of Flowers,* p. xvi.

70   *more than four thousand specimens*: Fletcher, ed., *A Quest of Flowers,* p. xxvi.

PART TWO: PERCEPTIONS OF PARADISE

75   *"One of the final and most complete embodiments of Tibet"*: Bishop, *Myth,* p. 19.

75   *"the horror of Chinese invasion and occupation"*: Lopez, *Prisoners,* p. 203.

76   *"It is time for the unveiling of Shangri-La"*: Lopez, *Prisoners,* pp. 203–4.

77 *Tibetan beggars he met to be racially "inharmonious"*: Meyer and Brysac, *Tournament of Shadows,* p. 520.

78 *avid readers of* The Secret Doctrine: Schell, *Virtual Tibet,* p. 228.

78 *a Buddhist-Theosophical temple opened in St. Petersburg*: Meyer and Brysac, *Tournament of Shadows,* p. 449.

79 *"a humbug, a bad painter"*: Meyer and Brysac, *Tournament of Shadows,* p. 472.

79 *"The place"*: *Heart of Asia* by Nicholas Roerich (Rochester, NY: Inner Traditions International, 1990), p. 58. From the first edition published in 1929.

80 *"not a bird, not an animal"*: *Altai-Himalaya: A Travel Diary* by Nicholas Roerich (Kempton, IL, Adventures Unlimited Press, 2001), p. 366 ff. From the first edition published in 1929.

80 *"Each night the freezing"*: *Heart of Asia,* p. 60.

82 *"The utopia . . . was an ideal fantasy world"*: Bishop, *Myth,* p. 217.

83 *"imagination will get you further than knowledge or first-hand experience"*: *New York Times,* July 26, 1936, Part IX, p. 3.

84 *a society of "Kelans," followers of the Panchen Lama*: The line of reincarnated Panchen Lamas is said to originate with the first king of Shambhala.

84 *an army of Kelans would rise up from among the living*: Bernbaum, *Shambhala,* p. 48.

84 *"madly rules like a wild elephant"*: Allen, *Search,* pp. 42–43.

84 *His writings*: Hilton may also have been inspired by a 1924 mystical potboiler titled *Om: The Secret of Ahbor Valley,* whose author, William Lancaster Gribbon, wrote under the penname Talbot Mundy. A Theosophist, Gribbon was a world traveler, ivory poacher, flim-flam man and, eventually, a successful and prolific author. His novel, now a cult classic, opens in 1920s India and involves a search for a hidden Tibetan valley in the "gorge of the Brahmaputra"—the Tsangpo Gorge—and a piece of jade with supernatural powers. Having found the valley, the protagonist, Cottswold Ommony, sees "the Tsangpo River, half a mile wide, tumbl[ing] down a precipice between two outflung spurs that looked like the legs of a seated giant. The falls were leagues away, and yet their roar came down-wind like the thunder of creation." Considering that Mundy had never been to the gorge, it's an uncannily accurate description of the real Falls of the Brahmaputra.

84 *beyuls are sacred places of mystical retreat*: Macdonald, ed., *Mandala and Landscape, pp. 288–91.*

85 *"Nepemako . . . a terre promise des Tibetains"*: Bernbaum, *Shambhala,* p. 276.

85 *They were going to Pemakö*: Eric Bailey had read Bacot's book when he went to the gorge in 1913 with Henry Morshead, and he was aware of the mythology of Pemakö. He had nevertheless been surprised to come across a village of Tibetan refugees living at about the eight-thousand-foot level in the lower gorge, a much lower elevation than Tibetans prefer. Their headman explained that

they were the leftovers of the large group of refugees escaping the armies of a Chinese warlord, but they had been unable to find Pemakö. The geographical location of the *beyul* was imprecise, he told Bailey. "All that was known was that somewhere on the Dihang-Lohit watershed [the lower Tsangpo, before it becomes the Brahmaputra] there was a holy mountain of glass, and around this holy mountain lay fertile fields," Bailey would recall forty years later in his memories. See *No Passport*, p. 35.

85   *the legendary Padma-shel-ri*: Sardar, "An Account of Padma-Bkod," p. 14.

85   *all religious activity in Tsari was officially banned*: Huber, *Cult*, p. 4.

86   *the yoga of "mystic heat" or "internal fire"*: Huber, *Cult*, pp. 87–90.

87   " 'The kingdom of Shambhala is in your own heart' ": Bernbaum, *Shambhala*, p. 24.

87   " 'only if their karma is ready' ": quoted in Allen, *Search*, p. 19.

87   *like "paintings stacked against a wall"*: Bernbaum, *Shambhala*, p. 49.

88   *a window clouded with an accumulation of karmic residue*: Bernbaum, *Shambhala*, p. 39.

89   *Lekdrup Dorje, "accomplished thunderbolt"*: *Dorje*, or thunderbolt, is a ritual implement that symbolizes empty awareness. Deities are frequently depicted brandishing a *dorje*, and lamas manipulate them gracefully while performing ceremonies.

89   *like trying to lick honey from a razor's edge*: The metaphor of poison for negative emotions is frequently used to differentiate between the three kinds of Buddhism. As anthropologist Carroll Dunham explains, "His Holiness the Dalai Lama has a very beautiful way of explaining the different paths in Buddhism: The Theravada Buddhist will [avoid acting on his desires, saying], 'I will retreat from the poison.' The Mahayana Buddhist will look for the antidote for it—'If the poison is hatred, I will use peace and loving compassion.' The Tantric Buddhist will consume the poison like a peacock, which according to Indian philosophy eats seeds of a plant that is poisonous to other creatures but in the peacock causes radiance in its feathers. The Tantricist transforms the poison. Transformation is critical" to achieve enlightenment.

90   *"house full of writers, film makers, archaeologists—interesting people"*: John Baker, personal communication. Puleston, who died at age ninety-five in 2001, was a leading figure in the fight to ban DDT spraying.

90   *"at the center of a bohemian fringe"*: McGowan, "Legend of the Falls," p. 28.

92   *Understanding the interplay*: Lopez, *Prisoners*, page 142 ff. Lopez disagrees with these theories, arguing that although some famous lamas were also painters, most Tibetan artists were rarely advanced tantric practitioners inspired by mystical states.

93   *"the eight magical powers"*: Lopez, *Prisoners*, p. 256n. This deity is the wrathful two-horned, nine-headed Buddha known as Yamantaka.

93   *"so obscurely encoded that access to it often seems barred to a thinking mind"*: Lopez, *Prisoners*, p. 256n, quoting from Detlef Lauf, *Tibetan Sacred Art*, p. 47.

96   *a list of seven place names in beautiful calligraphy:* The number of hidden lands varies from account to account. Some say there are eight, others twenty-four.

97   *Kyimolung can be thought of as a mandala:* Macdonald, ed., *Mandala and Landscape,* p. 134, from an essay by Charles Ramble. As Ramble explains, the general characteristics of sacred sites are that they were usually sanctified thanks to the action of a saint or wonder worker: the subjugation of a demon, for instance, or the ascetic's sacrifice of his body. In one sacred valley that Ramble visited, Dunglo Joonpa, north of the mountain Dhaulagiri, food is said to grow without effort, the water is like beer or milk, the earth like *tsampa,* and wood like meat. Also see Dowman, *Sacred Life,* pp. 216–20.

97   *"an elixir of forgetfulness:"* Dowman, *Sacred Life,* p. 218.

98   *anthropologist Fosco Mariani:* Mariani, *Secret Tibet,* pp. 401, 406.

98   *Features of the topography represent parts of her anatomy:* Dowman, *Sacred Life,* pp. 220–22. But as Dowman explains, "The actual identification of topographic features that relate to her body is a perplexing exercise . . . due to the variety of different indications given in the treasure texts and the lack of consensus among pilgrims who have used the guides."

99   *The Tsangpo itself is Dorje Phagmo's central meridian:* Dowman, *Sacred Life,* p. 221.

99   *twelve outer territories, forty inner ravines, and sixteen secret territories:* Sardar, "An Account of Padma-Bkod," p. 2.

102   *Dorje Drolo, the wrathful emanation of Padmasambava:* Dorje Drolo is a fearsome-looking being, usually depicted with his tigress consort. Chatral Rinpoche is not merely a reincarnation of the wrathful deity but a direct, spontaneous emanation of him.

104   *"over 14,000 feet below Gyala Peri and 16,000 feet below Namche Barwa":* Bailey, *No Passport,* p. 124.

115   *"canyoneering is a sport requiring a unique set of skills":* Fisher, *Earth's Mystical Grand Canyons,* p. 50.

PART THREE: BEYOND GEOGRAPHY

121   *"Hidden lands like* Padma bkod [Pemakö] *often appear as landscapes of paradox":* Excerpted from Sardar's unpublished doctoral thesis, *The Buddha's Secret Gardens,* p. 174.

121   *"an enclosed paradise":* Hilton, *Lost Horizon,* pp. 106–7.

122   *"green hell":* Sardar personal communication. "Green hell" is the way the Dalai Lama once described some of the more arduous hidden lands.

122   *the holy Padma-shel-ri:* The peak is described as a snow-covered mountain that resembles a mandala and is surrounded by eight valleys that fan out like a thousand-petaled lotus. A treasure finder named Rje drung 'Jam pa 'byung gnas, who led the exodus of refugees that Bailey and Morshead met in Mipi, explained that the mountain would protect his followers from evil. He called it

"the all-encompassing glorious citadel." He died before he was able to divine the mountain's location. See Sardar, *Secret Gardens,* pp. 161–62.

122   *quarrels had arisen between the tribesmen and the settlers:* See Sardar, *Secret Gardens,* p. 162n. Sardar received this account from the headman of Shinku, a village in Pemakö's Chimdro Valley.

123   *"It was a scene of the victory of nature over man":* Bailey, *No Passport,* p. 55.

123   *they took to boiling their yak-leather shoes to make broth:* Sardar, *Secret Gardens* p. 3.

123   *"an allegory for the path to enlightenment itself":* Sardar, *Secret Gardens.* p. 6.

123   *cobras exist to encourage mindfulness and leeches to draw away one's bad karma:* Sardar, *Secret Gardens,* p. 157.

125   *The gold-roofed temple:* Sardar, *Secret Gardens,* pp. 154–57.

126   *Dorje Drolo, a terrifying three-eyed figure:* Padmasambava appears in eight different forms. The wrathful emanation is Dorje Drolo, the form he took in Pemakö to subdue demons and spirits. The tigress is his consort, Mandarava.

127   *The southern gorge is home to a poisoning cult:* Chan, *Tibet Handbook,* p. 718.

128   *" 'I have made it to Pemakö. My life is complete' ":* Baker, "Exploring a Hidden Land," p. 23.

139   *"one of the most sacred and mystical regions in Tibet":* Chan, *Tibet Handbook,* p. 707.

140   *Walt Blackadar . . . successfully navigated the perilous rapids of Turnback Canyon:* Walters, *Never Turn Back,* p. 2. Blackadar became trapped under a log and drowned on a river he knew well, Idaho's Payette, in 1978.

141   *"the riverine equivalent of Mount Everest":* Walker, *Courting the Diamond Sow,* p. 20.

141   *a Sino-Japanese team made the first ascent of Namche Barwa:* Eleven members of the climbing expedition summited on October 30, 1992. The effort had spanned three climbing seasons—a reconnaissance in November-December 1990 and a summit bid in October 1991, during which one climber, Hiroshi Onishi, was swept away and killed by an avalanche while ascending to camp four at about 22,000 feet. A third team returned in 1992 to bag the peak.

142   *Takei's parents also mounted a later rescue mission:* The family lives in the city of Takamatsu on Shikoku Island, the whole of which is a spiritual sanctuary to the Japanese. Pilgrims circumambulate the island, visiting each of its eighty-eight temples, on an arduous thousand-mile walk that takes at least two months.

145   *a "battlefield" strewn with enormous trees like fallen soldiers:* Jenny Morris (Claire Scobie's pen name), "Red Lily." It should be noted that since 1997, Chinese logging policies have been reformed, not only in Tibet but also in neighboring Yunnan and Sichuan provinces. State planners have made the connection between timber clear-cutting, flooding, and loss of topsoil; they have put many loggers to work reforesting mountain slopes throughout the region. China now imports timber from Burma and Indonesia, where clear-cutting remains a problem.

146   *as they neared the summit, Storm cried out, "Found it!"*: Morris, "Red Lily."

146   *Baker could see they were adamant*: Apart from being more reliable than local porters and cooks in the gorge, Baker's Sherpas came with him as much to make a pilgrimage to Pemakö as for the work. Monpa and Lopa porters have been the bane of every expedition to the gorge, from Bailey's onward. The locals customarily stage a strike at the worst possible moment to extort higher wages.

148   *"Forty-three years!" he later wrote in a travelog about the expedition*: The Gillenwaters posted their narrative and photos on the Internet site www.hiddenfalls.org, which was still active as of this writing.

150   *"We've found the Falls of the Brahmaputra!"*: Gil Gillenwater, personal communication.

151   *caught "between the world of fantasy and romance and that of science and so-called reality"*: Bishop, *Myth*, p. 174.

152   *thirty or more miles of gradient that averages eight times that of the Colorado River's*: The drop of the Colorado River averages 7.8 feet per mile. Some stretches of the Tsangpo's inner canyon have a gradient that exceeds 250 feet per mile.

152   *"For a river of this size to descend 112 feet a mile was amazing"*: Kingdon-Ward, *Riddle*, p. 231.

154   *"somewhat narrow-minded pride for our deeply loved motherland"*: Personal communication with Wan Lin, Dr. Yang's assistant.

156   *hunting, butchering and even plowing or burning . . . are forbidden:* Huber, *Cult*, p. 5. Huber discovered the record of a nineteenth-century lama's invocation against hunting:

> You, faithful male and female patrons
> Of this empowered ground, the great ne of Tsari
> Do not feed yourselves by hunting birds and game animals.

157   *the takin will graze on magic grass:* Sardar, personal communication.

163   *"enough to make some informed judgments"*: Walker, *Courting the Diamond Sow*, p. 27.

170   *"Here, if anywhere were the Falls of the Brahmaputra"*: Kingdon-Ward, *Riddle*, pp. 234–35.

174   *"We don't need to film the whole falls"*: Baker, personal communication.

177   *"If there is a Shangri-La, this is it."*: The *Tribune* reporter, said Martin, "was looking to get Shangri-La. I told him, 'If one were to look at the images of the gorge, and the videotape of it, one would think that if there is a Shangri-La this is it.' I read his story and said, 'Wait, where's the rest of my quote?' "

180   *The* Geographic *dismissed Fisher:* "Trouble in Paradise," Sacramento *Bee*, March 4, 1999, p. F1.

181   *one of seven "explorers for the millennium"*: Fair disclosure: As a contributing editor of *Adventure*, I wrote about the Baker and Walter teams for this same issue.

185   *they had enlisted George Schaller*: The magazine never carried articles on the Walker expedition, marred by a death, or on Baker's, which was controversial.

189   *one hundred and seventy feet higher*: Bailey, op cit., pp. 105–9.

189   *The event took less than ten minutes*: International Center for Integrated Mountain Development report on the Yigrong Flood.

Select Bibliography

Allen, Charles, *A Mountain in Tibet* (London: A. Deutsch, 1982).

———.*The Search for Shangri-La* (London: Little, Brown and Co., 1999).

Bailey, Frederick M., *China-Tibet-Assam* (London: Jonathan Cape, 1945).

———.*No Passport to Tibet* (London: Rupert Hart-Davis, 1957).

Bernbaum, Edwin, *The Way to Shambhala* (Los Angeles: Jeremy Tarcher, 1980).

Bishop, Peter, *The Myth of Shangri-La* (Berkeley: University of California Press, 1989).

Cassaday, Jim, Bill Cross, and Fryan Calhoun, eds., *Western Whitewater* (Berkeley, North Fork Press, 1994).

Chan, Victor, *Tibet Handbook* (Chico, CA: Moon Publications, 1994).

David-Neel, Alexandra, *My Journey to Lhasa* (Boston: Beacon Press, 1986).

———.*With Mystics and Magicians in Tibet* (New York: Dover, 1971).

Dowman, Keith, *The Sacred Life of Tibet* (London: Thorsons, 1997).

Fisher, Richard D., *Earth's Mystical Grand Canyons* (Tucson: Sunracer Publications, 1995).

Fletcher, Harold, ed., *A Quest of Flowers* (Edinburgh: Edinburgh University Press, 1975).

French, Patrick, *Younghusband: The Last Great Imperial Adventurer* (London: Harper-Collins, 1994).

Hilton, James, *Lost Horizon* (New York: Pocket Books, 1933).

Holdich, Thomas H., *Tibet the Mysterious* (London: Alston Rivers, 1906).

Huber, Toni, *The Cult of Pure Crystal Mountain* (New York: Oxford University Press, 1999).

Kingdon-Ward, Francis, *Riddle of the Tsangpo Gorges* (London: Edward Arnold & Co., 1926).

———.*Himalayan Enchantment,* ed. John Whitehead (London: Serindia Publications, 1990).

Lopez, Donald, *Prisoners of Shangri-La* (Chicago: University of Chicago Press, 1998).

———. *The Story of Buddhism* (New York: HarperCollins, 2001).

Lyte, Charles, *Frank Kingdon-Ward: The Last of the Great Plant Hunters* (London: John Murray Ltd., 1989).

Macdonald, A. W., ed., *Mandala and Landscape* (New Delhi: D.K. Printworld, 1997).

Mariani, Fosco, *Secret Tibet* (London: Harwill Press, 2000).

Meyer, Karl E., and Shareen B. Brysac, *Tournament of Shadows: The Great Game and the Race for Empire in Central Asia* (Washington, D.C.: Counterpoint, 1999).

Morris, James, *Pax Britannica: The Climax of an Empire* (New York: Harcourt Brace Jovanovich, 1968).

———. *Farewell the Trumpets: An Imperial Retreat* (New York: Harcourt Brace Jovanovich, 1978).

Sardar, Hamid, *The Buddha's Secret Gardens: End Times and Hidden Lands in Tibetan Imagination* (Cambridge: Harvard University, Department of Sanskrit and Indian Studies, 2001).

Schell, Orville, *Virtual Tibet* (New York: Metropolitan Books, 2000).

Shapiro, Judith, *Mao's War Against Nature* (Cambridge: Cambridge University Press, 2001).

Swinson, Arthur, *Beyond the Frontiers* (London: Hutchinson & Co., 1971).

Vaurie, Charles, *Tibet and Its Birds* (London: H. F. & G. Witherby, Ltd., 1972).

Waller, Derek, *The Pundits* (Lexington: University Press of Kentucky, 1990).

Walker, Wickliffe, W., *Courting the Diamond Sow* (Washington: National Geographic Adventure Press, 2000).

Walters, Ron, *Never Turn Back,* (Pocatello, ID: The Great Rift Press, 1994).

Xiaolan, Mao, et al., *Flora and Fauna of the Namche Barwa Region* (Kunming: Science Press China, 19950.

ARTICLES

Bailey, F. M., "Exploration on the Tsangpo or Upper Brahmaputra," *The Geographical Journal*, October 1914, pp. 341–64.

Baker, Ian, "Exploring a Hidden Land," *Explorers Journal* (Explorer's Club of New York), fall 1997, pp. 19–24.

Fleming, Robert L., Jr., "A Summary of Biodiversity: The Great River Ecosystems of Asia Trust Region," published on http://www.future.org/greatbio.html.

Forestry Reconnaissance & Design Institute in Tibet, "The Master Plan on Yarlung Zangbo Great Valley State Reserve, 2000–2010," October 1999.

Gillenwater, Gil, and Troy Gillenwater, "1997 Tibet Expedition," posted on http://www.hiddenfalls.org.

Kaulback, Ronald, "The Assam Border of Tibet," *The Geographical Journal*, March 1934, pp. 178–90.

———."A Journey in the Salween and Tsangpo Basins, Southeastern Tibet," *The Geographical Journal*, February 1938, pp. 98–122.

Kingdon-Ward, F., "Explorations in Southeastern Tibet," *The Geographical Journal*, February 1926, pp. 97–123.

———."The Himalaya East of the Tsangpo," *The Geographical Journal*, November 1934, pp. 369–97.

———."Botanical and Geographical Explorations in Tibet, 1935," *The Geographical Journal,* November 1936, pp. 386–413.

———."Caught in the Assam-Tibet Earthquake," *The National Geographic Magazine*, March 1952, pp. 402–16.

Liang, Chen, "Chinese Explorers Get to the Falls First," *China Daily*, Jan. 29, 1999. p. 9.

———."Scientists Evaluate Fruits of Canyon Expedition," *China Daily*, Dec. 12, 1998, republished on http://www.chinadaily.com.cn, and in an advertising supplement to the *Washington Post National Weekly Edition*.

McGowan, William, "Legend of the Falls," *Middlebury Magazine*, winter 2000, pp. 27–33.

Morris, Jenny, "The Hunt for the Red Lily," *London Telegraph Magazine*, Oct. 25, 1997.

Sardar, Hamid, "An Account of Padma-Bkod: A Hidden Land in Southeastern Tibet," *Kailash,* vol. 18, nos. 3–4, 1996, pp. 1–22.

Schaller, George, et al., "An Ecological Survey of the Medog Area in the Yarlung Tsangpo Great Canyon National Reserve, Tibet," September 2000.

Waddell, L.A., "The Falls of the Tsangpo (San-pu) and of That River with the Brahmaputra." *The Geographical Journal*, vol. V, 1895.

Yichou, Yang, "The Grandest Canyon in the World: The Geographical Discovery of the Yarlung Zangbo River Canyon," *The Journal of Chinese Geography*, vol. 7, no. 1, 1997, pp. 105–10.

Yichou, Yang, et al., "Fight King Cobra" and other articles posted on http://www.100gogo.com.

———."On Foot Through the Great Gorge on the Yarlung Zangbo River," posted on http://shoe. wenzhou.com.cn/ChinaPictorial.

Acknowledgments

This book grew out of two articles about the exploration of the Tsangpo Gorge, the first in 1994 for *Men's Journal*, the second in 1999 for the premiere issue of *National Geographic Adventure*. Coincidentally, the same editor, John Rasmus, made both assignments. As the founding editor of *Men's Journal* and *Adventure,* and the former editor of *Outside* (where he and I worked together in the late 1970s), he has supported me on these and many other stories that have taken me around the world, and I owe him profound thanks. Thanks as well to James Vlahos, who helped shape the *Adventure* piece into final form, to photo editor Nell Hupman, and others on the staff who had a hand in its publication, not least Kalee Thompson and Katie McDowell. Had Caryn Davidson, *Adventure's* publicist, not urged me to propose this book in the first place, I would have never contacted my literary agent, Mike Hamilburg. I am deeply indebted to him for his constant encouragement.

I want to thank my editor at Broadway Books, Charles Conrad, for his patience, understanding, and suggestions. Thanks, too, to Claire Johnson and Alison Presley for fielding phone calls and e-mails; to Linda Steinman and Andrea Zalcman for their wise counsel; and to Rowland White and Kate Brunt of Penguin Books UK for editorial support and assistance in locating historical photographs at the Royal Geographical Society.

It is unusual for one author to share his story with another, even if they are writing about the same subject from different perspectives. For his generosity in doing this, I thank Ian Baker. He gave up many hours in interviews with me, by telephone and in person in Kathmandu, when he could have been writing his own account of exploring the Tsangpo Gorge. Among others who shared their experiences in the gorge, I am especially grateful to Hamid Sardar, as a scholar, linguist, expert on the gorge's spiritual and physical geography, traveling companion in Tibet, and interpreter of Tibetan history, religion, and culture.

Dozens of others added to my understanding of events in the gorge since it reopened nearly a decade ago. Thanks, in particular, to Gil and Troy Gillenwater, who shared with me their journals, personal insights, and photographs. Rick Fisher, who led the initial expedition to the gorge in 1993, gave generously of his time for the *Men's Journal* article. David Breashears and Gordon Wiltsie, who were in the gorge at the same time as Fisher's team, kindly shared their stories for that piece and again for this book. Both also allowed me to use their photographs.

I am grateful to John Milnes Baker, Richard Bangs, Jill Bielawski, Lukas Blucher, Simon Boyce, Jeff Boyd, Victor Chan, Diane Chang, Maryanne Culpepper, Steve Currey, Keith Dowman, Carroll Dunham, Yoshinobu Emoto, Donald Lopez, Charles Lyte, Minao Kitamura, Rebecca Martin, Peter Miller, Barbara Moffat, Tom and Jamie McEwan, Tomatsu Nakamura, Charles Ramble, George Schaller, Dale Vrabec, Wick Walker, Ron Walters, Roger Zbel, and Jiyue and Shaohong Zhang. Mrs. Jean Rasmussen, Frank Kingdon-Ward's widow, deserves special thanks for talking by phone with a writer who never seemed to find the time to come to England.

I have relied heavily on the scholarship of authors past and present who wrote about the gorge, the characters who explored it, and the complex mythology of Tibetan Buddhism. I cite them in the notes whenever I borrowed from their books, and apologize if I have missed giving credit where credit was due.

Finally, thanks to my wife, Virginia Morell, for her unfailing support throughout the writing of this book.

Index

Page numbers of photographs appear in italics.